A Railwayman's Odyssey

1930-1970
From Junior Clerk to Superintendent

A Railwayman's Odyssey

1930-1970
From Junior Clerk to Superintendent

Stan Hall

Ian Allan

Page 1: A stirring sight: a BR Class 9F 2-10-0, No 92133, in full cry at Wellingborough Midland Road with a heavy load of iron ore. These trains loaded to 24 wagons and originated at Wellingborough London Road (former LNWR). I believe the wagons were all unfitted and needed careful handling. The destination was Teesside. *Colin Boocock*

Pages 2 and 3: Surely one of the finest of Hubert Foster's superb photographs. 'Royal Scot' class No 6109 *Royal Engineer*, one of the very early rebuilds, overtakes one of Stanier's 2-8-0s, No 8177, at Blea Moor. *W. Hubert Foster/courtesy John W. Holroyd*

Page 6: A Midland Class 2F 0-6-0, No 3554, with a well-filled tender, heads north from Skipton with a heavy load. It was built at Derby in 1897. *Eric Treacy*

First published 2012

ISBN 978 0 7110 3750 2

Published by Stanley Hall

Distributed by Ian Allan Publishing Ltd, Hersham, Surrey KT12 4RG.
Printed in England

Visit the Ian Allan Publishing website at www.ianallanpublishing.com

Author's Note:
Nearly all the photographs in the book were taken many years ago and, owing to the considerable passage of time (50 to 80 years) since they were taken, there is substantial difficulty in contacting the photographers concerned. If any authors recognise their prints (which have been acknowledged where possible) and would like the usual payment for reproduction (if payment hasn't already been sent to them), please contact me, c/o Ian Allan Publishing.

It is fortunate that I kept substantial records of the whole 40 years covered by the book, but it is also inevitable that recourse has had to be made to memory in some instances. If any reader observes an error in the text I should be very grateful if I could be informed, again c/o Ian Allan Publishing.

Might I also mention that some of the material in this book appeared in articles written by me in *Steam World* magazine some time ago?

Finally, may I express my thanks and gratitude to Peter Waller, Alan Butcher and Ian Allan Publishing for their invaluable help in producing this book.
Stan Hall

Contents

One

HOW IT ALL BEGAN

My association with railways stems from a very early age. We lived less than five minutes from the former Midland main line at Bingley, about 14 miles north of Leeds, and it was my mother's habit, as she told me many years later, to wheel me in the pushchair to a nearby overbridge to watch what was apparently known locally as the Continental Boat Train pass through. It was many years before I unravelled the mystery of the train's intriguing title, but apparently one of the morning expresses from Glasgow St Enoch (or it may have been Edinburgh Waverley) to St Pancras conveyed through coaches for Tilbury for the continental boats. My mother rather liked trains, so perhaps I inherited my own love of trains from her.

This was about 1928, five years into the grouping. The LMS had adopted former Midland Railway locomotive types as standard, so there was little change in the railway scene at Bingley, but significant changes were not far away. The Horwich 'Crabs', known locally by the more dignified title of 'Moguls', were beginning to appear, especially from Carlisle, which had a large batch, and standard Class 7F 0-8-0s in the 9500 series were also to be seen from 1929 onwards. Most of the Midland freight sheds had half-a-dozen or so. At this time the former Midland lines were still full of 0-6-0s ranging from the extremely ancient to the relatively modern. Class 4F 0-6-0s were turned out by the hundred after grouping until 1928, No 4556 being the last one. Another 45 were built between 1937 and 1940: Nos 4562 to 4606 (Nos 4457-61 were built by Armstrong Whitworth in 1921 for the Somerset & Dorset Joint Railway

to the Midland '4F' design and taken into LMS stock in 1930). The 0-8-0s were intended to reduce double-heading. They were powerful machines but mechanically unsound. I knew nothing of this at the time, of course, but I do rather wish that my mother had jotted down their numbers. However, despite liking trains, she never knew one engine from another.

The Midland, in spite of being a powerful, wealthy and prosperous company, certainly loved its small engines, and none, well, hardly any, came smaller than its 0-4-4 tanks, Class 1P, which dated back to 1875 but looked older. Even though the Midland did not have an intensive commuter service compared with some of the other big companies, it still seems astonishing that the company never designed anything larger than tiny 0-4-4 tanks for its local passenger services, other than Deeley's unfortunate venture with his 0-6-4 n tanks, which had a distressing tendency to derail. They were rapidly removed to inoffensive corners of the Midland Division (no other Division on the LMS would touch them with a barge pole) and to very secondary duties, being sent for breaking up in the mid-1930s.

However, the 0-4-4 tanks were handy little machines and performed manfully, but after grouping the LMS transferred a number of the Lancashire & Yorkshire's very capable 2-4-2 tanks to other parts of the system including the Midland Division. About a dozen were sent to Manningham and Skipton for working the Bradford to Skipton and Ilkley locals, and they became part of the everyday scene for many years. Bradford had Nos

Above: A recent arrival on the Midland line —
an almost new LMS Standard Class 7F 0-8-0
No 9571, built at Crewe in 1929, at the head of a
light load just south of Bingley tunnel *circa* 1930.
I had my first introduction to trains at a very early
age, at the overbridge seen above the brake van.
We lived just a couple of minutes away and my
mother used to bring me 'to watch the trains'.
For me it was the beginning of a lifelong
love affair. These 0-8-0s were soon to be
concentrated on the Central Division of the LMS.
W. *Hubert Foster/Author's Collection*

Below: This is one of Eric Treacy's superb photos
and records a Midland Class 4F 0-6-0, No 3963
built at Derby in 1921, heading a Morecambe
excursion. Shed code 20D — Normanton. Note
the Stanier coach next to the engine, which dates
it to the later 1930s. This photo was taken from
the steps of a signalbox, one of Treacy's favourite
perches, in this case Marley Junction, between
Bingley and Keighley. *Eric Treacy*

10625-7/9-32/6/7; Skipton had Nos 10633/4. Holbeck also acquired some in later years. Stanier's funny little 0-4-4 tanks with stovepipe chimneys were also part of the local scene. Manningham had Nos 6400-04 for some reason. They were built at Derby in 1932 and must have been the last death-throes of the Midland's small engine policy. Only 10 were built. One wonders if Stanier knew nothing about them until they actually appeared. He would have been horrified.

Actually, the replacements weren't much better. The standard parallel-boiler 2-6-2 tanks, numbered 1 to 70, were built at Derby between 1930 and 1932 but were regarded as failures, being too sluggish, but the taper-boiler variety, numbered 71 to 209, were not highly regarded either. They too were sluggish. They were turned out at Derby and Crewe between 1935 and 1937. Virtually none of them worked north of Leeds, although one Sunday on our way home from church, much to our astonishment and delight we came across brand-new No 170 standing in the goods yard. We never knew why, but it was a sunny, summer's day and the engine was just simmering away with the driver sitting on the bottom step. Plucking up our courage, with our shining choirboy faces and neat clothes, we tentatively approached and asked if we could have a look in the cab. 'Nothing easier', replied the driver. 'Come on up.' It was a first for us and a day to remember, especially as we were told off when we got home for having dirty hands. No 170 was allocated to Manningham, but disappeared to Scotland later. This Sunday trek to church had become a weekly ritual as I had joined the parish church choir at my parents' 'suggestion'. Unfortunately, there weren't many trains on Sundays, at least until the war started, but more of that later.

Above: About 20 of these very serviceable former Lancashire & Yorkshire 2-4-2Ts were transferred to the Leeds (20A) motive power district after grouping to work local passenger trains, mainly north of Leeds City and Bradford Forster Square. One of them, No 10621, is seen fairly soon after grouping. It was built at Horwich in 1889. *Ian Allan Library*

The Leeds/Bradford/Skipton area had had its share of equally elderly 2-4-0s, but they eventually disappeared from the area by about 1933 (I can't remember seeing any there), although the class survived until after the war. I can recall seeing No 20002 at Nottingham about 1941 on one of my

Below: One of Fowler's parallel-boilered 2-6-2Ts, BR No 40063 (LMS No 63) rests at an undisclosed shed. Seventy of these engines (including No 1) were built at Derby between 1930 and 1932, but they were not highly regarded as they were considered sluggish. *Author's Collection*

Left: Bell Busk, north of Skipton, was one of Hubert Foster's favourite photographic locations. This is a splendid shot in August 1934 of a double-headed train composed of a motley collection of vehicles, and with a veteran ex-Midland 2-4-0 No 214, carrying express headlamps, piloting a Midland Class 4F 0-6-0. *W. Hubert Foster/ courtesy of John W. Holroyd*

Left: LMS Standard Compound No 929, shed code 33, stands in Bingley station on an express in around 1928, probably from Morecambe. The engine was built at the Vulcan foundry in 1927 and looks almost brand new in this photograph. The compounds were certainly aesthetically pleasing. *Author's Collection (probably W. Hubert Foster)*

Left: Several former LNWR 'Claughtons', displaced from the West Coast main line by the introduction of the 'Royal Scots', were transferred to the Midland Division to work the heavy Anglo-Scottish services. No 5932 *Sir Thomas Williams,* in commendably clean condition, seems quite at home with an Up express about a mile south of Bingley *circa* 1930. The 'Claughtons' were displaced by the arrival of the 'Patriots'. *Author's Collection*

days out. By that time it was 75 years old. These were the engines that the Midland had relied upon for its Anglo-Scottish services and were later used for piloting.

The LMS continued to rely on compound 4-4-0s for the Anglo-Scottish services, and double-heading was rife. Trials had been carried out shortly after grouping to see which, if any, of the pre-grouping express engines should be adopted as standard but the results were disappointing. Only the Midland Compounds performed efficiently, and it doesn't cast much glory on the front rank express engines of the other big players which formed the LMS that none of their designs was considered worth perpetuating. However, quite large numbers of former-LNWR 'Claughton' 4-6-0s were transferred to the Midland Division from about 1928 onwards after being displaced from their home ground by the new and much superior 'Royal Scots'. Nos 5944 and 6005 came to Holbeck shed in 1928, followed later by No 5912 *Lord Faber*, and eventually there were about a dozen of them. Kentish Town had about half-a-dozen and the Midland shed at Carlisle had four.

They had short lives as 'Claughtons'. The design had never really been considered satisfactory, even when some were given larger boilers in 1928, and the success of the 'Royal Scots' prompted the concept of a scaled-down version using these larger boilers on a more modern three-cylinder chassis.

Below: A footpath crossing about half a mile south of Bingley station was one of Hubert Foster's favourite spots for photography, especially as it was only about 10 minutes from his home. He captured this early 'Patriot', No 5971 *Croxteth*, on what appears to be the 12.0 noon from St Pancras to Glasgow St Enoch in *circa* 1932. The two LNER coaches were detached at Carlisle and attached to a train to Edinburgh Waverley, via Hawick. In the 1934 re-numbering, the engine was given the number 5500 and the name *Patriot*, in memory of the LNWR employees who were killed in the First World War. This name had originally been carried by a 'Claughton' class engine No 1914, which became LMS No 5964 and was withdrawn in 1934. No 5971 is seen here without smoke deflectors. These were fitted to all the 'Royal Scots' and 'Patriots' as a result of the recommendations of an MOT Inquiry into a serious derailment of an express at Leighton Buzzard in 1931. It was thought that smoke drifting down over the cab might have obscured the driver's view of the signals. *W. Hubert Foster/Author's Collection*

There was great excitement in 1930 when 'Claughton' No 5971 *Croxteth* appeared in new guise as a 'Baby Scot'. It had been 'rebuilt' at Derby in 1930 and was put to work on the Midland line. It was, in fact, to all intents and purposes a new engine, using only a few parts of the 'Claughton'. The design was an instant success and a further 41 'Baby Scots' were turned out from Crewe in 1932 and 1933. They were actually plated as rebuilds, presumably to suit the accountant, but in reality they were new engines.

Almost all the 'Claughtons' on the Midland were replaced in this way and the 'rebuilds' became Nos 5500 to 5541 under the LMS renumbering scheme of the time. This would be about 1933. Another 10 were added in 1933, Nos 5542 to 5551, and these were officially registered as new engines. The new

Above: An LMS 'Mogul' 2-6-0, Class 5P4F, No 42832, shedded at 12A — Carlisle — heads a semi-fitted freight through Bingley, past the 1930s signalbox and 'Treacle Alley' in 1948. They were later commonly referred to as 'Crabs' and re-designated 5F. A paved footpath leads from the town to the church and passes under the railway at this point. I spent countless happy hours here in the later 1930s. You could hear the signalbox bells and see the signals in both directions, and there was a low wall to sit on. *Author*

class became known as 'Patriots', after the first engine of the class, the former *Croxteth*, was renamed *Patriot* after the LNWR war memorial engine. It had been intended to build more 'Baby

Left: One of Herbert Foster's favourite spots was for photography was between Marley Junction signalbox and the road overbridge at Crossflatts, just north of Bingley. Stanier 'Jubilee' Class 5XP No 5565 *Victoria* is seen here with a long 12-coach Up Anglo-Scottish express, probably in the late 1930s. *Victoria* was a Holbeck engine for most of its life, and was built by the North British Loco Co in 1934. W. *Hubert Foster/ courtesy John W. Holroyd*

Scots' but the plan was taken over by events. The remaining unrebuilt 'Claughtons' were rapidly scrapped, the last one, No 5984, being withdrawn in 1935. Nor did the rebuilt ones fare much better. The first one, No 5986, was also withdrawn in 1935, and they had all gone a few years later except No 6004, which was reprieved by the war and surprisingly lasted in splendid isolation until well after it.

However, I was sufficiently literate and numerate for the next major change. By 1934, I was an avid observer of the railway scene at Bingley and spent many happy hours at the lineside near Bingley signalbox, at a spot known as 'Treacle Alley'. Don't ask me how it got its name, but it was part of a path that ran from the town to the parish church and went under the railway in a dank passage. It was a long passage too, as it passed underneath about four sidings as well as the two main lines. It was illuminated by a solitary gas lamp, which was a target for the attention of small boys who loved to extinguish the light so that they could scare old ladies who were on their way to the church. From the 'Alley' there was a good view along the line in both directions, and we soon learned that the

ringing of a bell in the signalbox denoted that a train would appear in the next few minutes. This heightened the excitement, of course. We quickly learned from older boys that when the signal arm dropped a train would soon appear, and we were alerted to the fact by the sound of the signal wires moving through the pulleys at the lineside.

We didn't know in those innocent days about the changes in the locomotive hierarchy of the LMS, and the younger ones among us had never even heard the name William Stanier. Imagine then our astonishment, when one of his new machines appeared on one of the Scottish expresses on a summer Saturday afternoon in 1934. It bore the number 5575. We gazed open-mouthed at this taper-boilered monster, this red 4-6-0 of such beautiful proportions, and we fell in love with 'Jubilees' at once. They were unnamed to start with, and it caused even greater excitement when they started to appear with names, which didn't happen until a couple of years later. What a splendid decision, which gave untold joy to generations of railway enthusiasts. This was especially the case on the Midland Division, where named engines were rare. And what names! Dominions and colonies to fire the imagination and swell our chests with pride of the Empire, followed by admirals, naval battles and warships to celebrate our national pride in the Royal Navy. The 'Jubilees' were both a history and a geography lesson. There were problems of pronunciation, of course. Udaipur, Seychelles, which we called Seychellees, Wemyss, Agamemnon, Leinster, to name just a few.

Before long the 'Jubilees' reigned supreme, but with such a large class, spread all around the LMS, it was going to take a long time to see them all.

Below: The 'Patriots' were very handsome and beautifully proportioned machines, seen to perfection in this official LMS photograph. Class 5XP No 5538 was named *Giggleswick* at the public school of the same name in 1938, and clearly polished up for the purpose. It was built at Crewe in 1933, nominally a rebuild of 'Claughton' No 6000, but was entirely new. The 'Claughton', LNWR No 15 and LMS No 6000, was built in 1920 and scrapped in 1933. *Ian Allan Library*

Above: Stanier Class 5P5F 4-6-0 No 5383 is seen at Plumpton Junction in BR days as 45383 shortly after leaving Ulverston with a local passenger train. This was a highly successful and versatile design, and continued to be built from 1934 to the early 1950s, eventually numbering 842 locomotives. They were fully at home on almost any type of train except heavy expresses. *Dr M. J. Andrews*

Below: A real veteran, a former Midland Railway Class 2F 0-6-0 No 3352 rests between duties at Skipton shed, date unknown. The LMS acquired 453 of these Johnson locos at grouping in 1923, and they seemed to go on for ever. *Courtesy John W. Holroyd*

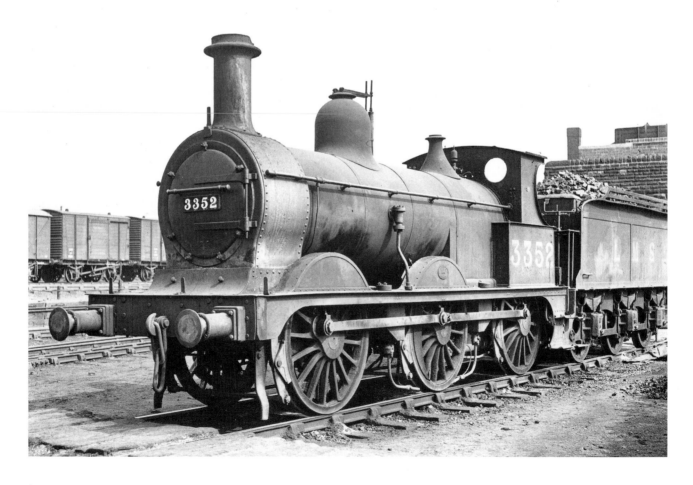

However, we did have three 'Patriots' by way of variety: Nos 5534 *E. Tootal Broadhurst*, 5535 *Sir Herbert Walker KCB* and 5538 *Giggleswick*. Broadhurst had been a director of the LNWR, and Sir Herbert Walker had spent part of his early career with the LNWR, although he was better known for his splendid and successful reign as general manager of the Southern Railway. Both names had a marvellous ring about them.

The years 1935 to 1937 were one continuous delight as more and more 'Jubilees' appeared. They hauled nearly all the Anglo-Scottish expresses. Saturdays in high summer were a source of intense interest and anticipation. Most of the expresses ran in duplicate, and there were relief trains too. Some of these brought in engines from Scottish sheds, and the passage of relief trains could be unpredictable. Owing to the frequent train service, they were often checked by signals and came past at low speed, giving us splendid views of unusual engines. Such excitement! It didn't do to be too far away from the lineside on a summer Saturday afternoon. The local library had a copy of *Bradshaw's Guide*, and it wasn't long before I learned how to use it and work out the approximate passing times through Bingley of all the timetabled expresses. We referred to them by their approximate passing times, eg 'What was on the five to five?'

During this period Stanier's mixed traffic 4-6-0s also started to appear. They bore the thrilling insignia '5P5F' on the cabside. We called them mixed-traffics and I never really cared for the later nickname of 'Black 5s'. It didn't do them justice somehow. Nos 5268-5272 were regular performers on the Birmingham–Carlisle and Glasgow fitted freights. For some reason at one period the Up evening train ran on the goods line from Marley Junction to Bingley, where the four tracks became two, and waited for a path. By walking through a couple of fields (farmers didn't mind in those days) it was possible to reach the lineside just opposite the engine and absorb every bit of detail, including that magic smell, a mixture of steam, smoke and hot oil. We called our hobby 'watching trains'. The term 'train-spotter' was surely of later vintage. That splendid journal of the RCTS (the Railway Correspondence & Travel Society), called *The Railway Observer*, referred to observers of the railway scene as 'railwayists', although I've come across the term 'railwayacs' as well. Train-watchers took in every detail of the railway scene; train-spotters were regarded as mere tickers of numbers.

About this time, 1935, I started to buy that splendid monthly journal *The Meccano Magazine*. It was a positive mine of information about engineering, scientific and transport developments, and always had a double-page spread about current railway affairs, including details of new engines and those withdrawn. It didn't take long to appreciate that the locomotive stock of the former LNWR was being slaughtered, especially its passenger engines. The Midland fared much better, especially for some reason its 0-4-4 tanks, which had started to be withdrawn as early as 1929. About 40 survived into BR days, and I think the last one to be withdrawn was No 1423, shedded at Bath, in 1960. It had been built about 1899.

Stanier's first brief had been to give the LMS a decent stock of modern engines for working express passenger trains, longer distance semi-fasts and express freight trains, and he accomplished this with his 'Jubilees' and mixed traffic 4-6-0s. They were intended to have the widest possible route availability. He soon turned his attention to tank engines used on commuter and suburban services. These were worked by a motley collection of generally elderly locomotives inherited from the pre-grouping companies. Such engines had very long lives, the Midland 0-4-4 tanks dating back to 1875 and the L&Y 2-4-2 tanks to 1889. The LNWR also had some very ancient-looking 2-4-2 tanks and 0-6-2 tanks, dating back to 1890 and 1898 respectively. They were generally adequate for the work they had to do. The company also had some slightly more modern, and larger, tank engines. Fifty 4-4-2 'Precursor' tanks appeared from Crewe in 1906, and 47 larger machines, 4-6-2s, came out in 1910. They were generally regarded as excellent machines, but they did not escape the slaughter of LNWR locos. They were all withdrawn by 1940/41.

The LMS had introduced a class of 2-6-4 tanks with parallel boilers in 1927 and they were very successful. They were numbered 2300-2424 and were turned out in batches until as late as 1934. Stanier produced a taper-boilered version in 1934, starting with a three-cylinder design for use on the LT&S, which had nothing larger than 4-4-2 tanks. These engines, numbered 2500 to 2536, were also an instant success, and a modified two-cylinder version was built in large numbers from 1936

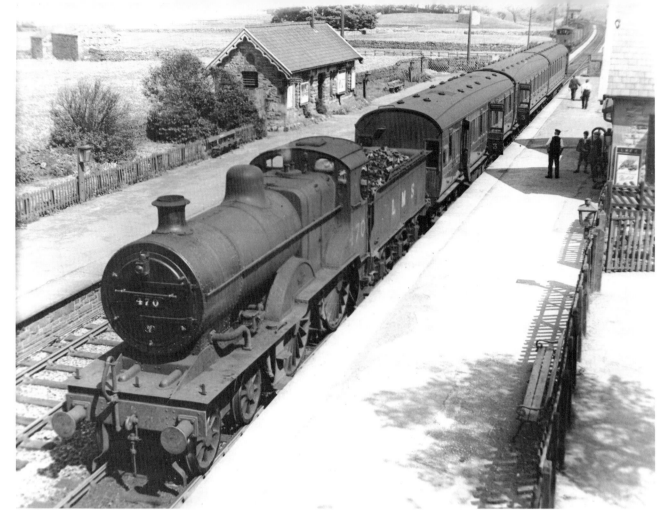

Above: A rural idyll, with Class 2P 4-4-0 No 470 basking in the sun at Hawes station and waiting the 'Off', before setting away to Garsdale and Hellifield (its home shed) in this undated view. Business does not appear to be brisk. The engine was rebuilt in its final form at Derby in 1922. Hawes was an end-on junction between the North Eastern Railway line from Northallerton and the Midland Railway from Garsdale. *Author's Collection*

Below: A pair of Fowler's very workmanlike parallel-boilered Class 4P 2-6-4Ts rest awhile from their banking duties at Shap summit, and await a path to return downhill to Tebay. They were built at Derby in 1933 and 1934 respectively. Even banking engines were kept clean in those days. *Eric Treacy*

onwards. The North British Locomotive Co built almost 100 in 1936, and Derby also built a large number the same year. Construction continued, although at a slower pace, until well into the war, and was resumed after it. The class was so successful that the LNER and the Southern also built some after nationalisation, and the design was adopted as the BR standard 2-6-4 tank, a great tribute to Sir William Stanier's design. Very few of the pre-war 2-6-4 tanks came to the Midland Division, the great majority going to the Western Division as replacements of the 'Precursor' and 46-Ts. The Central Division received about 50 in 1938/39. Manningham received Nos 2545 and 2549, which tended to be used on the Bradford-Leeds portion of the St Pancras and Bristol expresses. North of Shipley the reliable L&Y 2-4-2 tanks continued to hold sway.

Private locomotive builders received large orders from the LMS in the 1934-37 period to assist with the modernisation of LMS stock. The money for this was provided by the government under a guaranteed loan scheme at a low rate of interest to relieve unemployment and stimulate industry generally. Armstrong Whitworth received very large orders for '5P5F' mixed-traffics, delivering 347 in 1935-37, possibly the largest order ever given to a private builder. Indeed, Armstrong Whitworth were not primarily locomotive builders, although they had turned out 50 Class 4F 0-6-0s for the Midland in 1921. Vulcan Foundry and North British also benefited from the government's scheme. Naturally, I knew nothing of this at the time, but enjoyed picking out details on the maker's plates.

Finally, it was the turn of the freight fleet to receive attention. Express freight trains through Bingley were now in the hands of Horwich 'Moguls' and 4-6-0 mixed-traffics, but the slower freights were still entrusted to 0-6-0s of all vintages. Strangely, double-heading was unusual, but speeds were low and loads moderate. This is not to say that Midland and standard '4Fs' were incapable of reasonable speeds. That was not the case, because they were widely used on excursion trains and summer specials. Excursion trains to Morecambe were big business, and one of my earliest memories is of being taken to Morecambe on a Sunday School outing, and being intrigued by all the primroses and rabbits in cuttings. I also remember falling over in the sea fully dressed. I don't remember what teacher said! The Morecambe excursions were usually formed of non-corridor stock, which brought its own problems. Many excursionists spent most of the day drinking, or so it seemed, and Promenade station had very

Below: The first of a batch of Stanier's Class 4P two-cylindered tank engines, No 2537, which first appeared in the mid-1930s and continued to be built in their hundreds until replaced by the very similar BR design in 1952. A highly successful and very attractive design.
Ian Allan Library

Above: A reminder that Hellifield was once an important and busy junction. Looking in the Up direction, probably in the late 1930s, we can see the engine shed, North Junction signalbox, the coaling stage, and the commodious station, with bays at both ends. The station had a wide range of facilities, including a large refreshment room. Many of the Scottish expresses stopped here to cater for passengers from Lancashire via Blackburn and Clitheroe. *W. Hubert Foster/ courtesy John W. Holroyd*

Below: Still at Hellifield, LMS Standard Compound 4-4-0 No 929 stands outside the shed in what appears to be pristine condition, probably just delivered from its makers the Vulcan Foundry in 1927. It carries no shed plate. *W. Hubert Foster/courtesy John W. Holroyd*

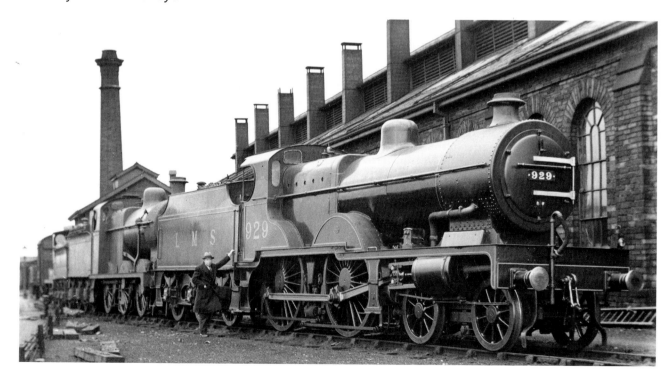

Above: No 6978, an ex-LNWR 4-6-2T is one of the same class as Nos 6969 and 6973, which were shedded at Hellifield in the early/mid-1930s. They were used to assist expresses 'on the steeper parts of the Carlisle road'. The class was introduced in 1910. *Author's Collection*

extensive Gentlemen's toilets, as was the practice at similar seaside resorts up and down the country. These excursion trains wended their way homewards at quite a gentle pace, first stop Hellifield, which also had commodious toilets for very good reasons. I think that mother shielded my eyes as we entered Hellifield station so that I wasn't terrified by the mad rush. It must have been quite a job getting everyone back in the train, but time was not of the essence. The worst part of the journey for some was being held up at Settle Junction, before Hellifield, whilst a couple of expresses and fitted freights passed to and from the Carlisle route. I always hoped that we would be stopped there, but I hadn't been drinking.

I was intrigued by two strange-looking machines which were often to be seen outside Hellifield shed and which turned out to be of LNWR origin, or so older schoolboys told me. They were 4-6-2 tanks Nos 6969 and 6973, bearing 20G shedplates. Apparently they had been transferred there to assist expresses on the steeper parts of the Carlisle road, sometimes coupled in front, and sometimes in rear, and became redundant when the Class 5XP 'Jubilees' appeared between 1934 and 1936. They were withdrawn shortly afterwards. These LNWR tank engines were used regularly on banking duties from Oxenholme and Tebay.

However, back to new engines for heavy freight.

As readers of *Meccano Magazine* we already knew that something big was on the way, so when the first 2-8-0s, numbered 8000 onwards, appeared occasionally through Bingley in 1935 we were not surprised, but nevertheless we were greatly impressed. Only a dozen were built in 1935, but Vulcan Foundry received a big order and produced about 70 in 1936. Crewe took over at a more gentle pace and there was a small annual programme which continued right through the war. No 8125 was the last one to appear in 1939. They were all shedded on the Midland Division to reduce double-heading and improve freight train loads and speeds. The standard Class 7F 0-8-0s on the Midland were then transferred to the Central Division to replace life-expired 0-8-0s of L&Y vintage, which were being withdrawn.

After 1937, the frantic excitement of the last few years subsided somewhat. The huge building programmes for 2-6-2 tanks, 'Jubilees' and '5P5F' mixed-traffics were complete and no more new types appeared. One event which we knew nothing about was the closure of the Midland shed at Durran Hill, Carlisle, on 15 February 1936, with all its diagrams being taken over by Carlisle Kingmoor. This gave access to a much greater selection of engines from that end of the line than had previously been the case. By the end of 1937, Kingmoor had 14 'Jubilees', which all worked to Leeds at times. The 8.5am all stations from Carlisle to Hellifield, then semi-fast to Leeds, was a regular Kingmoor turn, monopolised by No 5716 *Swiftsure* for quite a while. Holbeck also had 14: Nos 5560/2/8, 5598, 5619-22, 5658-60 and 5724-26. Despite that, compounds still appeared occasionally on the Anglo-Scottish expresses, but they were now mainly employed on the Leeds/Bradford to Morecambe/Carnforth trains.

The annual week at the seaside, or in the Lake District, provided plenty of railway interest as the journeys were almost always taken by train. Unfortunately all my records of those journeys and holidays have long since disappeared, but I can remember a number of highlights. Holidays at

Colwyn Bay were always a delight. When playing on the sands palled, there was always the busy North Wales main line just behind the shore to provide interest, and I recall seeing an ancient-looking LNWR tank in the middle of four coaches, ie pushing two and pulling two. Hiking holidays in the Lake District, which were undertaken every Whitsuntide, provided excitement for that portion of the journey over the West Coast main line between Carnforth and Oxenholme. Our train was waiting in the Windermere platform at Oxenholme for a while, this would be 1938, and I was hoping

Below: Ais Gill summit, with Wild Boar Fell in the background. The Compound, No 1132 of Carlisle Kingmoor, has just piloted, in this late 1930s view, a southbound 'Jubilee'-hauled express to Ais Gill, and was then detached and put into the Up loop to await its return to Carlisle. The train engine was Holbeck's No 5594 *Bhopal.*
W. Hubert Foster/courtesy of John W. Holroyd

A Railwayman's Odyssey

Above: Back at Bell Busk. A 'Patriot', No 5992, heads a Down Anglo-Scottish express with two teak LNER coaches next to the engine. The train is likely to be the 12.00 noon from London St Pancras to Glasgow St Enoch, which is shown in the public timetable as conveying 'Through carriages to Edinburgh Waverley', No 5992 seen in the photograph became No 5515 in the 1934 renumbering, and was named *Caernarvon* in 1939. 'Claughton' No 5992 was officially listed as being rebuilt in October 1932, but the engine seen in the photograph was a new build in October 1932, and the Claughton No 5992 was withdrawn in the same month. *Author's Collection (probably W. Hubert Foster)*

Below: An official view of 'Coronation' class streamlined Pacific No 6222 *Queen Mary,* which caused me such excitement when it rushed past at Oxenholme in 1937 whilst our train for Windermere stood at the other side of the island platform. This was the LMS response to the LNER. *Real Photographs*

A Railwayman's Odyssey

and hoping that a Pacific would come along. I was standing in the corridor anxiously looking up and down the main line when I heard the sound of a down express approaching. Then this silver and blue apparition burst into view — No 6222 *Queen Mary*. I was overjoyed. On the way home from that holiday it had been arranged that we would join a Keswick-Leeds return excursion at Penrith. We arrived at the station by bus from Pooley Bridge with some time to spare, to be greeted by No 6210 *Lady Patricia* and No 6212 *Duchess of Kent* on successive trains. I couldn't get home fast enough to tick off all three. At Arnside 4-6-4 tank No 11113, remembered both for its bulk and its intriguing number, was seen on the Hincaster Branch. But there were disappointments. During our family holidays at Morecambe I was never allowed to go to Hest Bank on the West Coast main line. The nearest I got was Happy Mount Park, from where you could see the trains in the distance but were too far away to read the numbers. Talk about the torments of Tantalus! A school friend had spent his entire holiday watching trains at Hest Bank and made us intensely envious with his stories of Pacifics and 'Scots'. I got to Hest Bank

by myself two or three years later, but that's another story.

I wouldn't want to give the impression that we had no other interests than watching trains. During the summer months we played cricket in the park and on bits of spare ground, and we cycled all over. In the winter months there was Meccano and the model railway. It was only a Hornby tinplate set, but with a bit of ingenuity and imagination you could achieve almost anything. There were also war clouds looming, to provide more interest, or at least that's how we saw it as boys. And it would change the railway scene. But again, that's another story.

Below: Whilst waiting at Penrith for our train home after the same holiday, what should roar through the station but 6212 *Duchess of Kent,* one of the 'Princess Royal' class of Pacifics. *Ian Allan Library*

A Railwayman's Odyssey

Two

TRAIN-SPOTTING IN WARTIME — THE EXCITEMENT

The Railway Scene at Bingley

July 1940, school holidays. The old churchyard at Bingley. A splendid place to watch trains. The churchyard had been unused since the beginning of the century and it ran down to the edge of the railway line, from where there was a very good view of the line in both directions. And the wall was just the right height for sitting on comfortably. You could see the signals in both directions too. An ideal spot and quite private; no angry verger coming along to chase you off. A few pals and I spent many happy hours there that summer, playing among the old graves and climbing trees when there were no trains about.

It seems strange in retrospect. There we were enjoying ourselves, yet 250 miles away in the south of England the most astonishing air battles were taking place which ultimately determined whether we grew up speaking English or German. But here, in the north of England, life seemed to carry on much as usual, so far as schoolboys were concerned.

Even the railway scene hadn't changed much since before the war. There weren't as many expresses, but there were occasional troop specials which often brought unusual locos from strange sheds. They were exciting. The Anglo-Scottish expresses had declined to one each way per day — the 10.0am St Pancras to Glasgow St Enoch and Edinburgh Waverley and a corresponding Up train. In addition we had a 10.30am Leeds City to Glasgow and a return working at 3.50pm from

Below: 'Jubilee' Class 5XP 4-6-0 No 5619 *Nigeria* pauses at Carlisle Kingmoor shed (12A) between duties in around 1937. She was one of the Holbeck (20A) group of 'Jubilees' for many years, but had not yet received a domed boiler in this photograph. *Railway Correspondence & Travel Society*

Glasgow. There were two night expresses in each direction but we never saw those. Occasionally we might hear them (I could hear them from my bedroom but I was usually fast asleep) and wonder what the engine was, thinking that it would be one that we 'wanted'. All these trains were usually hauled by '5XP' 'Jubilees', of which Holbeck (20A) had a large stud, or one of the three 'Patriots' there: Nos 5534 *E. Tootal Broadhurst*, 5535 *Sir Herbert Walker KCB*, and 5538 *Giggleswick*. Perhaps I ought to explain the significance of the designation '5XP'. The figure '5' denoted the power, in a range from 1 to 7, 7 being the most powerful. 'XP' meant designed to work express passenger trains. They were painted red too. Very exciting to small boys (of all ages).

However, there were other trains that were '5XP' hauled. The 8.5am all-stations except Saltaire from Carlisle to Bradford Forster Square must have ranked as one of the slowest trains in the country. It called at no fewer than 31 stations, of which 21 are still open, in its 105-mile, four-hour journey, and often had a Carlisle Kingmoor (12A) 'Jubilee'. It returned from Forster Square at 12.57pm on a

Below: Stanier Class 4P 2-6-4T No 42154 halts in front of Wennington Junction signalbox. The line from Leeds and Bradford to Morecambe and Carnforth divided here, and most trains from Leeds and Bradford carried two portions, dividing here. In the opposite direction; the portion that arrived first was set back into a dead-end platform line where the second portion backed on to it. Wennington station and the signalman could be quite busy at times, but the Morecambe line closed many years ago and Wennington is now a sleepy little unstaffed halt. *Ian Allan Library*

A Railwayman's Odyssey

stopper to Hawes, but I believe the loco came off at Hellifield and worked forward later. It wasn't a very exciting journey for a '5XP'. Then, the last train from Morecambe (at 6.50pm) to Leeds, attaching a portion from Carnforth at Wennington, frequently had a 'Jubilee'. It followed the 3.50pm Glasgow to Leeds from Skipton, and after we had seen those two expresses pass, it was time to go home. In those days we had what was known as 'double summertime', when the clocks went forward an extra hour, so there were some very long, light evenings. Finally, there was a wartime extra MWFO — the 1.40pm Forces Leave train from St Pancras to Stranraer Harbour, which passed through Bingley just on 8.0pm. Between Leeds and Carlisle it called only at Skipton. For some reason we always expected this train to have something special at the front end, but it usually had a Holbeck '5XP'.

There is no doubt that '5XP's were the favourite engines, and fortunately I have fairly comprehensive records for the second half of 1941. However, Holbeck did not have a monopoly of the expresses north of Leeds, no doubt influenced by wartime conditions. 'Jubilees' from other Midland sheds, such as Kentish Town (14B), Bristol (22A), Derby (17A) and Millhouses ((19B) were often seen, and occasionally Scottish engines caused excitement, such as No 5584 *North West Frontier* from Polmadie (27A) on the 3.50pm from Glasgow on 18 July and No 5692 *Cyclops* also from Polmadie on a relief to the Up Glasgow-London on

1 August. In fact, this continued a peacetime tradition; the second part of the Up 'Thames-Clyde' on Saturdays had often had a Scottish 'Jubilee'. Probably the outstanding 'Jubilee' sighting that summer was No 5564 *New South Wales* from Willesden (1A) on the afternoon St Pancras-Glasgow on 5 September.

However, what were among the most exciting events of all that summer, and completely unexpected, were the appearance of 'Royal Scots', No 6104 *Scottish Borderer* on the morning Leeds-Glasgow express on 24 July, followed next day by No 6162 *Queen's Westminster Rifleman* (Preston — 10B) on the afternoon St Pancras-Glasgow. This really had us all jumping up and down. Nothing like this had ever happened before. No 6162 was seen several times that week, and from then on the 'Scots' began to put in occasional appearances. No 6107 *Argyll and Sutherland Highlander* (12A — Kingmoor) was recorded on 9 November 1941 on the Down afternoon Scottish express. Perhaps it was a trial to see if 'Scots' could take heavy loads unaided, because, with the heavy wartime loads over the Settle-Carlisle line, double-heading was not uncommon; in fact it was quite a regular

Below: 'Royal Scot' class 4-6-0 No 6104 *Scottish Borderer* is seen here in its early life without smoke deflectors. They were fitted in the early 1930s following an accident.
Locomotive Publishing Co

Above: The rebuilding with larger boilers of 'Jubilees' Nos 5735 and 5736 (*Comet* and *Phoenix)* in 1942 caused great excitement among the local train-watchers. The two engines, originally built at Crewe in 1936, were transferred to Holbeck (20A) for working the Scottish expresses over the hilly Settle & Carlisle line. The plan to make these changes had been developed before the outbreak of war, and was by no means a straightforward operation, which is possibly why no more 'Jubilees' were modified in this way. *Ian Allan Library*

Below: Standard Compound No 1098, built at Derby in 1925, is seen at one of Hubert Foster's favourite locations — the four-track section between Bingley and Marley Junction in probably the early 1930s. It is conveying a motley collection of carriages, 14 or 15 in all, and the guard's brake van at No 6 may suggest that this is a train for Morecambe and Carnforth.
W. Hubert Foster/courtesy of John W. Holroyd

Right: A Midland Class 2F 0-6-0, No 3554, with a well-filled tender, heads north from Skipton with a heavy load. It was built at Derby in 1897.
Eric Treacy

A Railwayman's Odyssey

Above: A timeless scene: a local train waits in a platform at a country station whilst two or three passengers alight. The station is Ormside on the Settle & Carlisle line between Appleby and Kirkby Stephen, which one of the quietest on the line with a very sparse train service. It closed to passengers on 2 June 1952, along with the adjacent and equally quiet Crosby Garrett. A commodious house was provided for the Stationmaster and his family. The engine, No 720, is a Class 3P 4-4-0, rebuilt at Derby in 1923 and shedded at Holbeck (20A). It survived until after the war. The passengers have the luxury of travelling in Mr Stanier's very comfortable corridor coaches. *Author's Collection*

occurrence on the Down afternoon express. The assisting engine was usually a Hellifield or Lancaster Green Ayre compound, and looking back I wonder if the pilot engine was taken off at Ais Gill and worked back light. The Up expresses were rarely seen double-headed through Bingley, but possibly they were sometimes assisted as far as Ais Gill as in Midland days. During 1942 'Jubilees' Nos 5735 *Comet* and 5736 *Phoenix* were rebuilt with 250lb taper boilers and allocated to Leeds. This was another completely unexpected development, and had us all agog. They were often seen on the afternoon Glasgow-Leeds express, which conveyed a string of loaded milk tanks from Appleby, forming quite a heavy load. This was the precursor to the eventual rebuilding of all the 'Royal Scots' and many 'Patriots'. Several of the rebuilt 'Scots' came to Holbeck.

The other mainstays of the passenger train service through Bingley were the Leeds to Morecambe and Carnforth services, leaving Leeds at 6.10am (used by us for exciting train-spotting trips to Carnforth and Hest Bank), 10.40am and 5.42pm. There was also an 8.33am from Bradford Forster Square to Morecambe. Compounds had a virtual monopoly of these services. Holbeck (20A) had about a dozen, whilst Manningham (20E), Hellifield (20G) and Lancaster (20H) had about half-a-dozen each. Local services were mainly in the hands of ex-L&Y 2-4-2 tanks, supplemented by Class 2P 4-4-0s. One

exception was an early evening train from either Morecambe or Carnforth which roared through Bingley non-stop behind a Class 3 Belpaire 4-4-0 of Midland vintage. As it approached, the engine seemed to rock from side to side and it created a slightly alarming spectacle with its coupling rods flashing round and round, and smoke and steam shooting out of the chimney. I believe they were Holbeck engines. They were built by the former Midland Railway, and originally there were 80 of them, a mixture of superheated and saturated, but by 1940 their number had dwindled to about half. They were originally numbered 700 to 779.

We must not, of course, forget the 'Ressie', the 5.13pm Residential Express from Bradford Forster Square to Morecambe Promenade, which it reached at 7.5pm. This train, and its return working which left Morecambe at 7.42am, was of ancient lineage, and had been provided to convey Bradford's wealthy wool merchants to their seaside homes each evening. How times change. In Midland Railway days, at the turn of the century, the evening

Below: Carlisle's fleet of Hughes/Fowler 2-6-0s were a regular sight on the Carlisle-Leeds section in the 1930s and later. No 2830, built at Horwich in 1929, heads a semi-fitted freight through Bingley, at some time in the 1930s. *W. Hubert Foster/ Author's Collection*

train accomplished the journey in just under an hour and a half, calling only at Shipley to attach a portion from Leeds, and at Keighley. Similar timings applied right up to 1939, but the two portions were then joined together at Skipton. There is no longer a 'Ressie', mainly because there are no longer any wealthy Bradford wool merchants, or if there are they live at Baildon or Ilkley. If you want to travel from Leeds to Morecambe today you might find yourself in a rackety 'Pacer', rather like an old bus body on a four-wheeled wagon chassis. What a comedown! *Sic transit gloria mundi*, as our Latin teacher would have said, glaring at us.

There were lots of freight trains, usually hauled by one of the ubiquitous Class 4F 0-6-0s, but '3F' and even '2F' Midland 0-6-0s were often to be seen. On the faster freights, Hughes/Fowler 2-6-0s had been regular engines for many years, supplemented by Stanier two-cylinder 4-6-0s, Class 5P5F, which later became known as mixed-traffics, and later still as 'Black 5s'. You can tell someone's age-bracket by the name they give to those engines. Saltley's Nos 5268-72 were regular performers on the Birmingham-Glasgow fitted freights and associated return workings. Those workings continued until the end of steam, but towards the end '9F' 2-10-0s were used. However, in 1941 we had no concept of anything as gigantic as a 2-10-0 (although they were to be seen towards the end of the war).

Our Wanderings Begin

During the long summer holidays of 1941 we travelled far and wide, but the precursor was a visit to Leeds on Saturday 5 July. Leeds was a good station on which to train-spot, as all the LMS trains came in from the west end, either into the Midland side or the LNWR side. The Midland part used to be called Wellington and the LNWR part was Leeds (New), but just before the war the Midland side was rebuilt and renamed Leeds City (North). The LNWR side became Leeds City (South). You could observe everything from the far end of the Midland island platform, Nos 5 and 6, or from the long platform at City (South), which I think was No 11.

We took our packet of sandwiches and a bottle of pop in a haversack, and went to Leeds on the train. The whole day was spent either on platforms 5/6 or on 11, and there seemed to be a constant procession

of trains. Undoubtedly the LNWR side provided most excitement, because almost every engine we saw there was a stranger to us. Farnley Junction's stud of 'Jubilees' was a real delight, supplemented by others from Edge Hill and other Lancashire sheds. We didn't see any 'Scots', which became common on the LNWR section in later years. Altogether, we saw 84 engines, of the following classes:

Class 2P 4-4-0	5	Class 4F 0-6-0	4
Stanier 2-6-4T	3	0-6-0T	2
'Jubilees'	17	Hughes 2-6-0	2
Compounds	14	Class 3F 0-6-0	1
Stanier 2-6-2T	5	L&Y 2-4-2	7
'Patriots'	1	L&Y 0-6-0	1
Class 3P 4-4-0	4	Std 0-8-0	1
Stanier 0-4-4T	2	Stanier 2-8-0	1
5P5F 4-6-0	14		

We came home tired, hungry and dirty, but very happy. We'd seen 17 'Jubilees', which came from the following sheds:

Edge Hill (8A)	1 (No 5671 *Prince Rupert*)		
Derby (17A)	2	Bristol (22A)	2
Millhouses (19B)	1	Farnley Junc (25G)	3
Holbeck (20A)	7	Newton Heath (26A)	1

Exactly half of the engines we saw were Staniers, which indicated the massive change which had taken place in LMS locomotive stock in those few hectic years before the war.

Although our main interest was the LMS, there were plenty of LNER locos to be seen coming in from York and from the Harrogate direction, which in those days was on the main line from Northallerton. We saw two of the very handsome 'Shire' class 4-4-0s, including No 234 *Yorkshire*, which I believe was the prototype for a Hornby Gauge 'O' model. We also saw no fewer than 10 'Hunt' class 4-4-0s, which reflected the hunting counties served by the LNER system. Although there were no Pacifics, a couple of 'V2' 2-6-2s put in an appearance, Nos 4817 and 4818, the latter bearing the lengthy name *St Peter's School, York, A.D. 627*. Gresley's green engines were very attractive and gave us the incentive to visit York a couple of weeks later, to see a stream of Pacifics.

Above: Another of Hubert Foster's pictures taken on the line between Bingley and Marley Junction. 'Jubilee' No 45606 *Falkland Islands* cruises along with a light load of LMS coaches, possibly the early evening Morecambe 'Residential'. The engine carries the shed code 24L — Carnforth. The very neat track and ballast merit our admiration. *W. Hubert Foster/courtesy John W. Holroyd*

Below: Hubert Foster spent much of his spare time at Bell Busk, where he had a relative. Here is a picture of the signalbox and station. The station closed in 1959, but at one time dealt with large crowds visiting Malhamdale, for which it was the railhead. *W. Hubert Foster/ Author's Collection*

A Railwayman's Odyssey

Carnforth Becomes a Mecca

As soon as the lengthy summer holidays started (which in my case lasted about seven weeks) our travels began in earnest, my parents having agreed, with what appeared to be some misgivings, that I was now old enough at fourteen to go off train-spotting with some friends and not get ourselves locked up by the police as spies. In fact, no one ever bothered us as we stood at the lineside or on station platforms earnestly recording the movements of all sorts of trains, including troop trains and munitions specials. Fresh-faced boys in schoolcaps didn't look like spies. Common sense ruled the day. Cheap Day return tickets were still, surprisingly, available and were not withdrawn until 5 October 1942.

Wednesday 30 July 1941 took us to Carnforth. This was like a visit to paradise. We had hardly alighted from the train (the 6.10am from Leeds), which arrived in the F&M bay platform at Carnforth, than we were greeted by the hugely impressive sight of two 'Scots' double-heading a long parcels train standing in the Up Wessie (LNWR) platform. That was just the beginning of

a stream of '5P5F' 4-6-0s, 'Jubilees', 'Scots' and Pacifics, hardly any of which had we ever seen before. The only representatives of the once proud and mighty LNWR were 0-8-0s, which chugged through gently at quite low speed on big loads.

We knew when an important express was due, because there was a long pause in the stream of freight trains. The expresses then came in a comparative flood, starting with the 11.0am Birmingham to Glasgow and Edinburgh at about 2.30pm, followed by the Down 'Royal Scot', the 10.5am Euston to Perth and the 10.25 Euston to Carlisle (with Barrow and Windermere portions). This had been preceded about an hour earlier by a similar flurry of activity on the Up road, with the

Below: One of Mirfield's Class 4P Fowler 2-6-4Ts, No 2405, is being fettled up ready for its next job. It was built at Derby in 1933. This was a very successful design, and a worthy forerunner to Stanier's taper-boilered version. *Author's Collection*

Above: The Lancashire & Yorkshire Railway had a huge stud of these sturdy 0-6-0s, like many companies in the 19th century. They were built in the company's works at Horwich from 1889 onwards and, as numbered by the LMS they ran from 12086 to 12619. Many survived until the 1950s. They were classified by the LMS as 3F. Here 12362 (renumbered 52362) heads a long train of sheeted open wagons along what appears to be the West Coast main line. It was built at Horwich in 1897 and was shedded at 23B — Aintree. *Courtesy John W. Holroyd*

Below: 'Royal Scot' class 4-6-0 No 46156 *The South Wales Borderer,* in unrebuilt form in early BR days, takes a semi-fitted train load of vans past Farington Junction, on the West Coast main line just south of Preston. This was one of our favourite train-spotting locations in 1941/42 because you could also see the former L&Y route from Lostock Hall towards Liverpool which went over the LNWR main line. *Author's Collection*

Birmingham, the 'Royal Scot' and the Perth. These were very long trains by today's standards, often loading up to 15 coaches. After this spell of intense excitement there was a lull before the procession of freights started again. We always knew when a non-stopper was coming on the LNWR side, because it would be announced by the continuous ring of a bell as a warning to stand clear.

We spent 10 hours at Carnforth, and were very reluctant to leave on the 7.8pm train home. I can't remember visiting the famous refreshment room, but I expect we went in for a cup of tea and a meat pie. Sandwiches and meat pies were the staple diet. We couldn't wait to return to Carnforth again, and we were back there a week later.

However, having had our fill of the LNWR for a while we decided we'd have a change. We had heard of the attractions of Mirfield from the local train-watching fraternity so decided to give it a try. We cycled there from our homes in Bingley, a distance of about 20 miles, via Bradford, then a long pull up Manchester Road, which was cobbled and had tram lines in those days, and on through Heckmondwike. It was a route we came to know well on repeat visits in the next two or three years, and provided a cheap day out. The following Sunday we visited Low Moor and Mirfield sheds (Sunday was usually a good day for unofficial shed visits) and had our fill of L&Y Class 3F 0-6-0s, L&Y 2-4-2 tanks, L&Y saddle tanks and standard Class 7F 0-8-0s. Freight sheds were usually fairly easy to get round on Sundays, but we never tried them on weekdays. There were too many intimidating-looking men around in bowlers.

The lure of the LNWR West Coast main line was too strong to resist for long but, on the next occasion, we went to Hest Bank and played cricket on a level grassy patch on the foreshore. When a train was heard approaching the bat was flung to the ground and everyone raced up the slope to the lineside. We had a field day — two 'Patriots', 13 'Jubilees', 10 'Scots' and six Pacifics — No 6208 *Princess Helena Victoria* (5A Crewe North), *No 6221 Queen Elizabeth* (27A Polmadie) and four 'Cities', Nos 6235/6 and 6242/3, respectively *Birmingham, Bradford, Glasgow* and *Lancaster* (all 1B Camden). What heaven! The 'Cities' had been built at Crewe in 1938 and 1939, and more of them were turned out at fairly lengthy intervals right up to nationalisation. The ones we saw were, of course, still in their streamlined cladding. I was particularly fond of the non-streamlined 'Duchesses' Nos 6230-34; they were massively impressive.

We Discover Farington Junction

However, it was back to school all too soon, but we had a final fling at Autumn Half-Term 1941. I can't recall how we discovered this particular spot, but there was a small patch of waste ground surrounded by houses overlooking the LNWR main line just south of Preston near Farington Junction. It was immediately north of an overbridge carrying the L&Y line from Lostock Hall towards Liverpool, and on the Up side of the LNWR main line. The visit took place on 1 November 1941. It entailed another early start for the train to Skipton, then a Skipton to Manchester train as far as the quaintly named Rose Grove. Here there were large marshalling yards and an engine shed. A quick five-minute change into the 9.7am all-stations to Preston via the Padiham loop (long since gone) and we disembarked at Preston Junction station (also long since gone, together with the L&Y direct line into Preston from Bamber Bridge). Finally, a mile walk through the streets. Our feet had wings, fuelled by the anticipation of forthcoming excitements.

The journey from Colne to Preston Junction was our first real excursion into L&Y territory. It was one long stream of goods yards, carriage sidings, large stations and marshalling yards, but only one engine shed (Rose Grove). Colne was our first surprise, with its very extensive carriage sidings, followed quickly by Nelson (at one time the largest cotton spinning town in the world), Burnley, Accrington and Blackburn. At each one there were L&Y 0-6-0 saddle tanks and trip engines, usually L&Y 0-6-0s. I seem to remember that Accrington's shed (24A) was on the Manchester line, and Blackburn was served by Lower Darwen shed (24D), also on a Manchester line. Neither was visible from the Preston line. Today, Colne station consists of a single unstaffed platform at the end of a long single line, and the journey to Preston is not for the faint-hearted, bouncing up and down in a 'Pacer'. Some of the mills may still be there, but they no longer spin cotton, and the row upon row of workers' terraces no longer house mill workers. It is a sad decline, but evolutionarily inevitable.

My records of the day are incomplete, but they reveal that we saw the following:

L&Y 2-4-2T	9	L&Y 0-6-0ST	2
5P5F 4-6-0	8	2-6-0 Hughes	4
Std 4F 0-6-0	1	Std 4-4-0 2P	3
L&Y 0-6-0	8	L&Y 4-6-0	1
2-6-4T Stan.	9	2-6-0 Taper	1
Mid 3F 0-6-0	1	Std 7F 0-8-0	5
L&Y 0-8-0	3	LNW 0-8-0	2
2-6-4T PB	1	2-8-0 8F	1
Compound	2		

Details of express passenger engines have unfortunately been lost. Here is a moral for younger readers. Keep your records carefully — you may need them 70 years later!

I recall it being a very cold day and we took refuge in a guard's brake van parked next to the buffer stops in Lostock Junction sidings, just by the bridge, and had our 'lunch' there. Railway trespass is severely frowned upon these days, because it is so often accompanied by vandalism and stone throwing, but like most boys we were reasonably well behaved and generally tolerated.

By 1941 the L&Y Section of the LMS had lost almost all its former L&Y express passenger locos. Just 10 Hughes 4-6-0s remained, all shedded at Blackpool. One of W. A. Stanier's masterpieces, the '5P5F' 4-6-0s, had almost completely replaced them. The same was true of the LNWR main line, in that nearly all its former LNW express engines had gone, except for the lone survivor No 6004, reprieved by the war. A few 'George V' 4-4-0s and 'Prince of Wales' 4-6-0s remained, mainly to be seen on secondary duties on cross country routes south of Crewe, and in North Wales. I only ever saw one 'George V' No 25350 (formerly *India* but without nameplates), and that was at Crewe. It was a Chester engine. 'Prince of Wales' locos were a little more common, several being shedded at Stafford (5C). Most of the others were at Bletchley. The 'Royal Scots', followed by Stanier's 4-6-0s

Below: Only four 'Claughtons' survived until the outbreak of war: Nos 5946, 6004, 6017 and 6023. The class of 130 engines suffered wholesale withdrawal in the mid-1930s in the Stanier onslaught, to be replaced nominally by the 'Patriots' and by the 'Jubilees'. No 5948 *Baltic* pictured here in all its pristine glory, succumbed in 1937. It was built in 1917 and received a larger boiler in 1928. They were handsome-looking engines, but the only one I ever recorded was the unnamed 6004, seen on a visit to Liverpool during the summer holidays of 1942.
(no attribution)

A Railwayman's Odyssey

and Pacifics, were worthy replacements, but it has always been a source of considerable surprise to me that the LMS did not reboiler more 'Jubilees' to bring them into power Class 6 and reduce the amount of costly double-heading. Would it be scandalous to suggest that what the LMS needed were 50 of the LNER's 'V2s'?

Changes in LMS Motive Power 1941-42

There was very little new building in 1941, the priority being maintenance and repairs. Also, many of the workshops were engaged in armaments production. So far as I can tell, only 10 new engines were built in 1941 — Class 8F 2-8-0s Nos 8136 to 8145, built at Crewe. Fifty prewar Stanier 2-8-0s had been requisitioned by the War Department (WD) and were replaced in 1942 by another 50 from the North British Loco Works, Nos 8176 to 8225. North British and Beyer Peacock also built a large batch of 2-8-0s in 1940/42 which were taken over by the WD for use overseas. Subsequently, Stanier 2-8-0s were built in large numbers in other companies' workshops, as well as at Crewe. They were a highly successful design. The only other new building which I can trace was a batch of 10 2-6-4 tanks at Derby in 1942, Nos 2663 to 2672.

Needless to say, in view of extra wartime demands very few engines were scrapped in the first few years of the war, and quite a large number which had been withdrawn before the war but not

Above: The LNWR 'Prince of Wales' class of 4P 4-6-0s fared a little better. The first one appeared in 1911, and building continued both in Crewe and at contractors (with a break during the war) until 1922, by which time there were 245 members of the class. Continuing the LNWR tradition, 102 were named. They were numbered 5600 to 5844 by the LMS. As with the Claughtons, almost the entire class was withdrawn in the mid-thrties, and only 16 remained in stock by 1939. Six locos which had been withdrawn but not scrapped were reinstated. During the war, almost all the survivors were located at Bletchley, with a few at Stafford, but after the war, they were fairly quickly put to the cutter's torch. Loco 25797, seen here at Slaithwaite on an express from Leeds to Manchester, was one that had been withdrawn, but reinstated. It survived the war by a couple of years. It was unnamed. *Ian Allan Library*

broken up were reinstated to traffic. There were several L&Y 0-6-0s and 0-8-0s, and a number of 'Prince of Wales' class 4-6-0s. Without doubt, one of the oldest engines around was No 20002, a Midland Railway Kirtley double-framed 2-4-0 Class 1P, which dated from 1866. It was shedded at Nottingham and we were fortunate to see it there on one of our 1942 excursions. I believe it wasn't withdrawn until 1948.

The Scene at Bingley in 1942

Apart from changes already mentioned, 'Royal Scots' continued to appear at intervals. The year started well with No 6161 *King's Own* (Crewe — 5A) on the daytime Anglo-Scottish express on 19 January. It returned the following day on the corresponding Up express. This was a regular diagram. However, even more of a surprise was the appearance a week later of No 6104 *Scottish Borderer* (Kingmoor — 12A) on the 8.5am Carlisle to Bradford Forster Square stopper and its return working, the 12.57pm to Hawes. Was this the first appearance of a 'Scot' at Forster Square?

New 2-8-0s began to be seen, and there was a regular daily working from Motherwell (28A). These became more frequent when American troops and supplies began to arrive on the Clyde. Motherwell had quite a sizeable stud, and Grangemouth (28C) had several. I believe that these were the first 2-8-0s to be allocated to a Scottish shed. Later in the year, Scottish engines provided another diversion from the usual procession of engines from Midland Division sheds. Derby took over some of the responsibility for the heavy general repair of Standard Class 2P 4-4-0s and Standard Compounds from Scottish sheds, and the engines travelled light to and from their home sheds. Examples were No 598 from Ayr

on 27 September and No 1179 from Corkerhill on 17 November. They appeared at roughly weekly intervals, completely unannounced, and always caused great excitement.

Another interesting working produced L&Y Class 7F 0-8-0s on a working from Rose Grove via Colne. These trains conveyed a huge load of empty coal wagons, often numbering over 100, which must have produced some interesting operating problems en route, and especially in the Leeds area. As they passed through Bingley it was impossible to see the engine and the brake van at one point — just a mass of empty wagons.

Further Wanderings in 1942

We discovered the delights of Crewe and went there several times, becoming expert at finding our way between Manchester Victoria and London Road. The journey started by bus to Bradford, then

Below: Ex-L&Y 0-8-0 Class 7F No 12921 is seen here at its home shed of Lostock Hall in 1936. It was built at Horwich in 1917 and withdrawn in 1937. There were about 130 of these powerful-looking engines, but only about 30 remained at the outbreak of the Second World War. *Midland Railway Trust Ltd*

the 8.15am express from Exchange, which picked up a Leeds portion at Low Moor. In a similar manner to the trip between Colne and Preston, the journey was punctuated by a succession of marshalling yards, goods sidings, carriage sidings, important stations and engine sheds, every one a scene of bustling activity. You became expert at leaning out of the window without getting your head knocked off and without getting an eyeful of smuts. Interest began at Low Moor engine shed, followed by Halifax goods yard and sidings, Sowerby Bridge engine shed and sidings, Mytholmroyd marshalling yard, then Rochdale. In memory, Rochdale was a large and busy station with an overall roof and no doubt a refreshment room, bookstall, telegraph office and lots of waiting rooms and offices. It was surrounded by goods yards and sidings and a carriage depot. There were branches to Oldham (currently temporarily closed and to be incorporated into Metrolink) and to Bacup (long since gone). How very different today. Rochdale is a microcosm of a half-century of industrial change, reflected in the railway scene.

The Delights of Manchester

There was, of course, plenty of interest at Manchester without going on to Crewe. At Victoria there was a constant procession of local passenger trains to and from the terminal platforms, always headed so far as memory goes by Stanier's splendid 2-6-4 tanks. Then, there were plenty of trains to and from the through platforms, including departures to Preston and Blackpool, and expresses to Liverpool Exchange via the L&Y route. These were hauled mainly by Stanier '5P5Fs', but the star performer was the 9.30am from Victoria to Glasgow Central. This was hauled by one of Newton Heath's (26A) 'Jubilees' and lent a bit of glamour to what was

Below: Railway enthusiasts visiting Manchester Victoria station were greeted with a constant procession of Stanier's two-cylinder 2-6-4Ts. No 2634, pictured here, was an Accrington engine, and was built at Derby in 1938. *Ian Allan Library*

otherwise a bustling workaday station, which had lost part of its roof in the 1940/41 bombing. Passengers for Edinburgh had to change at Preston into the 9.40am from Liverpool Exchange, which conveyed portions for both Edinburgh and Glasgow and followed the Manchester train about 10 minutes later.

Manchester Exchange was also worth a visit, which entailed a walk along the well-known longest platform in the country. Apart from local trains to former LNWR stations to the west, there were trains to and from North Wales which brought engines from North Wales sheds. If you were lucky, you might even see a Great Western engine. The GWR penetrated the fastness of the LMS as far as Manchester, thanks to some quid pro quos in the 19th century. Finally, the prestige trains from Liverpool Lime Street to Newcastle also called there. They were trains with first rank rolling stock and restaurant cars. However, they could also be seen passing through Victoria before climbing the bank to Miles Platting and on to Stalybridge, Huddersfield and Leeds. Freight trains needed banking up Miles Platting bank and there were usually a couple of L&Y 0-6-0s simmering gently away in Victoria awaiting their next job. It seems

Above: The Hughes four-cylinder 4-6-0s were always a pleasure to see, being well proportioned and elegant, but it is said that they were heavy on coal and maintenance. When costs became more important in the 1930s, owing to increasing road competition, the Hughes locos could not compete with Stanier's new engines flooding into service under his 'scrap and build' policy. The Hughes' 4-6-0s were largely withdrawn in the mid-1930s, with only nine remaining at the outbreak of war, all shedded at Blackpool, out of a class of 55. They were comparatively modern, being built between 1921 and 1925, but the war gave the survivors a reprieve for a few years, No 10455 being the last of the class to be withdrawn (in 1951). No 10412, rebuilt in 1921 from an earlier class, is seen here with a light load on a stopping passenger train service between Preston and Manchester. *Eric Treacy*

strange to think that in the thick of the war it was possible to travel from Liverpool to Newcastle in greater style and superior comfort than 60 years later. But not as frequently.

Finally, one mustn't forget the 10.40am from Liverpool Exchange to York, the L&Y's prestige train, which ran via Rochdale, Wakefield Kirkgate and Normanton. In later years it was hauled by a Bank Hall 'Jubilee', usually No 5717 *Dauntless*. It must be borne in mind that this was the L&Y Section main line to York and Goole, and very busy indeed with freight trains.

And Eventually to Crewe

Naturally, Crewe demanded our attention. We soon discovered a better way of getting there than by changing stations in Manchester. We caught a train from Bradford Exchange to Huddersfield, thence to Stalybridge and on to Stockport. In those days, Stalybridge was an important junction, and the LMS trains travelled to Stockport over the former LNWR line to Denton Junction which avoided Guide Bridge. Two of the curiosities of the Huddersfield to Stalybridge section were the little branch to Delph, which curved off the main line just beyond Diggle, and the branch to Oldham, which curved away from Greenfield for the four-mile run to the oddly named Glodwick Road and Clegg Street stations. Even odder, Oldham also had Mumps, Central and Werneth stations. Was there ever a town with so many stations with such peculiar names! Lees shed (26F) was situated on the branch from Greenfield and one of its Fowler 2-6-2 tanks, numbered 56 to 61, usually stood quietly in the bay platform to connect with the train from Huddersfield.

At the north end of Crewe station there was a long footbridge that gave access to Crewe North shed. The shed was completely out of bounds, but the footbridge gave a good view of not only the passenger station but also, and more important so far as we were concerned, of the goods avoiding lines which ran at a lower level and tunnelled under the main lines. From time to time a string of dead engines would be dragged from the works to the South shed (5B). These engines came from

anywhere on the LNWR system and were a major attraction. The south end of the station also needed a quick visit from time to time, but on one occasion, greatly daring and without tickets, we jumped on a train bound for the south with the intention of alighting at Stafford, crossing over, and getting the next train back, hoping that there would be no ticket inspection on either train. It worked and we saw all the engines outside Stafford shed including some very interesting LNWR veterans. Stafford was as far south as we ever travelled.

But we hadn't quite finished with the West Coast main line yet. A friend and I decided that we would explore the main line from Preston to Crewe, and we spent a few nights in the youth hostel at Longridge. Each morning we caught the bus into Preston and went forward to Crewe on the next available train. This route too was full of freight trains, most of them apparently standing in goods loops with an LNWR 0-8-0 at the front end. Springs Branch engine shed (10A) and the very extensive marshalling yards at Bamfurlong, just south of Wigan, captured our interest, and they

Below: C. J. Bowen-Cooke produced the LNWR 'George V' class of 4-4-0s in 1910, and 90 were built between then and 1915. All were named, and they were regarded as good engines for their size. They were superheated. Ten remained in service at the outbreak of the Second World War, but were withdrawn soon after the war's end. They mainly worked along the North Wales Coast. I only ever saw one — No 25350, a Chester engine, at Crewe. The engine in the photograph is No 5377 *Grouse* (LNWR No 1733), withdrawn in 1937 along with many others in that and the preceding year during one of Stanier's purges. *Ian Allan Library*

were followed fairly quickly by the engine shed (8B), yards and sidings at Warrington. There were plenty of former LNWR engines of various types to delight us.

A Visit to Liverpool

One of our group of schoolboy train spotters, Bob Evans, had been evacuated from Liverpool to Bingley. Today he would be described as 'streetwise' and during the summer holidays of 1942 he suggested that we should have a look at the railways in the vicinity of Edge Hill. So off we went. Until then, we had had little experience of wartime bomb damage other than in Manchester, although we had been quite impressed by the burnt-out buildings on the south side of Deansgate. I say 'impressed' deliberately. As schoolboys we were not dismayed or astonished, but took it in our stride. After all, we had read all about the bombing during the winter of 1940/41 and we expected to find a lot of damaged and destroyed buildings in cities. By contrast, the northern part of the West Riding where we lived had escaped very lightly. Edge Hill, on the other hand, was a wasteland, but the railways were still functioning and Bob knew the area well. He had lived at Wavertree, near the engine shed. We had a splendid day with our guide, and picked up some of the more obscure and ancient (to us) LNWR engines, such as Class 1P 2-4-2 tanks, Class 2P 0-6-2 tanks, quite a lot of Class 2F 0-6-2 tanks, and several 0-8-2 tanks and 0-8-4 tanks. Edge Hill had about 15 of the latter, the remainder being in South Wales. It was a good day.

The reader may be wondering how I managed to finance all these excursions. It happened like this. The West Riding War Agricultural Executive, known as the Warag, was responsible for converting as much grassland into arable land as possible, and employed tractor drivers and assistants to carry out the work. Older schoolboys were encouraged, voluntarily, to sign on as assistant tractor drivers and I did so. I was attached to a driver and we went all round the area within a radius of about 10/15 miles of Bradford, ploughing and harrowing etc. It was very enjoyable and exceedingly well paid, because it included travelling time and expenses. I cycled everywhere on the very quiet roads of the day and there was plenty of time off for train-spotting expeditions.

Finally, back to the Midland

We had not yet explored the railways south of Leeds, but decided it was time to head off in that direction. Destination — Nottingham and Derby. At that time the Midland main line went via Normanton and Cudworth, and virtually the whole route from just south of Leeds to Rotherham was thronged with collieries, coke ovens, marshalling yards and sidings. A delight for the railway enthusiast, but environmentally awful. There were large marshalling yards at Normanton and an engine shed (20D), then a mile or two further along at Goose Hill Junction the Lanky main line turned off towards Wakefield. Before long Royston shed (20C) could be seen on the left-hand side just before the yards and sidings at Cudworth. A little branch train ran from here to Barnsley Court House. The former Hull & Barnsley Railway also ran into Cudworth and had its own platform. I seem to recall that at one time H&B passenger trains ran through to Sheffield Midland.

We changed at Chesterfield and spent some time there, and I can visualise even now the continuous procession of heavy freight trains on the goods lines behind the station, drawn by '3F' and '4F' 0-6-0s, '8F' 2-8-0s and the Garratts which were there in profusion. All 33 of them were shedded at either Hasland (18C), just a mile up the line and easily visible from the train, or at Toton. We had learned quite a bit about railway geography by now, and knew that the St Pancras expresses via Nottingham turned off the Erewash Valley main line before reaching Toton. Only the stopping trains went via Toton, so we boarded one. It was an advantage to travel on such a train, because there was such a lot to see. The route was full of collieries and trains. It seems unbelievable now, but at that time there were no fewer than 30 signalboxes in the 20 miles between Clay Cross and Toton. A total of 36 collieries were served either directly or on branches. There was an amazing tangle of lines in this area, because practically all the collieries were also served by the former GNR, and some by the former GCR. It suited the colliery owners to have two or even three companies serving them, because it provided competition on rates.

There were four tracks all the way from Tapton Junction, just north of Chesterfield, to Toton, and they were full of trains, mostly headed by '2F', '3F' and '4F' 0-6-0s. Westhouses shed was on a spur off the main line and Toton shed was obscured by rows

Above: LMS Garrett No 4998 was one of three prototypes built by Beyer Peacock in 1927, Nos 4997-99 (later Nos 7997-99). Thirty more were built in 1930 by the same firm, and were originally 4967-96 later being renumbered numbered 7967 to 7996. Most of the class were allocated to Toton (18A), but a number went to Hasland (Chesterfield) (18C). They were introduced to avoid the double-heading of coal trains, using pairs of 0-6-0s (mainly Classes 3F and 4F), working south from Toton, although Garratts could be seen at Washwood Heath (Birmingham), Peterborough and even at York. *Author's Collection*

Below: Ex-Midland Class 4F 0-6-0 No 3870 heads a train of what appear to be empty coke wagons along the Erewash Valley in 1946. It was built at Derby in 1918 and survived until 1963. *H. C. Casserley*

and rows of wagons, but there was plenty to see and pencils were nearly red hot. We were also nearly hoarse shouting out numbers to each other, but fortunately it was a quiet train and we had a compartment to ourselves. However, we did better on the way into Nottingham, passing the extensive marshalling yards at Beeston and the large engine shed (16A). This is where we saw No 20002 in steam. After a short break (tea and a meat pie) we set off for Derby and discovered something else to our discomfiture. For some reason, Derby was an 'open' station and tickets were collected at the last stopping station before reaching it. I can't recall what explanation we gave for travelling from Bingley to Derby via Nottingham and Trent, but it was possibly a recognised route. There were many

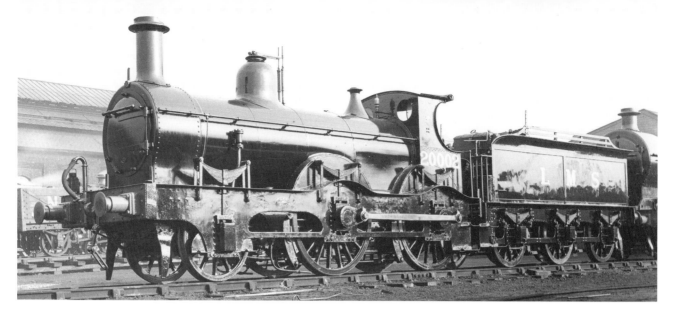

such permitted variations, as I learned later. It was also a good way to view Derby shed, and all the engines awaiting or following general overhaul.

Finally, the End of my Schooldays

I left school at Easter 1943, but during the holidays there was time for another couple of visits to Manchester and a trip to Derby and Nottingham, before I joined the railway and became a proper railwayman. The daily express passenger scene was now firmly in the hands of Holbeck's 'Jubilees', including the two rebuilds *Comet* and *Phoenix,* with help from Kingmoor and occasionally other Midland sheds. It wasn't until August that Holbeck received the first rebuilt 'Scots', No 6103 *Royal Scots Fusilier* and No 6109 *Royal Engineer,* but by then I was firmly in my stride as a junior booking clerk at Keighley, the story of which forms the next chapter.

I might mention here that I joined the RCTS (the Railway Correspondence and Travel Society) in 1942. Its monthly journal, *The Railway Observer*,

Above: When I saw No 20002, a Kirtley engine, at Nottingham in 1942 it was already 76 years old, and I next saw it in Derby Works in preservation in 1956. This photograph was taken outside Derby Works in 1935. According to my records, its original number was 158, and it was renumbered 2 in the 1907 renumbering scheme, having 20000 added in LMS days. *Midland Railway Trust Ltd/Author's Collection*

was (and still is) a mine of information and I still have the issues of 1942, which have helped me with this chapter.

Below: No 185, seen here, might be considered a younger brother of No 20002. It was designed by Johnson and built by D bs & Co in 1876.
It was part of the '1282' class, renumbered in 1907. It was finally withdrawn in 1948, as No 20185, when it was only 72 years old. *Midland Railway Trust Ltd/Author's Collection*

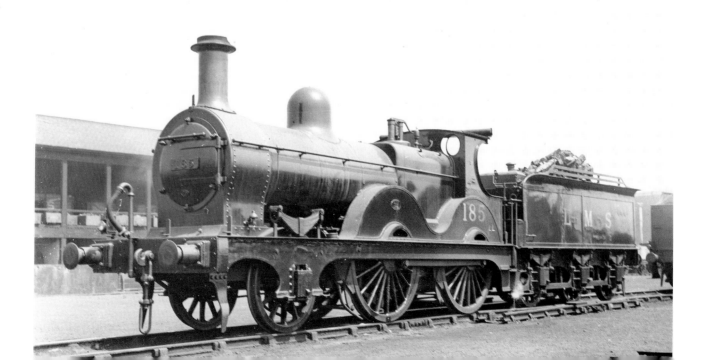

Three

THE START OF A RAILWAY CAREER

I BECOME A JUNIOR CLERK

I know it doesn't sound like a very auspicious start, but life taught me subsequently that it's better to start at the bottom, because that's where you learn what railways are all about, and what makes them tick. Whilst I was at school I had never thought of 'going on the railway' indeed I never really thought about the future at all. The future was next week, or next month. I was just 17 and it was Easter 1943. I expected to be called up to the armed forces at 18 and the idea of planning a career never entered my head.

Then came one of those defining moments that set the course of your whole life. A determining moment, as they say. The local paper carried an advert which was worded 'Vacancies for Temporary Junior Railway Clerks to replace staff in HM Forces'. It sounded just right. It would fill in the year before call-up, and I would get paid (not much!) for being among trains. This sounded very attractive, as I had just spent several years being among trains without getting paid for it. And there would be plenty of time to think about a permanent career when I was eventually 'demobbed'. The idea that I might not survive never entered my head.

So, I sent in my written application, went for educational and medical exams and waited. A couple of weeks later there came a letter headed 'London Midland and Scottish Railway Company'. My heart missed a beat. I read on. It said that it was from the Chief Commercial and Chief Operating Manager's Departments, Office of Superintendent of Organisation and Staff, Derby. I was even more impressed. I learned later that the whole of the commercial and operating staff of the LMS were

dealt with from this one office. It might have seemed like gross centralisation, but it worked. When I got down to the meat of the letter it stated simply, 'Please report to the Station Master at Keighley prepared for duty on the morning of Friday April 30th.' That was a bit optimistic, as the letter was dated only two days earlier, but the postal service worked well and I had one day's notice to prepare myself for 'the great leap forward'.

There I was. One day a grubby schoolboy who spent long hours in a gloomy building which always smelled strongly of furniture polish and disinfectant. The next day, I was a RAILWAYMAN, destined to spend long hours in a railway station booking office which smelled strongly of soot. There was a reason for the sooty smell. At Keighley station, the offices were on the overbridge, and the booking office was located nicely above the Down main line. The chimney of the pilot engine of a double-headed express standing in the station positioned itself precisely beneath the booking office. The night expresses were often double-headed and they stood for several minutes whilst they unloaded mails and parcels etc. But I was now a railwayman, and inordinately proud of my calling. I received my Railway Service lapel badge, to be worn at all times when on duty, and I polished it so hard that it began to wear away. Needless to say, that badge is still there today in the souvenir box.

In those days Keighley was a well set-up and prosperous town, whose main industries were textiles and machine engineering. The station, which was very near the town centre, had four

platforms. Platforms 1 and 2 served the main Leeds to Carlisle/Morecambe line, whilst platforms 3 and 4 served both the Oxenhope Branch and the LNER trains which came in from Bradford and Halifax. It was very busy, both with passengers and parcels traffic of all descriptions.

Anyway, to get back to my story, I duly reported in shiny shoes to the Stationmaster, Mr Richardson, who had a separate office on the bridge. I had visions of his being some stony-faced old gent rather like my headmaster, but in fact he was kindness itself. He was probably in his late fifties. He then introduced me to the Chief Booking and Parcels Clerk, John Barnes, always referred to as

Above: Surely one of the finest of Hubert Foster's superb photographs. 'Royal Scot' class No 6109 *Royal Engineer*, one of the very early rebuilds, overtakes one of Stanier's 2-8-0s, No 8177, at Blea Moor. No 6109 was rebuilt in July 1943 and No 8177 was one of a large batch built by the North British Loco Co, dating from 1942.
W. Hubert Foster/courtesy John W. Holroyd

Below: Canon Eric Treacy did not scorn the lowly freight. A perfect picture, taken near Kildwick, shows an LMS Class 4F 0-6-0 No 4404, on a Class B Goods, throwing out plenty of smoke for pictorial effect (by pre-arrangement?). This was another Leeds Holbeck (20A) engine. *Eric Treacy*

Mr Barnes. It didn't seem to be the custom to call superiors 'Sir' in those days, just plain 'Mr'. John Barnes was an exceptionally fussy person who seemed permanently worried about something, but he too was kindness itself and a very decent chap indeed. He was a stickler for things being done correctly, and I learned something else about railway life. Everything you did was covered by huge books of regulations, which was fine provided you knew where to look. JB also had his own office.

In the booking office itself there was a grizzled old senior clerk who looked to me to be about 90 but was only 59 (oh, the arrogance of youth!), then there was a middle turn clerk who dealt with paybills, accounts and correspondence. Finally there were two clerks who manned the booking office windows and the enquiry counter, and who worked early and late turn alternate weeks. We worked a 48-hour week, which for shift workers meant six 8-hour days. We also worked regular Sunday turns. These were much sought after because they were paid at the rate of time and three-quarters (ie 14 hours' pay). The night turn was worked by a clerk from the parcels office. In the pecking order, booking clerks were superior to parcels clerks but were paid the same rate.

My first day was a culture shock. I had entered a world of grown-ups and attractive young lady clerks (I had been to an all-boys' school) and would soon have to carry responsibilities, but for a start I was given a chair, placed at a large table and told to help with the 'month-ends'. I had no idea, of course, what they meant by month-ends, but I discovered that it was one of those railway rituals in which the accounts are done covering all tickets issued the previous month. The accounts books, known as Traffic Books, were huge, and had a line of entry for each type of ticket, of which there were several hundred, in the ticket racks. Then there were vertical columns for each day of the month, in which each day's total transactions were recorded. Those columns were totalled daily and in theory equalled the cash receipts. At the month end, the total number of tickets issued, and their value, was calculated for each line of entry, and entered in the final column.

If you are still with me, the total of the final column had to balance with the total of each separate day's transactions, and it was a heart-

Below: One of the better LMS products of the 1920s: parallel-boilered 2-6-4T No 2341 in splendid condition. The locomotive was built at Derby in 1929 and shedded for some time at Nottingham (16A). *Ian Allan Library*

stopping moment. Needless to say, I didn't balance first time, but I was made to work at it until I had balanced. I seem to recall that it took me several days and it taught me the value of careful calculation and accurate addition. Booking clerks became geniuses at mental arithmetic. Two adults and three children at 11s 7d (eleven shillings and seven pence to younger readers) became child's play. John Barnes would not let us use pencil and paper to work it out; it had to be done in our heads. Quite right too.

After a few weeks' learning all the tickets and fares, and the accountancy procedures, I was ready to go solo. I lived at Bingley at the time and Keighley was the next station, so I was given a pass to travel on the train. The trains were very convenient too for the shifts, and there was a bit of give and take among the clerks to fit in with the train service. Although LNER trains used the station, all the staff belonged to the LMS. However, we had a separate booking window for LNER tickets (and LNER accounts too), which led to a certain amount of confusion in passengers' minds when they came to the wrong window and were directed to the next one along. It also created a certain amount of scuttling to and fro for the clerk. If there was a queue of passengers at each window, the clerk had to be adept at keeping each queue moving, and it was quite an art, believe me. One can understand passengers' confusion. If they were going to Liverpool or Manchester, which were plainly LMS stations, it must have seemed logical to present themselves at the LMS ticket window, but the tickets were LNER tickets because the journey started on that company.

The Oxenhope branch was a very minor part of our activities, although we had a thriving business in singles to Ingrow (the first station on the branch), for which the fare was 2d. Don't scoff — you could buy a bar of chocolate for that. The branch trains were worked push-and-pull by elderly ex-Midland 0-4-0 tanks, mainly Nos 1275, 1277 and 1366. Keighley had a small sub-shed under the supervision of Skipton (20F), which also housed a few Class 3F 0-6-0s. Nos 3295 and 3558 spring to mind. The branch has, of course, taken on a new lease of life as the Keighley & Worth Valley preserved railway.

There was also a large goods depot, with extensive sidings and warehouse facilities and its own Goods Agent. Shunting went on non-stop. Sorry to say, the site now contains a Sainsbury's supermarket and car park, but it could have been worse. It might have been a scrap yard. There was an equally large LNER goods depot on a short stub of line from its passenger line from Bradford Exchange and Halifax. Its imposing warehouse still remains and now houses an electricity undertaking. These two goods depots give some indication of the enormous amount of goods traffic handled at Keighley in those days.

The LNER goods depot was at the end of a steep falling gradient several miles long. One day, a goods brake van ran away from a station up the

Below: One of the many ancient looking Class 2F 0-6-0s of Midland Railway vintage is seen here at Harpenden in 1936. This locomotive was subsequently transferred to Skipton shed (20F) and is believed to have been located at the Keighley sub-shed; the latter also had some Class 3F 0-6-0s and some 0-4-4Ts.
Midland Railway Trust Ltd

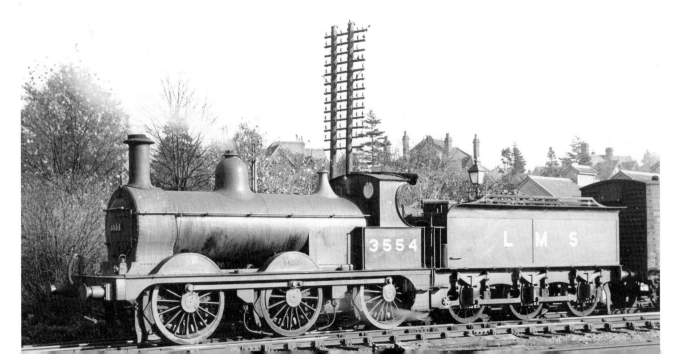

line. It gathered speed and careered down the hill at an ever-increasing rate. The signalman at GN Junction signalbox received the 'Vehicles running away' bell signal and had the presence of mind to set the points towards the goods depot and away from Keighley passenger station. The runaway raced into the goods yard and, fortunately or otherwise, into an empty siding. With little perceptible reduction of speed it smashed through the buffer stops as though they were cardboard, through the wall and into the street below, where it finally came to rest, fortunately without hitting anyone. Such runaways were, I believe, not unknown and the good citizens of Keighley tended not to linger in that area.

Above: Class 3F 0-6-0s of varying vintage were common all over the Midland Division of the LMS. Here No 3299, with a heavy load of coal wagons, takes the curve at Ambergate before heading northwards. Its home shed was 18D Staveley. *Locomotive Publishing Co*

Below: The LNER penetrated the LMS system as far as Keighley, but this fine picture taken on 4 September 1945 of an ex-North Eastern Class D20 4-4-0 was taken at Leeds City. The NER was one of the few pre-grouping companies that believed in giving its locomen a decent cab. *E. R. Wethersett*

Keighley station had a refreshment room on platform 2, and on early turn it was the custom to nip down there during a quiet spell for a cup of Oxo or Bovril. The premises were presided over by Miss Pierce, a formidable lady of indeterminate age, who was the manageress and could quell us young bloods with a mere glance. Meat pies were the staple diet and were taken back to the office to be warmed up in a little stove so that the juices flowed. No, we never had any tummy troubles. Such things hadn't been invented in those days.

It wasn't long before I set my sights on becoming a stationmaster, and Mr Richardson gave me every encouragement to learn about signalling. There were six signalboxes at Keighley — Thwaites Junction, Station South, Station Junction, North, West, and GN Junction. The last two were on the Oxenhope branch. My usual resort was the Station South box, but occasionally I cadged a lift on the footplate to travel to GN Junction box when a relief signalman I was friendly with worked there. I have to say that most signalmen were very kind and helpful when they found that you were really serious at 'learning the block'. Among the staff, railways were a much less formal place in those days than they are today and you could walk along the lineside to your heart's content. In fact, by becoming a railwayman you felt that you owned the place. It was one big railway family and, I think, a reasonably happy one too. It certainly was for me. I loved every minute of it. Often, after early turn I would visit one of the signalboxes, or have a trip up the branch with the driver, or help to load and unload parcels on the platform, or even go out with one of the parcels delivery men. There were four delivery rounds at Keighley, two of which were motor vans and two were horse-drawn. The latter were used on the town rounds, for which they were very suitable as they called at nearly every shop, either to collect parcels for dispatch, or to deliver them.

One of the more arcane activities on the station was the weekly ritual of emptying the toilet door locks, which were of the penny-in-the-slot variety. Each platform had Gents' and Ladies' toilets so it was quite a time-consuming activity. The Chief Clerk himself performed the activity, but he had to be accompanied by the early turn clerk because the railway company didn't trust anyone not to slip a few pennies into their pockets, not even its Chief Clerk. The Gents' toilets caused no problems, but the Ladies' were a different matter. Accompanied by the Ladies' Waiting Room Attendant, the Chief Clerk would stride boldly into the waiting room to the palpable astonishment of its occupants, followed meekly by me, blushing somewhat and holding out my little cash bag as an indication that I had no evil intent. He would them hammer peremptorily on any door that showed 'Vacant' and call loudly 'Anyone in?' If silence ensued, he would open the door with his master key so that the cash compartment could be unlocked and the pennies retrieved. For my part, I tried to make myself as inconspicuous as possible and hope that none of my friends would see me. By the end of the proceedings the cash bag had become very heavy indeed, and all the contents had to be carefully counted when we got back to the booking office.

The railway companies were obsessed with ensuring that every penny was properly accounted for. In the rough and tumble of booking tickets, mistakes were bound to happen from time to time and no matter how careful you were, you might occasionally find that when you cashed up at the end of your turn you didn't balance. It was usually only a matter of coppers but you were not allowed to cover your shame by making up the shortage out of your own pocket. That was definitely forbidden. Nor were you allowed to pocket any surplus. Small surpluses were hidden away at the back of the ticket date-stamping press and retrieved to cover losses.

About every six months we would have a sudden unannounced visit from the auditors, who would take immediate charge. You had to cash up straight away, then the auditors would examine the books and make sure that all the ticket pro-numbers in the racks corresponded with the entries in the books. They also knew all about the dodge of hiding away small cash surpluses and if they found anything there they would look over their glasses at us with mock disapproval. We would look back with injured innocence. They were more concerned with fraud of a more serious nature. It was one of the railway customs that auditors ticked the books with a green pencil. When the senior clerk checked them daily he used a red pencil.

I mentioned earlier that I used to travel to and from work by train. The train service at Keighley had a punctuality record that would make today's railwaymen green with envy (apart from the Down night sleepers which sometimes suffered from enemy action further south). Barring accidents,

Right: A stunning, BR official photograph, of Pacific No 6241 *City of Edinburgh,* shorn of its streamlining, setting out from Carlisle Citadel station with an Up Perth express, shortly after nationalisation. It was built at Crewe in 1939.
British Railways

Below: Rebuilt 'Royal Scot' class 4-6-0 No 6108 *Seaforth Highlander,* in beautiful condition, picks up speed after the Skipton curve and passes Snaygill (and the 220 milepost). This is another of Eric Treacy's near perfect compositions, and was probably taken from the signalbox steps.
No 6108 was rebuilt in May 1948, and this picture must have been taken shortly afterwards. It was one of Holbeck's substantial stud.
Eric Treacy

A Railwayman's Odyssey

they were on time. We did have the occasional accident. I was going to work one morning on my usual train, the 5.50am all-stations from Bradford Forster Square to Skipton (6.7am from Bingley) when we ground to a halt at Marley Junction, midway between Bingley and Keighley. Marley had connections between the main and goods/slow lines. We sat there in silence for some time (nobody told you anything in those days, of course) but eventually we moved forward at low speed towards the next signalbox, Thwaites Junction. Naturally everyone was looking out of the window with some impatience to see what was up. Nearing Thwaites the line had a fairly sharp left-hand curve and we spotted on the outside of the curve a neat row of fish vans all lying on their sides and still apparently coupled together. It looked as though one of the night expresses, the Edinburgh sleeper which did not stop at Keighley, had come through a bit fast and flung the fish vans off when rounding the curve. Of the sleeper there was no sign. It would have been brought to a stand by the application of the vacuum brake when the train parted, but quickly put right and sent on its way. That's how things were done in those days. Top priority — get trains moving.

There was a rather more serious accident the same year on 11 October 1943 when the Down Edinburgh sleeper came to grief at Steeton, the next station beyond Keighley. The signals were at danger because the signalman was shunting a goods train from the Down main line back into the sidings, but the express failed to stop and ploughed into the wagons. The engine veered off to the right across the Up main line and came to rest on its side, together with its tender and the first vehicle, a parcels van. Four coaches were derailed. However, there were no fatalities and only four people were taken to hospital, of whom only one was detained, with rib injuries. Two of the goods wagons were thrown into the Stationmaster's garden. The local newspaper reported that the stationmaster's wife made as many cups of tea as possible, until a mobile canteen arrived from a local ordnance

Below: I hadn't been at Keighley for long when this accident happened on 11 October 1943. The engine was a 'Jubilee' class, No 5581 *Bihar and Orissa* of Carlisle Kingmoor (12A), and the driver had passed Steeton's Home signal at Danger. The signalman was also at fault, because he was shunting a goods train from the Down main line back into the sidings and should not have accepted the express with the overlap of the Home signal occupied by the goods train. Fortunately, casualties were remarkably few, and only one person was detained in hospital. The line was open again by next morning. *Author's Collection*

Above: The rebuilt 'Royal Scots' were very photogenic. Hubert Foster captured this one at Bell Busk as No 6133 *The Green Howards passes* with the Up 'Thames-Clyde' express. The Class 6P engine was rebuilt in July 1944. *W. Hubert Foster*

Below: In 1943 the War Department was planning ahead to the railway situation in Europe after D-Day in June 1944. They required several hundred 2-8-0 heavy freight engines, in the expectation that there would be a serious shortage of serviceable steam locomotives in northwest Europe at that time. R. A. Riddles,

of the LMS, designed an 'Austerity' 2-8-0 steam locomotive, based on a simplified version of the LMS 2-8-0. In 1943 the North British Locomotive Co produced 545 engines and the Vulcan Foundry, of Newton-le-Willows, built 390. They were numbered in the 77xxx sequence. After the war, almost all of them were returned returned to Britain, except for 184 which were retained by Netherlands Railways. The LNER bought 200, and the British Transport Commission purchased 533 in 1948. BR numbered them 90000 to 90732. No 77170 is seen here at Doncaster in May 1947, still carrying its WD number and air brake equipment. *A. B. Crompton*

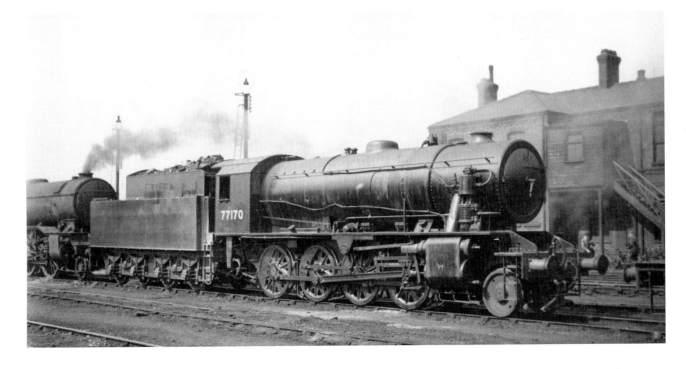

factory with plentiful supplies of tea and cakes. The line was expected to be reopened by next morning. Once again — top priority. According to my records the express engine was Class 5XP 'Jubilee' No 5581 *Bihar and Orissa,* a Carlisle Kingmoor engine. It ought to be mentioned that the signalman also made an error in accepting the express when his quarter of a mile clearance beyond his Home signal was in fact not clear but was occupied by the goods train.

Holbeck 'Jubilees' practically monopolised the expresses, and included the two rebuilt locos, Nos 5735 *Comet* and 5736 *Phoenix.* However, there were exceptions, such as Nos 5640 *Frobisher* (19B Millhouses) and 5607 *Fiji* (14B Kentish Town). Carlisle Kingmoor 'Jubilees' and '5P5F' 4-6-0s were seen quite often, and later in 1943 rebuilt 'Royal Scots' started to appear, beginning with Nos 6103 *Royal Scots Fusilier* and 6109 *Royal Engineer.* Both were shedded at Holbeck and were splendid-looking engines without the smoke deflectors, which were fitted later. Goods trains provided more variety, and locos from Midland Division sheds south of Leeds were often seen.

Rather more unusual were Class 7F 0-8-0 No 9543 from Wakefield (25A) and one of the 'Austerity' 2-8-0s, No 7323 from Wellingborough (15A). Even more exciting was the appearance on the railway scene of the American-built Class S160 2-8-0s on heavy freight trains. They looked very strange to British eyes, with all their innards on the outside. It was a good time to be a train-spotter.

During virtually the whole of my stay at Keighley from April 1943 to March 1945 there were regular programmes of special trains bringing mainly American troops and their equipment from Scotland to the Southern and Western Regions,

Below: This very strange-looking locomotive with all its bits and pieces hanging out became quite a common sight on Britain's railways in the months leading up to D-Day. They were 2-8-0s of American origin, desgnated Class S160, and were used on our railways whilst waiting to be transported to France following D-Day. They were not uncommon passing through Keighley. They belonged to the US Transportation Corps. *C. C. B. Herbert*

A Railwayman's Odyssey

both in the big build-up to D-Day and afterwards. Trainloads of guns and tanks were commonplace, usually hauled by LMS Class 8F 2-8-0s. Engines of this class were being turned out in large quantities by all four companies. These special programmes could amount to as many as a dozen trains in a single day. What excitement! All stations en route were informed by special notice of the detailed timings of these trains so that signalmen could regulate them appropriately. There were other specials of a more sombre nature during late 1944 when ambulance trains were received at Keighley, bringing civilians injured in the V-1 and V-2 raids on Southern England, for dispersal to hospitals in the area.

I don't remember there being any specials for holidaymakers. 'Holidays at Home' was the rule

Below: Another of Hubert Foster's superb photos taken at Bell Busk. Stanier Class 8F 2-8-0 No 8652 heads a trainload of coal towards the northwest. It was built by the Southern Railway in 1943 to assist with heavy wartime freight traffic; the design was built by all four mainline companies during and immediately after the war. Its home shed was Stourton (20B).
W. Hubert Foster/courtesy John W. Holroyd

Bottom: This is one of the electric multiple-units that ran between Lancaster Green Ayre, Lancaster Castle, Morecambe Promenade and Heysham. The system was installed by the Midland Railway in 1908. The centre three coaches are normal steam stock, used for strengthening purposes at times of heavy traffic.
W. S. Garth

during 1943 and 1944. In any case, large parts of the country — near the east and south coasts, and in Scotland — were out of bounds for non-residents. However, there were no such restrictions on the Lancashire resorts, and Morecambe was the favourite resort for Keighley people. We had three trains in the morning, at 6.49am, 9.2am and 11.16am, and people just had to cram in as best they could. Those train times are imprinted on my memory. I must have said them thousands of times. There was no time for niceties, with the enquiry office heaving with people, especially service personnel returning from leave to all points of the compass in Britain. Anywhere on the LMS system was comparatively easy, but East Anglia was a regular destination as a result of the extensive building of bomber airfields there. You winced when someone asked for a remote station there. Change at Queensbury (possibly), Bradford Exchange, Peterborough, March, Ely and probably a couple more places. Or maybe go via Leeds, Nottingham, Saxby, Bourne, Lynn, Melton Constable, etc. I hate to think at which tiny country station some of my enquirers might have ended up after the last connection had gone.

I must admit I really enjoyed being busy, with a queue at each window and half a dozen people at the enquiry counter. Then there was the telephone. If it got too busy the middle turn clerk would help out, but they were reluctant to do so unless shouted at. When all the day staff went home at about 5.30pm the enquiry office door was locked and you were on your own. My busiest day was undoubtedly the Friday before Keighley Feast in July 1944. As is well known, all the Lancashire and Yorkshire mill towns had a week during the summer when all the mills stopped and the towns

virtually closed down. Lancashire had its Wakes weeks, Yorkshire had Feasts or Tides. The year 1944 was no exception, because it was accepted that the workers needed a break. In addition to the residents, Keighley had a large number of workers evacuated from the London area to work in the local ordnance factories and they received a warrant entitling them to free travel to and from their homes in the southeast. Esher and Ewell seemed to be two popular destinations. The rush of passengers started in the mid-afternoon, and from then on I was at it hammer-and-tongs until well after 9.0pm. When I cashed up I had taken over £600, which doesn't sound much, but a monthly return to King's Cross or St Pancras was only £2.0s.9d and Morecambe was 11s 8d. Probably equivalent to about £30,000 at today's fares. No, I didn't balance, but I was only a bob or two out.

In those days the buses closed down for the day about 9.30pm. It was some sort of wartime economy measure. However, the last train to Skipton did not leave until 10.53pm, and on Friday and Saturday nights there seemed to be a mass invasion of Keighley by the younger people of Silsden, the next station along the line. They came by bus, but that was rather early to go home from Keighley's cinemas and dance halls, so they came down to the station for the last train. In droves. Fortunately, the fare was 6d, so it was very easy to issue lots of tickets in a very short time. Keighley was a 'closed' station, and passengers had to have a ticket to get onto the platform. The passengers were very well behaved and there was little or no rowdyism in those days. People still respected authority. However, the main purpose of the last train was not only to provide a late departure from Bradford Forster Square but also to connect at

Right: Another of Wethersett's excellent pictures: LMS Class 4F 0-6-0 No 4128 is seen on 7 September 1945 near Luddendenfoot with a trainload of empty coal wagons en route to the collieries. *E. R. Wethersett*

Shipley with the 4.5pm from London St Pancras. It was a notorious late runner and in those days the Bradford to Skipton train almost *always* waited to connect, a comical idea today. I've known that train sit in Shipley station until well after midnight, which meant a long wait for Silsden passengers at Keighley. But it was wartime and people were very stoical.

In December 1944 I was called up for a week to attend an aircrew selection board in the Grand Hotel at Scarborough. I had been in the Air Training Corps for four years by then and had been mustered

as aircrew, but the requirement for aircrew in the trainee pipeline had reduced considerably and the pipeline was being thinned out. However, I passed the various aptitude tests and returned to the railway, but from then on I was in a sort of limbo,

Below: On the same day, Wethersett also captured this photo of ex-LNWR 0-8-0 No 9094 at the same location, but heading in the opposite direction with a trainload of coal.
E. R. Wethersett

Above: Various somewhat elderly, but still serviceable, ex-Caledonian Railway engines — 0-6-0s and passenger tanks — were loaned to the West Riding and possibly elsewhere later in the war. Treacy spotted this one, 0-4-4T No 15130 with a two-coach train, at Marley Junction, one of his favourite locations.
Eric Treacy

waiting for the calling-up papers to arrive. If it didn't happen soon, the European War would be over. A couple of months later a vacancy arose for a Booking and Parcels Clerk at Bingley, only five minutes from home. I needed to learn parcels office work and accounts so it was decided to transfer me there. My couple of years at Keighley had been hugely enjoyable. In the meantime, I had become an adult clerk at age 18, officially a Class 5 clerk.

There were only three clerks at Bingley passenger station, two of whom worked early and late turn, with the third clerk being the senior clerk on middle turn. He was Class 4, one grade up. When I became a fully-fledged Class 5 railway clerk, my salary went up from £55 per annum to £80, plus war advance. The Class 5 salary scale increased by £10 each year until you were 32 years old, and many clerks remained in Class 5 until well in their 40s or even 50s. When the Class 4 Senior Clerk retired at Keighley, his successor came from Nailsworth in his mid-50s. He was a good chap too. Prewar conditions on the railways had brought about retrenchment and promotional stagnation.

The Stationmaster at Bingley, Mr Hamer, was also the Goods Agent, and there was quite a large goods yard. There were two signalboxes, one at Bingley and the other at Marley Junction. I became friends with one of the signalmen at Bingley, Cliff Nicholls, and went there frequently in my off duty hours to work the signalbox and 'learn the block'. He helped me enormously and I shall always be grateful to him. That's how the railway was in those days. If you wanted to get on you made the effort in your own time and there were older railwaymen willing to help you. Many young clerks did it. As I said earlier, the railway was a big family affair.

I was on late turn on VE-Day and a few days beforehand I had searched the various cupboards in the office for anything to decorate the station with. I came across a pile of bunting which we draped over the station frontage. It had been left over from the Coronation in 1937, or so I was told. I also came across a bag of cricket gear, and being very keen on cricket, although not much good at it (an awful admission for a Yorkshireman), I approached a chap I knew in the Goods Department who was. He had been a member of the prewar Bingley LMS cricket team and between us we formed a new team. We played several evening matches that year against other club teams. In between, a few of us played during the evening in the goods yard, with the wickets chalked on a wall. Happy days indeed. The railway companies were very keen to encourage social activities, but I'm not sure it extended to playing cricket in the goods yard!

My 19th birthday passed and I was still in limbo. Then VJ-Day went by and I was beginning to feel forgotten. But someone must have found my name because I was called to the RAF in October 1945. Aircrew were no longer needed and I finished up on the ground staff. In Aden. I didn't see or hear a train for well over a year. But there were other excitements to compensate.

Four

BACK FROM HM FORCES, AND BACK TO WORK

After nearly a year in Aden I embarked on a troopship, the *Empire Test,* towards the end of February 1948. I wasn't really sorry to leave. Aden was very hot and humid. Sticky. There had been one day of rain in the whole year. But it had been an interesting posting and life was quite comfortable in the Sergeants' Mess. Aden was a duty free port, so cigarettes and drinks were very cheap, and there was always something interesting going on in the harbour.

But the nearest railways were hundreds of miles away, although I did see an engine once. On my fortnight's leave I chose to go to a leave station in Asmara, in what had been Italian Eritrea. This was up in the mountains, at about 7,000ft and a welcome change from sea level in Aden. We flew there in a Wellington bomber, refuelling at a small island, Kamaran, in the Red Sea. Fortunately I had acquired a camera and was able to take plenty of photos. There were several of us in the Sergeants' Mess at the leave station and we spent the morning in the town playing snooker, then visiting the ice-cream parlour. In the afternoon we borrowed bikes and toured around. Asmara was undamaged in the war and was quite a fine city with a strong Italian influence, including a palace built for Mussolini.

One day we went on an organised tour down the mountain passes to Keren, the scene of some fierce fighting with the Italians in 1940 or 1941. And there stood a small steam engine outside the engine shed. There was also quite an imposing railway station. Keren was on the line from the port of Massawa on the Red Sea, which climbed up to Asmara, before dropping down to Keren and on to Kassala in Sudan. I can't imagine why I didn't visit the railway station in Asmara, but probably I didn't know there was one.

The sail home from Aden took three weeks, but we had a comfortable billet on the poop deck at the back of the ship, and were well fed. Most of the time seemed to be spent either looking over the ship's rail or playing housey-housey, but eventually we arrived at Liverpool and were shepherded onto a train for Kirkham to be demobbed. This being shepherded onto a train was quite novel, not having experienced it for two years. Then home to Bingley in civvies.

Reporting back

There I was, back home towards the end of March 1948 with about eight week's leave, which I think was made up of six weeks' demob leave and a fortnight's outstanding leave from 1946. However, first things first. I called in to see Mr Hamer, the Stationmaster at Bingley, to report back, and he informed District Office at Leeds City. In due course I was called to see the District Operating Superintendent at Leeds, Mr Hibbert, for a chat about my future, and I said I wanted to be a stationmaster. He was a really nice chap. 'Good,' he said, 'there are plenty of small stations in my district, so learn the Rules and get yourself passed out.'

He was right. There were plenty of small stations. From memory, the Leeds District at that time stretched from Methley, south of Leeds, to Morecambe and Heysham in the west and Garsdale in the north. Most small stations had oil lighting at

Above: A Manningham (20E) favourite: ex-L&Y 2-4-2T No 50621 waits at Skipton to take the 4.30pm local train through to Barnoldswick on 2 June 1952. It mainly conveyed schoolchildren. This engine was the pioneer of the class, as L&Y 1008, and was built at Horwich in 1889. It survived until 1954. *Harold D. Bowtell/ Author's Collection*

Below: A splendid photograph of the southern approaches to Skipton, with a pair of ex-LNER Class J39 0-6-0s climbing up the Ilkley branch with a goods train for the North Eastern Region on 23 June 1950. *H. Weston*

Above: A reminder of the terrible winter of early 1947, when it was essential to clear at least one line as soon as possible. This is the scene at Dent. *W. Hubert Foster/courtesy John W. Holroyd*

that time, as electricity hadn't yet reached the more remote areas, but events were to change things. The railways had been nationalised on 1 January 1948 and the new Regional boundaries placed the Leeds and Bradford areas, together with the line as far as Snaygill, near Skipton, in the newly created North Eastern Region. Henceforth, my promotion was to be in that Region until I reached a certain level. Most of the Region had been LNER territory and it didn't go down well with a die-hard LMS man like myself. However, for operating purposes there was to be no change and a system of 'Operating Areas' was established, so that the Leeds City and Wakefield District Offices continued to control their areas as before. The Control organisation and the telecommunications system could not be altered for several years.

Now I had several weeks in which to get used to being in civvy street, and one of my first acts was to buy with my gratuity a Dawes lightweight bicycle, aluminium framed and with a Sturmey-Archer three speed, all of £30. It was worth every penny, and cycling was a real pleasure on the quiet roads of 1948. My Uncle Edgar was the youth hostel warden at Malham and he had taken me on

holiday walking in the Lake District several times before the war, having no children of his own. So I had a week's walking with him, staying at youth hostels, where Edgar knew all the wardens. I remember climbing Scafell Pike, which seemed so easy in those days.

I also watched an exciting cricket match at Bradford Park Avenue over three days — Australia v Yorkshire. It was a sticky wicket and Yorkshire were all out for 71 and 89. That's not as bad as it sounds, as Australia, who swept all before them in 1948, were all out for 101 in their first innings, and had been reduced to 20 for 5 in their second. At that point, the excitement was intense in the crowded ground, but the Aussies managed to pull round and beat Yorkshire by four wickets.

And as a portent of things to come, I attended my first Ministry of Transport public inquiry into a

railway accident at Winsford, several miles north of Crewe, which occurred shortly after midnight on 17 April 1948. The 5.40pm Glasgow to Euston, hauled by Pacific No 6207 I noted, was halted in section between two signalboxes at 12.10am when the communication cord was pulled by a soldier who wanted to nip off home smartly. The following train, the Up Postal, 6.25pm from Glasgow behind Pacific No 6251, was allowed to proceed into the occupied section in error and crashed into the rear of the standing train at 40/45 mph. Sixteen passengers were killed outright and eight were fatally injured. They had all been travelling in the last two coaches, which were severely damaged. And thus began for me a lifetime's interest in signalling and accidents.

However, a few weeks later I was notified that I would be starting work at Shipley on 24 May 1948

and I duly presented myself to the Stationmaster, Mr Wright, at 9.0am. He might easily have been a template for Captain Mainwaring in the well-known TV series *Dad's Army,* because like him he was irascible and henpecked. And yes, we never saw his wife at the station. There were four Class 5 clerks, rostered on four rotating weekly shifts, roughly early, late and nights, with a 12.0 noon to 7.0pm shift. The other shifts were 6.0am to 1.0pm, 4.0pm to 11.0pm and 11.0pm to 6.0am. As was usual on the railways, the night-man would always come on duty a little early and he would stay until 6.30am. There were very few trains on the night shift, so the clerk dealt with correspondence and entered parcels for delivery on to the appropriate delivery sheets. There were two parcels vans, which delivered parcels in the mornings and collected them from shops and business premises

in the afternoon. Lyons Cakes, Palethorpes sausages and Vitacream linger in one's memory.

In those days, Bradford was still the woolopolis of the world, and mainline trains to St Pancras and Bristol started from Forster Square. There were quite extensive carriage sidings at Manningham for that purpose. The trains reversed at Leeds City, so they were hauled between Bradford and Leeds by 2-6-4Ts. We had trains to St Pancras at 7.26am, 9.15am, 10.37am, 12.18pm and 9.35pm, and to Bristol at 7.42am, 4.52pm and 9.12pm. There was also a 9.25am from Bradford to Bristol which strangely at that time did not stop at Shipley. It also went to Kingswear on Fridays and Saturdays during the summer timetable, the forerunner of the 'Devonian'. The afternoon gap in the timetable to London was met by changing at Leeds into the 'Thames-Clyde Express'. Passengers for Scotland took a local train to Skipton and changed there into one of the expresses from Leeds or St Pancras. The two overnight trains were heavily used for mails and parcels. By 1948 the railways were restoring their holiday extra trains, and Morecambe was well served from Bradford and Shipley on Saturdays. There were also Friday night trains to Bournemouth and Paignton. Those with long memories of summer Saturdays will remember the Heads of Ayr to Leeds express and the 9.0am Glasgow St Enoch to Sheffield, often hauled by a Scottish 'Jubilee', which caused great excitement among the fans.

Below: Double-headed Class 5 4-6-0s Nos 44919 (pilot engine) and 44765 slow down for the Shipley curve with the Up 'Thames-Forth' express on 12 June 1951. A typical West Riding background. *Author*

The Clerical Grading Structure

Class 5 was the lowest grade for salaried staff, and the salary increased by small annual increments until the age of 32, subsequently lowered to 28. The grading structure was altered several years later.

Salaried staff in the Traffic Department comprised mainly clerks, stationmasters, goods agents, inspectors and controllers, and District and HQ staff. Salaried staff retired at the age of 60 and were compulsory members of a superannuation fund, which provided a lump sum on retirement and a pension of roughly half the retiring salary. These were quite generous benefits, although a fund member paid 5% of his salary into the fund. However, at the age of 22, as I was then, thoughts of retirement were well over the horizon and out of sight. It is interesting to note that the LMS Superannuation Fund had its roots in the LNWR Fund, which was established with similar benefits in the late 19th century.

In LNWR days the company required complete obedience, unswerving attention to the job and a high standard of performance. Discipline was strict but being a member of the salaried staff gave one complete job security. Two world wars had changed people's attitudes, and jobs on the railway were not so eagerly sought after the Second World War as they had been previously; in fact there were always vacancies in some wages grades. Basic rates of pay were uncompetitive in the labour market, but the 24 hour, seven days a week, operation of the railway provided plenty of jobs with extra pay for night work, Sunday work and overtime. There were rarely any unfilled vacancies in such posts. Most railway staff were glad of the opportunity to increase their take home pay. Staff in wages grades were porters, signalmen, drivers and firemen, ticket

collectors, platelayers, etc and had rather different conditions of service from salaried staff. The jobs were not pensionable and retirement was at age 65. Wages were paid weekly on a Friday whilst, on the LMS, salaries were paid fortnightly on a Thursday.

I Become the Stationmaster's Clerk

The weekly/fortnightly wages and salary paybills were compiled at stations and depots by ordinary Class 5 clerks, who had to know all about conditions of service, together with income tax and other 'stoppages'. They were based on timesheets or timebooks. At Shipley the paybills were compiled by the night shift clerk, a good arrangement as there was little interruption or disturbance. Whilst I was there, there was a rearrangement of duties. The clerical night shift was withdrawn and a new post was created of Stationmaster's Clerk. This was a middle turn job and included the paybills. The Stationmaster must have liked me, and asked me if I would like to become his clerk (probably because I could type, albeit with two fingers). It didn't take me long to say 'Yes'. No more nights or late turns. I could remain on the Sunday roster. But more important

Above: The Rebuilt 'Royal Scots' were firm favourites of Canon Eric Treacy, and he captured this one just north of Saltaire station with the 10.25am express from Leeds to Glasgow St Enoch. The engine has already acquired its initial number ('4'), but the tender still proudly exhibits its LMS parentage. It was rebuilt in May 1948, and appears to be straight out of the shops. The station, about a mile north of Shipley, was under the control of the Stationmaster at Shipley, and a clerk from Shipley had to visit the station daily to check the books and bring back the daily takings. The total staff was two porters, one on each shift. Saltaire was not a commuter station in those days, and almost the entire population of Saltaire worked in Salt's Mill, although at Bank Holidays the station was thronged by passengers from Bradford visiting the local beauty spot of Shipley Glen. If it suddenly rained in the afternoon they came back to the station in droves for single tickets to Bradford Forster Square. I think there was always a clerk there on Bank Holidays. Saltaire is now a World Heritage Centre; people in 1948 would have scoffed at the idea. *Eric Treacy*

A Railwayman's Odyssey

Right: LMS Compound 4-4-0 No 40931 takes day-excursionists back home from Morecambe, along the electrified route to Lancaster Green Ayre station, on 11 September 1950. Morecambe was very popular with West Riding people, for both a week's holiday and for day, half-day and evening excursions. *Ian S. Pearsall*

to me was the opportunity to learn about the operational aspects of a stationmaster's job, and Pongo (as the Stationmaster was unkindly referred to for some unknown reason) knew that I was attending the Train Signalling classes and was keen to get on in the service. And perhaps most important of all was the increased opportunities it gave for meeting my girlfriend in the evenings for a bit of courting. When you are 22 and in love, a week on late turn is an eternity!

One of the peculiarities of the layout at Shipley was the existence of a small booking office at the entrance to platform 1 (the Skipton platform), which allowed passengers to obtain a ticket without having to go to the main booking office in the angle of platforms 2 & 3, a journey which required a tiresome tour of the grotty subway twice. Over the years, the opening hours of the satellite booking office had been reduced until the only train for which the office was open was the 8.44am to Morecambe, for which there were usually a few takers. It was a cold, dank office but I also used it for compiling the paybills on Mondays, which was a lengthy job. Needless to say, I lit the stove on Mondays. The title 'booking' office was a relic of the very early days of railways when passengers booked a journey. Another thing that John Barnes at Keighley had impressed on me was that you did not sell a ticket. You issued it, and it remained the property of the railway company. There were legal implications such as tickets being non-transferable.

Whilst I was at Shipley we ran what was, I believe, the first postwar Sunday excursion to Morecambe. I was on duty that day and the queue

of passengers was both amazing and gratifying, but I was somewhat taken aback when Bradford (the starting point of the train) phoned up and said that the train was at bursting point when it left them. They were sending it non-stop to Morecambe and were going to run a second train to pick up intermediate passengers. Everyone was taken by surprise, but in those days we had plenty of resources to fall back on and could quickly respond. Spare coaches for excursion trains were often elderly ex-Midland non-corridor stock, and special stops had to be inserted in the longer distance trains 'For lavatory purposes' as the Weekly Special Traffic Notice accurately described it. This usually applied on the return journey for the comfort of those passengers who had spent some time at the bar before joining the train. Morecambe Promenade station had commodious Gentlemen's conveniences. I'm sure there is an unfilled niche for a book on the history, design, construction and development of conveniences on railway stations. As a social study, of course.

In-House Training
There was adequate on-the-job training for the job you were going to do, but if you were ambitious you needed to know about the rest of the railway. The railway companies had always been very good in this respect and provided a range of evening classes in both Passenger and Goods Station Work and Accounts. They also provided classes in Train Signalling, called 'Block' classes as they dealt mainly with the Block Signalling arrangements. They were purely voluntary, but there was an exam

Left: Back nearer home again, at Bingley where I lived for the first 25 years of my life, Stanier 2-8-0 No 8159 (20A — Holbeck) passes the signalbox with an Up Class B goods train on 26 April 1948. I learned my 'Block' there with a friendly signalman, Cliff Nichols, who allowed me to work the box under his supervision. Quite unofficial, but that's how we all did it, and it was tacitly encouraged. *Author*

at the end of each winter and the results were entered on your staff history. Good results were likely to improve your chance of promotion, so there was some incentive both to attend the classes (in your own time, of course) and to do well in the exams. Indeed, there was always a bit of friendly competition amongst us to see who got the best marks. Another incentive! So the first winter I enrolled for all three (thanks to an understanding girlfriend). The Signalling Class was held at Leeds Central passenger station, the Passenger Class at Bradford Bridge Street Goods Depot and the Goods Class at Bradford Adolphus St Goods Depot, in one of the offices. All three of these large edifices were demolished years ago, but at the time they were part of the everyday scene, as were Bradford Valley Goods Depot, Forster Square station and Exchange station, with all their associated sidings layouts. Who would have imagined in 1948 the major changes which were to engulf our railways? They seemed so solid and permanent.

The instructors for these classes were volunteers from among the normal staff, but they received some sort of financial recognition. The railways also ran more advanced courses in Railway Operating and Commercial Practice, but owing to the more limited demand they were often correspondence courses, but very valuable nonetheless. You had to do mini essays in answer to the various questions and one of my early acquisitions was a portable typewriter, which cost £25 — a month's salary. It's a good job that I was still living at home in Bingley.

I Become a Summer Temporary Relief Clerk (TRC)

Such posts were advertised to staff every year to provide cover for annual leave, especially at smaller stations which couldn't cover by resident staff working overtime. They were still Class 5, even though a TRC had to have a wide experience and knowledge to be able to go to any station in the district and take charge of a job without any training. Fortunately, every detail of station working was written down somewhere, and was the same at every station, so you could walk straight into a station and start to issue tickets. What wasn't written down was where to find the key to the booking office and where was the safe key hidden? Often the door key was kept in the signalbox if it was adjacent, but TRCs were nothing if not resourceful. It was very good training.

That was one of the reasons for applying for such vacancies. The other was financial, so there was quite a lot of competition for TRC vacancies. Each TRC had a 'home' station, and was paid travelling time when working away from the home station, which was almost always. The train was used when practicable, using a free duty pass covering the district, or a bus could be used if quicker (keep the bus ticket). In the case of more remote stations or depots there was a limit to the amount paid for travelling, lodging allowance being paid instead, even though you didn't necessarily lodge. And train travelling time was paid even if you did it more quickly on a bicycle. I did a lot of cycling in those days and the roads were so quiet.

Above: Viewed from a few yards further north, another Holbeck engine, Rebuilt 'Royal Scot' No 46145 *The Duke of Wellington's Regiment (West Riding)* with what appears to be a full train of BR Mark 1 coaches forming the Up 'Thames-Clyde' express, approaches Bingley in the early 1950s. A goods train can be seen standing on the Up goods line, waiting for the express to pass. Bingley was a regulating point in both directions, and the signalman had to watch his margins for goods trains in front of expresses very carefully. *W. Hubert Foster/courtesy John W. Holroyd*

Below: This photograph was taken 10 minutes later. Now that the express has passed, the goods train can safely follow it. Stanier Class 8F 2-8-0 No 48126 takes its load of coal wagons gently from the Up goods line on to the Up main line. The wagons are all loose-coupled and it is necessary to avoid 'snatches', which can break couplings. The engine was built at Crewe in 1940, and was one of the first 2-8-0s to be shedded at Holbeck (20A). It was soon followed by others. *W. Hubert Foster/courtesy John W. Holroyd*

On top of travelling time, expenses were paid as well (and they were tax free). Midday meal allowance (three shillings) was paid if you were working more than one mile from your home station. In addition, breakfast allowance was paid if you had to leave your home station before 8.0am (which was quite often). Finally, dinner allowance was paid if you returned to your home station after 6.0pm. This all gave scope for what today would be called 'creative accounting', even if it was all legal.

On one occasion I was relieving for a fortnight in the Yard Master's office at Hunslet Sidings, not a very accessible location, and I imagine my official travelling time was sufficient to push me into the lodging allowance bracket (also tax free). I think I cycled there every day, only about 15 miles and just over the hour. There were two clerical posts there and both needed coverage, so a TRC pal of mine also relieved there. We had a great time. The Yard Master was a very nice chap, and just glad that he had received some cover. Neither of us had been in a Yard Master's office before, but, ever resourceful, we soon caught on. The paybills were one of the big jobs, because in addition to the yard staff there were several signalboxes. It was the practice at Hunslet Sidings to do the paybills on Sundays when it was quiet and I can recall cycling there on a fine sunny day along very quiet roads at 8.0 o'clock in the morning and through the almost deserted streets in Leeds and Hunslet. We both got stuck in to the paybills and were finished by lunchtime. Sunday pay was calculated as a minimum of 8 hours at time and three-quarters = 14 hours. It all sounds very mercenary but courting was becoming serious and one needed to save up for the consequences of such development. However, the excitement of the week, apart from courting, was pay day, with a couple of hundred men hammering on the paying-out window, waiting for it to open and anxious to get the money home to their wives so that the latter could do the weekend shopping. Wives called the financial shots in those days!

A Typical Day in the Life of a Relief Clerk
Actually, there were no typical days for TRCs. You went where you were sent within a defined area, often at a day's notice if you were covering a sudden sickness vacancy. However, if we take Monday 3 April 1950 as an example, I was booked

to go to Woodlesford station and then on to Methley station later in the day. I may well have cycled there as I needed to be at Woodlesford by 8.0am. There were few passengers to book, and the porters did most of the work. My job was to do the daily accounts for the previous day, then cash up and take the previous day's takings (not a lot) to Methley, the next station down the line. The Stationmaster at Methley also covered Woodlesford.

I doubt that Woodlesford had seen many passengers ever since the early 1920s when buses started running into Leeds, all of 6 miles away, but there was quite a good train service, especially for commuters (I think we called them office workers in those days). There were trains to Leeds at 7.18am (from Knottingley), 7.58am (from Cudworth), 8.25am (from Knottingley) and 8.37am (from Sheffield). All stopping trains, of course, no doubt well filled from stations further out.

Much of the work at Methley seemed to be completing colliery waybills for wagons of coal being turned out by the hundred by collieries in the area. Every so often a shunter or goods porter would come into the office with a fistful of declaration notes from a colliery, listing wagons, destinations and tonnage. As I remember it, the clerk then made out the wagon labels and gave them to the shunter, then made out waybills, which were sent off to each destination station by railway post, for each wagon. The destination station needed to receive those waybills as an advice that such a load was on its way, and also as proof that the wagon transit had been paid for (most important — the railways made lots of money from carrying coal). All internal correspondence, waybills, etc went by train. It was handed to the guard, who collected it from each station and handed it all in at a main centre, where it would be sorted and sent on to destination. It was quick, convenient and, most important, cheap. The latter was an important feature, as the railway generated massive quantities of internal mail. Important items could be registered and sent forward under signature.

We didn't calculate the carriage charges for coal — that was done by a central office, and needed to be. The history of the setting of carriage charges for coal traffic was extremely complicated, mainly arising from 19th century inter-railway competition for carrying such lucrative traffic. There was a time in about the 1870s when colliery owners in South Yorkshire proposed building their own railway to

London because they thought the railway companies were charging too much. Parliament was not impressed and refused to sanction it (the railway companies had many members of both Houses of Parliament).

A few weeks later I relieved at Kirkstall station for a whole fortnight, on middle turn (there was only one clerk's post). This was a very easy job; in fact, clerks at most small stations were not overworked. I can't remember how I passed my time but I do recall that there was plenty of rhubarb grown in the area, some of which went by train. Indeed, there was a group of sidings at Hunslet Marshalling Yard known as 'Rhubarb End'. We were having a fine spell of weather and I used to walk across to Kirkstall Abbey and have my sandwiches there. I may even have popped into Headingley cricket ground too, which was just up the road. I had been a member since 1945, so entrance was free.

Above: In 1948 the East Coast floods destroyed or damaged several underbridges on the East Coast main line north of Newcastle. For a short while, some expresses were diverted via Leeds and Carlisle, which caused great excitement locally. Everyone had heard of the 'Flying Scotsman', and Treacy was soon in action. He chose Marley Junction as the best spot from which to photograph the Down train, and produced this splendid picture of 'A4' No 25 *Falcon.* The original is in my possession. *Eric Treacy*

Below: Hubert Foster was also quickly into action and chose Bell Busk from which to photograph the Up train, which came behind two LMS engines to universal disappointment. Hellifield's (20G) elderly 4-4-0 No 40459 never thought it would have the honour of piloting the 'Flying Scotsman'. The train engine is a Class 5 4-6-0. I photographed the train at Shipley, and the approach road to the station, from which there is a good view of the line, was absolutely solid with people, hoping for a repeat of of the previous day's streamliner. What a let-down! *W. Hubert Foster/courtesy John W. Holroyd*

Above: LMS Class 5P5F 4-6-0 No 5050 heads a train of LMS Stanier coaches approaching Marley Junction. The engine was shedded at Carnforth (11A) and the train appears to be marshalled in two portions, signifying a train from Leeds to Carnforth and Morecambe that will divide at Wennington. It is difficult to date this photo, although the sans-serif type of lettering on the locomotive may give a clue to experts in that field. *W. Hubert Foster/courtesy John W. Holroyd*

Below: A strange headcode for an express passenger train: one of Holbeck's semi-experimental trio of Class 5 4-6-0s with Caprotti valve gear, No 44756 built in 1948, was fairly new in this photograph. Judging by the rake of vehicles, it is possible that the locomotive was under test. It was photographed approaching Marley Junction. *W. Hubert Foster/courtesy John W. Holroyd*

A Long Day

One day, whilst I was at Kirkstall, the Staff Office rang up in a panic. Could I drop everything at Kirkstall and go to Armley GN? The late turn clerk had failed to turn up without notice. So I told the Stationmaster at Kirkstall, and he said it would be all right. Thus, I set off for Armley GN. This was off the beaten track for me, and was the first time I had been at a former LNER station, but I found it without too much difficulty and sought the Stationmaster, who took me into the booking office and left me to it, saying encouragingly, 'You'll be all right.' This was being thrown in at the deep end with a vengeance! It was a big office, and dealt with parcels and goods traffic as well. There were just rows and rows of drawers, with racks above them. Nothing labelled, of course. I quickly hunted around so that at least I could issue tickets. (Where's the safe? Where's the safe key? Where's the float? Where, where, where?) As I mentioned, this was the first time I had ever been to a former GN station, but when a passenger asked me for a return to Keighley (change at St Dunstan's) I felt at home. It all made one very resourceful. It was a long, long day, but I was young and it was financially rewarding.

Below: One of the sturdy and long-lived ex-Lancashire & Yorkshire 2-4-2 tank engines, of which there were a goodly number in the Leeds/Bradford area, engages in a spell of shunting at Leeds City station on 29 August 1951. No 50689 was a Manningham (20E) engine. *Author's Collection*

A Change of Job and Temporary Promotion

Each summer a number of temporary jobs were created at larger passenger stations to cover annual leave, and they were advertised on the periodical vacancy list. One which particularly took my eye was a Temporary Class 4 post at Leeds City enquiry office (one step up). I applied for it and was appointed, perhaps as a reward for good marks in the evening class exams. The vacancy lasted three months and the office was open from 8.0am to 8.0pm. It had three sections — train enquiries, reservations and telegrams.

Reservations were something new to me, but quite straightforward. We had charts for each train showing the disposition of coaches, and the internal layout of seats, rather like theatre reservations. A passenger would specify the date of travel, the train, the class, smoking or non-smoking, window seat (nearly always first choice), sometimes near the toilet or dining car, and back or facing the engine. We had to be very careful with the latter; trains from Bradford Forster Square reversed at Leeds. Some passengers felt quite strongly that they wanted their backs to the engine. Perhaps they felt safer that way. Apart from those trains which started at Forster Square, we did not reserve seats on intermediate trains. Proper attention to detail was required, and before you marked the chart you repeated the passenger's request so that there was no misunderstanding. You also made sure you marked the chart, or double booking could result and then there would be a commotion on the train.

I spent some time on the Telegrams desk, and that was quite fun. I quickly learned how to calculate

the number of words — eg how many words for Mrs E. G. Dodds, 28 August 1950? I think it was nine words for one shilling plus a penny for each extra word. We made out a telegram form, and then stuck it in a holder and pushed it into a pneumatic tube,which went straight to the post office. If you had made an error in charging, the post office would ring up and give you an earful. Many of the telegrams were bets on horses, and some were in code. No, I never bet on a tip! The subject matter covered the whole range of human activity, happy, sad, boring, etc but the lovey-dovey ones could be a hoot, especially if the sender was giggling in an embarrassed way as you counted up the words. If you were feeling especially cruel that day you would point at a particular word and pretend to be unable to read it, then you would both giggle. We only did inland telegrams — others were referred to the Cable and Wireless office. But I enjoyed the face to face contact with passengers.

The Pace Quickens

At the end of summer I went back on relief, but this time I was appointed as a permanent relief clerk, home station Bradford Forster Square. No more travelling expenses, but instead a 10% commuted allowance. I was still Class 5 and one of my first jobs was at Baildon. Yes, another easy posting, and I came across an old record book showing numbers of passengers year by year and going back to George Stephenson. Up to about 1924 there were many thousands, but a couple of years later there

had been a catastrophic slump. The motor bus had arrived, which many people found more convenient, and was probably cheaper. That situation was repeated throughout the railway system and led to some closures about 1930 when the railways had received powers to run bus services. They chose to do so by acquiring shares in existing bus companies.

However, for the last couple of years I had been spending a lot of spare time in signalboxes, especially with my mentor, Cliff Nicholls, at Bingley, and I had been working hard at the Rules. I felt it was time to put in for a Rules Exam. This might not sound important, but in the railway world it was a vital step, because unless you passed the Rules many Operating Department jobs were closed to you, including stationmasters' jobs. You had to demonstrate that you had a good working knowledge of the Rules, and could apply them. That last bit was important. So I applied for a Rules Exam and was called into the District Office for a

Below: In the spring of 1949 LMS Pacific No 46237 *City of Bristol,* a Camden (1B) engine, awaits its next duty at Carlisle Citadel station. Its streamlined casing has been removed, but the sloping smokebox top denotes its lineage. Much of the station roof and the ornate glass screen were subsequently rebuilt. *Author*

Above: The caption on the back of this photograph refers to its being an Up express for Leeds, which would denote the 4.0pm from Glasgow St Enoch to Leeds City. The pilot engine is a Carlisle Kingmoor compound No 1141, which will probably be detached at Ais Gill from which point the train engine, a Class 5XP 'Jubilee', will work forward unaided to Leeds. Both engines could do with a good clean. *H. Gordon Tidey*

face to face examination by one of the senior men there. These exams lasted as long as it took, but if you started off well and had the right answers you were on your way. The exam covered the Rule Book, the Train Signalling Regulations (known as the Block Book) and the General Appendix which, as its name implies, covered all those instructions about train working, loading, accidents, bad weather and a host of other items not covered in the Rule Book or the Block Book. Nothing was left to chance on the railway. And the questions were not of the 'What does Rule 67 say?' variety, but rather, 'What would you do if such and such…?'

Into the Stationmaster's Grade — a Milestone
After a couple of anxious hours, the examiner smiled and said 'Congratulations'. I was on cloud nine, and he said, 'Now you can start applying for stationmasters' posts in Class 4.' What a relief! I felt like a real railwayman. It was early in 1951 and a Summer Relief Stationmaster's post was advertised, Class 4, Leeds Central District GN. Nothing daunted, I applied and was appointed. The District Superintendent wanted me straight away, and I took up my new job in March. It was, of course, a uniform job, and I was duly measured for a suit (with two pairs of trousers), an overcoat, and a long, black mac, in those days the ultimate symbol of authority out on the line. Also the most prized possession: the uniform hat with the magic words thereon and the gold braid. It wasn't delivered straightaway and before it had arrived, fate intervened.

I had started scanning the vacancy list for Class 4 stationmasters' permanent vacancies but I had a specific requirement. This was 1951 and there was a severe shortage of houses. Those to rent were like gold. Stationmasters' positions frequently came with a house, but as many small stations were out in the country, the houses were often oil-lit with few amenities which, so far as my fiancée was concerned, ruled them out. However, after about a couple of months a vacancy at Battyeford, i/c Bradley was advertised. There was no station house, but a railway house was available only a couple of minutes from the station.

It sounded like an interesting job. I applied for it, was interviewed by Mr Birch, the District Operating Superintendent at Wakefield, and was successful. I now had a foot firmly planted on the promotion ladder and, on 21 May 1951 I took up my new job. A new chapter in life had started, at the age of 25.

Above: Class 5 4-6-0 No 4883, one of a batch of 60 built in 1945, looks brand new in this photograph taken at the engine's home shed, Carlisle Kingmoor (12A), as it is being coaled. *W. Hubert Foster/courtesy John W. Holroyd*

Left: A long-time Holbeck favourite, 'Patriot' class 4-6-0 No 5535 *Sir Herbert Walker KCB* works back north with a train of empty milk tanks from Cricklewood in 1948. *P. Ransome Wallis*

Below: Shortly afterwards it was selected for rebuilding and appears in the original BR livery for express passenger train locomotives. *(no attribution)*

Five

THE FIRST STEP ON THE LADDER — STATION MASTER AT BATTYEFORD

The Perk of a Station House

Most small stations had a house for the Stationmaster, which was either part of the station buildings themselves, or in the grounds of the station. They were built during the 19th century when it was thought necessary for the stationmaster to be near the job (even when in bed). But there was another reason. In those far off days, the Stationmaster was expected to be on duty for every train that stopped at the station, but in between trains he could go into the house for his meals and probably have a nap. After all, there was nothing much else to do, (although the Stationmaster at Bell Busk found time to have about a dozen children). And he might spend an hour in the village pub in the evening between trains; stationmasters were expected to be part of the community.

Many stationmasters' posts had 'On Call' duties, usually on alternate weeks, which they would share with an adjacent stationmaster. 'On Call' meant being available for any emergency, and the responsibilities were an accepted and expected part of a railway operator's life. They were paid for, usually by a commuted allowance of 5% of annual salary. If you were called out in an emergency you were paid overtime. As it happened, there were no 'On Call' responsibilities at Battyeford. My salary at Battyeford was £340pa, quite a step up from my Class 5 clerk's salary, which had progressed to about £260, but I had lost all my perks and was probably worse off, being one of the penalties that often accompanied promotion on the railway. The house at Battyeford was not immediately available for occupation, so until the autumn I travelled backwards and forwards each day from my parents' home at Bingley. The train service fitted in quite well, via Leeds.

This was 1951, and houses to rent were like gold, so I was glad to get the tenancy of this railway house. It was a substantially built end-terrace house, three bedrooms but no bathroom, with an outside toilet which had a propensity to freeze up in winter. Ah, the delights of bathing in a tin bath in front of the Yorkist stove, but we were young, and in any case we tended to visit our parents quite frequently. They had bathrooms. The Yorkist oven was great for storing nappies, after our first-born arrived in 1955.

There was a railway canteen at Mirfield in the goods yard, which was still going strong and serving excellent two-course tasty meals at reduced prices, all cooked on the premises of course, and puddings with lots of nice, thick custard. Most railway centres had a staff canteen; they had been built during the war, particularly to cater for shift workers. I used it most days, cycling there and back. There was quite a sizeable marshalling yard at Mirfield, hence the need for an engine shed (25D), which had mainly LMS Standard 0-8-0s, ex-WD 2-8-0s and elderly but still serviceable L&Y 0-6-0s and 2-4-2 tanks.

Battyeford was actually part of Mirfield township, but it was on the ex-LNWR Spen Valley line, known as the 'New Line' because it had been opened in about 1900 to enable the LNWR to bypass the congested area through Mirfield, between Thornhill LNWR Junction (at

Ravensthorpe) and Heaton Lodge Junction. I was also nominally in charge of the station at Bradley, about a mile from Battyeford and virtually a suburb of Huddersfield, but it had closed the year before I arrived. It was on the four-track section of the former LNWR main line between Heaton Lodge Junction and Huddersfield and had no fewer than four signalboxes within a mile of each other.

Wartime Train-spotting at Mirfield

Fortuitously, I knew the area quite well. As a schoolboy I had discovered somehow that Mirfield was an especially good place to go train watching, because if you got within reach of the Spen Valley line you could see trains from both the Western and Central Divisions. During the early war years a group of us often cycled there during the school holidays and we found a spot a couple of fields beyond the engine shed, and near Heaton Lodge Junction, from where we could see both lines. It would be impossible today, owing to the growth of

Above: The Class 2 2-6-0s were introduced by the LMS in 1946; one of the class, No 6406, a Farnley Junction (25G) engine, sports parcels train headlights with a very light load, leaving Leeds City station in this undated photograph. I passed through here every weekday from May to September 1951, travelling between home at Bingley and Battyeford, my new station. *Eric Treacy*

Below: Mirfield shed, which I could see from my back door, had a number of these very useful ex-L&Y 2-4-2Ts. No 10748, a Wakefield (25A) engine, takes a three-coach train through typical West Riding territory. The locomotive was built at Horwich in 1896 and withdrawn in 1950. *Author's Collection*

lineside trees, now the curse of today's railways. We took sandwiches and a bottle of pop and happily settled down for the day.

In those days there was a constant stream of goods trains and plenty of passenger trains on the L&Y Section through Mirfield, which also carried Western Division expresses, but the less frequent trains on the ex-LNWR Spen Valley line provided even more interest because they tended to come from far-flung sheds on the Western Division of the LMS, which to us at the time were just names. When we noticed that a train was approaching on that line one of us had to sprint across to the other side of the field to be sure of getting the engine number and the shed number. It was all great fun. There were plenty of standard and ex-L&Y 0-8-0s on the Lanky, and ex-LNWR 0-8-0s on the Spen Valley with their distinctive **puff-puff** puff-puff beat. To our eyes those LNWR engines looked fairly ancient even then; we were not to know that they would last for another 25 years and easily outlive the more modern LMS standard 0-8-0 engines. L&Y 0-8-0s had been withdrawn in large numbers in the later 1930s, but quite a few had not been broken up and were quickly reinstated for wartime use. The last one, No 12857, was

withdrawn in December 1951. I shall use the LMS numbering for this section.

Local passenger trains then were in the hands of the ubiquitous and dependable ex-L&Y 2-4-2 radial tanks, but there were several standard engines to be seen. Low Moor (25F) had Class 2P 4-4-0s Nos 585/9 and 676, together with compounds No 1185 (remembered fondly as the Hornby model), plus Nos 1190/9. Wakefield (25A) had Nos 586/7. Longer distance passenger trains and the expresses were in the hands of 'Jubilees' and 4-6-0 mixed-traffics from a variety of sheds, but mainly in Lancashire and Yorkshire. Any hopes we might have had of seeing ex-LNWR 'Princes' and 'Georges', or even the ex-L&Y Hughes 4-6-0s, failed to materialise. And it never entered my head that I might one day in the not too distant future be Stationmaster at that wayside station that we could just see up the Spen Valley line.

Life at Battyeford Station

Until I became a stationmaster I had been one of the boys and having a good time without too many responsibilities. They were indeed happy times and very sociable. As a Class 5 clerk you had only yourself to think about, but now I had entered the world of the bosses, and I soon realised it could be a lonely life and that I had a role to play. I was now 'in charge', with all the responsibilities that that entailed.

Battyeford station was a typical wooden-built LNWR station, with a booking office, waiting rooms and toilets on each platform. This was quite extravagant by today's standards, but typical of its era. The station was staffed by two porters, one on each turn, and was closed on Sundays. This meant a bare week's wage, and staff were hard to come by. Fortunately, the hours suited married women, and the work was not too arduous, as the Stationmaster did the hard work, such as climbing up and cleaning the gas globes, and changing gas mantles, especially on the overbridge. One of my lady porters was mad clean on scrubbing floors (we had bare boards in the booking hall and waiting rooms). Don't ask me why, but she made an extra effort when the station inspections were due, which helped us to gain the Best Kept Station award in 1953. It never entered my head then, that within 10 years I would be doing the judging, but at least I would know what to look for.

Supervision of Signalboxes

The greater responsibility of the job was looking after five signalboxes, all of LNWR design, four of which were on the four-track Heaton Lodge Junction to Huddersfield section. Heaton Lodge Junction signalbox itself was a former L&Y signalbox on the old L&Y main line from Wakefield to Sowerby Bridge, Rochdale and Manchester Victoria. My signalboxes, all within a few hundred yards of each other, were Heaton Lodge Sidings, Spen Valley Junction and Bradley Junction, all three-shift boxes, and Holliday's Sidings, which was open on a single shift only, to enable the sidings to be serviced by the local trips. There were two fans of sidings at Heaton Lodge Sidings, one on each side of the main line, and they were a relic of the old days when traffic was exchanged there between the L&Y and the LNWR. Now they were used only for stabling freight wagons, or for freight trains which for some reason couldn't immediately be worked forward to the Manchester area. On the 'New Line', from Spen Valley Junction to Farnley Junction, there was a three-shift signalbox at Battyeford adjacent to the station.

All told I had 15 signalmen including relief under my charge, and some, probably most, were old enough to be my father; in fact, one looked old enough to be my grandfather. How to get on with them was a steep learning curve, and you had to work it out for yourself, but practically all of them were decent railwaymen who knew the job and got on with it. The standard instructions laid down that I had to visit them once a week to check that all was in order, and that the signals and the block signalling instructions were being dealt with correctly. My many long hours in signalboxes when I was a clerk, and when the signalmen felt that they had no need to cover up anything slightly irregular just because I was there, had given me a very good insight into the way in which signalmen interpreted the instructions. That experience now stood me in very good stead. I knew what they were up to, and what I needed to be on the lookout for, and it helped me to gain the signalmen's respect.

These signalbox visits entailed a very pleasant walk down the line, but on Fridays I had to pay out the wages, as well as pensions to retired railwaymen. This involved going down to the bank in the town escorted by the early turn porter to collect the money, which was quite a substantial

Above: This is a splendid photo of LMS parallel-boiler 2-6-4T No 42412 (25B — Huddersfield) coming off the 'New Line' through Battyeford, onto the Leeds-Mirfield-Huddersfield line at Spen Valley Junction. This was one of the signalboxes under my control. The four tracks were paired and referred to as 'North' and 'South' rather than Fast and Slow. *Ian Allan Library*

sum. We always believed that the purpose of the escort was not for security but to act as a witness to testify that I hadn't run off with the money if it happened to be stolen from us. The railway company trusted no one! Paydays were quite busy. Having obtained the money, I had to put it in pay packets together with the payslip, and then deliver the pay packets to the signalboxes for the men who worked in that particular signalbox.

The Battyeford staff came to the station for their wages and pensions, but I cycled or walked down the line with the payouts for the others. Retired people who had been attached to Bradley were paid by me at the station signalbox at a specific time because the station buildings had been demolished and there was no other cover. Those retired people loved to come in the signalbox, sit down and have a chat, and no one thought anything about it. They would have needed a Personal Track Safety certificate these days, as the signalbox was at the end of the former platform which stood between the two pairs of lines. But they had all had anything up to 50 years' service and they knew a thing or two. It couldn't happen today, of course, but it was a lot less dangerous than crossing the road to get to the station. However, it wouldn't have looked good

in an MOT Accident Report, but it was the method which I inherited and I was told by the local Inspector that it was acceptable. 'Not to worry', he said. In any case, the signalbox had all the modern electrical controls on the signalling.

The Train Service
The passenger train service at Battyeford was mainly in the morning and evening peaks, such as they were, and the passenger traffic was quite light: mainly workers to Leeds and Huddersfield. Parallel-boilered 2-6-4Ts from Farnley Junction and Hillhouse handled most of the trains, which were all-stations Leeds-Huddersfield, but the 5.25pm to Leeds worked through from Manchester and was hauled by a 'Jubilee' from Edge Hill (8A). I can't recall it ever being late in two years. Among

the 8A engines seen at Battyeford were No 5596 *Bahamas*, No 5633 *Aden*, No 5647 *Sturdee*, No 5670 *Howard of Effingham*, No 5681 *Aboukir* and No 5721 *Impregnable*. I always saw this train away before I went home, and felt quite important giving the right-away to a train hauled by a 'Jubilee'! However, even the local trains could occasionally spring surprises. On 6 July 1953, the 4.45pm from Leeds turned up behind a Class 4F 0-6-0 No 4134 of Rowsley (17D), and later that month a compound, No 1119 of Llandudno Junction (6G), hauled the train on two consecutive nights. '4Fs' were rare but compounds were virtually unknown.

Freight trains usually provided more interest. They were hauled by Class 5s, '8F' 2-8-0s, LNWR 0-8-0s and occasionally a taper-boiler Stanier 2-6-0, from a great variety of Western Division sheds, including Aston, Crewe South, Shrewsbury (and occasionally Swansea), Mold Junction, Edge Hill, Warrington, Widnes, Speke Junction and Patricroft. Up trains often stopped for water, then slowly edged through the station, preparing for the steep falling gradient to the dive-under near Spen Valley Junction. Practically none of them were fully braked. Down trains came through full-blast, attacking the uphill gradient. Freight trains were referred to by their starting or terminating points in the west, eg 'The Mold Junction' or 'The Oxleys', because they all started or terminated at Leeds.

Above left: Another of the class, No 42310, calls at Battyeford with a Leeds-Huddersfield all-stations train, shortly before the passenger train service was withdrawn, and the station closed, in October 1953.
Author's Collection

Below left and above: The high spot of the day at Battyeford was the arrival of the 5.25pm all-stations service to Leeds, nearly always in the charge of an Edge Hill (8A) 'Jubilee'. The train was aa all-stations service from Manchester, but the engine would work back on an express, possibly a double-header as many on the Diggle route were. Two regulars were No 5647 *Sturdee,* seen here with an Euston-Heysham express at Kings Langley in this undated photograph, and No 5681 *Aboukir,* also on the West Coast main line with a Liverpool-Euston express at Sutton Weaver in 1948.
R. F. Deardon / R. Whitfield

Right: Class 8F 2-8-0 No 48457 (8A — Edge Hill), on the 12.5pm freight from Leeds Neville Hill to Liverpool Edge Hill, takes water at Battyeford on 10 September 1951. Most freight trains took water here.
Author

We had two non-stop expresses — the 4.0pm Manchester to Leeds, almost always with a Class 5, and the 5.0pm Liverpool to Newcastle. The latter was without doubt the star turn of the day. It was always double-headed with any permutation of Class 5s, 'Patriots' and 'Jubilees', and possibly 'Scots', and stormed up the hill breathing fire and smoke as it roared through the station with its heavy train. I could see the railway line from my back door and often watched it go by. I don't want to keep harping on about punctuality, but you could set your watch by this train and I knew exactly when to stand outside the back door. Even in winter it was quite a sight. There were other double-headed expresses, which went via Mirfield, including the 9.55am Newcastle–Liverpool (often including an Edge Hill 'Royal Scot') and the 10.40pm mail from Leeds to Swansea (which started from York). On 10 March 1953, the 9.55am from Newcastle had two 'Scots', Nos 6169 (9A) and 6153 (8A) — superpower indeed.

Bank and Summer Holidays provided extra interest with a programme of holiday reliefs and excursion trains. The empty stock for some of these was often stabled in Heaton Lodge sidings and it was the Stationmaster's job to label these and see that they got away to time as far as possible, although this depended on the timely arrival of the light engine. Blackpool and Belle Vue were the favourite destinations for day excursion trains, with specials to Scarborough working through from Huddersfield and beyond. In those far-off days, whole towns in the textile areas closed down for the holiday week, and a cavalcade of special trains would take them away to the seaside, and bring them back a week later. Those who stayed at home would have a wide choice of day excursions.

Fire Drills

Dating from the mists of the 19th century it was the practice for each station or depot to have a fire brigade and a monthly fire drill, a very necessary precaution at a wooden station like Battyeford, although the local fire station was only a few minutes away. I believe that at one time the railway company had to pay for calling out the town fire brigade, so it was a way of keeping costs down. The companies were very good at that! The drill consisted of attaching a fire-brigade-style hose pipe to the main valve on the station platform and running it out to its full length, then rolling it up again. Sounds a bit like a Will Hay film, I know. The porter remained at the valve ready to turn the water on whilst I ran along the platform with the nozzle. We had to time the operation and send a return to the local fire officer, which probably took longer than the drill itself. In due course we received a payment — 6/- for the captain (me), which doesn't sound much but was equal to a couple of hours' pay, and 3/- for the porter.

Every so often we had to have a wet drill (as opposed to the normal dry drill), when we actually turned the water on. This was great fun and I think we received a slightly higher payment. One day I decided we would hose down the wooden walls of the station to get rid of dust and cobwebs. The water came out of the nozzle with a great rush and splashed all over the place, which meant that we

Below: Another Edge Hill Class 8F, No 48513, moves slowly through Battyeford station after taking water, in preparation for the falling gradient towards Spen Valley Junction in September 1953. *Author's Collection*

had to clean all the windows afterwards, but fortunately no damage was done. I don't think the District Engineer was too pleased. He was responsible for the routine maintenance of the station and had to send workmen to repair such things as broken windows, burst pipes, etc.

Minor Repairs

One Monday morning the porter who opened the booking office for the first train, the 5.50am to Leeds, noticed that one of the windows had been broken, as though someone had been trying to get in. So even in 1952 there were burglars about and we had to call the Railway Police to investigate. We also had to ask the Engineer to send someone to do the repair that day. Eventually a man came and was in no hurry to finish the job. It would have been far cheaper for the Stationmaster to have sent for a local man to do the repairs but that was forbidden. The authorities thought that it was too open to fraud and obviously didn't trust even their stationmasters. Their job was to see that everything was carried out in strict accordance with the laid down regulations, set out in voluminous books as well as the Rule Book etc, and that the utmost economy was observed. That left little scope for individual initiative or enterprise; those were the prerogative of District Offices or HQ.

The Importance of Signal Lamps

All the signal lamps in my domain were oil-lit, and they were filled and trimmed weekly by the lampman from Mirfield. Most signalboxes had a

Above: Some years later, on Friday 12 May 1961, with an almost deserted shed yard at Mirfield, two of Newton Heath's (26A) Class 5 4-6-0s, Nos 44735 and 44895, provide plenty of power for the Newcastle to Manchester Red Bank parcels train, which is returning the previous night's newspaper vans. At that time the newspaper traffic was still big business for BR. *Gavin Morrison*

lamp room nearby, usually a small corrugated iron structure, just large enough to contain a metal-covered bench on which the lamps were cleaned and trimmed, and a wooden stand on which 40 gallon drums of lamp-oil were stored. From time to time lamps went out, either through lack of oil, a dirty wick or a high wind, or a combination of all three. If a lamp went out during the day, and if the signalman could tell that it had done so (not all signals had light repeaters in the signalbox) the lampman could usually be contacted, but if it happened after he had gone home it was often difficult to contact him (telephones had been invented but lampmen didn't usually have one) and staff at Mirfield station were rather disinclined to call him out. Rather than leave the lamp out until he came on duty the following morning, the signalman would phone the Battyeford porter and ask her to knock on my door and tell me what had happened.

A lamp out at night meant that drivers had to be stopped and cautioned, causing delays. I was young and keen, and I must have been a bit mad too, because I generally responded and went out whatever the weather to relight the lamp. Most of the lamps were reasonably accessible, and many of them were on gantries, which at least gave you a safe place to stand while you tended to the lamp. However, the LNWR, in true LNWR style, didn't believe in mollycoddling its staff, and didn't provide a safety platform on straight signal posts. Battyeford's Up starter, an important signal, had co-acting arms, ie, a low arm so that the driver could see it when looking ahead below the platform awning, and a high arm so that he could see it some distance away when looking above the station buildings. The signal stood on the viaduct over the road, and for clearance reasons the post was fixed on the outside of the viaduct wall. I must have been mad to go up it — it was an unobstructed fall on to the road miles below, there was no safety platform at the top of the long ladder, there was quite a wind blowing, and I had to go up the ladder twice; once to fetch the lamp down so that I could relight it (impossible to do at the top) and a second time to take the lamp back. Still, I had the old-fashioned view that you should never ask anyone to do something that you would not do yourself.

Fog — the Railwayman's Enemy

In those days, fog was a constant problem in autumn and winter, and because all the distant signals were oil-lit they had to be 'fogged'. The arrangements were carried forward from year to year with little change. The local permanent-way inspector provided men from the gangs on the basis of two men for each fogging post, ie a first call and a relief, working 12-hour shifts. The men were supposed to turn out without being called if fog came on, but it was often necessary to arrange for them to be called, usually by the ganger or a platelayer living in the area who was rostered as a caller-up. The fogsignalmen had to be examined annually in their knowledge of the fogsignalling rules, and that duty fell to the Stationmaster. I had about 30 fogsignalmen, so it was quite a task. As can be imagined, the rules could be somewhat complex to cover different situations.

The fogsignalman's job was to maintain a detonator on the line all the time the Distant signal was at caution, and remove it when the signal moved to the off position. On the four-track sections he fogged both lines and had a machine which placed a detonator on the far line so that he didn't have to cross any lines. This was a vital job. Each signalbox had a 'sighting point', about 200 yards from the signalbox, and when it could no longer be seen owing to fog, the signalman had to report to the Control Office and tell the controller that he had sent for the fogsignalmen. Until they took up their posts the signalman had to apply special fogsignalling regulations concerning the acceptance of trains from the previous signalbox, in effect by keeping a longer clear stretch of line ahead of the approaching train in case it should run by his signals. Drivers had a particularly difficult job in fog. They had no means of knowing whether there was a fogsignalman on duty at any signal, so they had to look out and find it in the fog, reducing the speed of their trains if necessary. The 'crack' of the detonator meant that the Distant signal was at caution.

Most 'Stop' signals were not fogged, because the driver knew that if the Distant signal was at Clear, all the other signals worked from that signalbox would also be at Clear — the locking frame in the signalbox would enforce it. However, where an Outer Home signal had been provided ¼ mile before reaching the Home signal, special instructions applied in fog and fogsignalmen were appointed at such signals if there were sufficient platelayers available.

The Supply of Detonators

A two- or three-day fog caused an enormous number of detonators to be exploded, and a supply was kept in a disused waiting room at the station. Replacement supplies had to be ordered from main stores and inevitably took some time to arrive, so the spare stock was considerable as it would have been very embarrassing if the supply had run out. The spare stock was kept in cartons containing probably a gross, and the cartons stretched from the floor to the ceiling. Remember that this was a wooden building. If it had caught fire the explosion would have broken every window in Mirfield. There should really have been a secure brick building away from the station acting as a detonator store, but these were robust days and you would have been told to 'stop worrying and wasting my time' if you had asked District Office to have one built. After all, it had been like that for half a century. But an old gunpowder van would have sufficed.

Six

BATTYEFORD — THE AXE FALLS, AND I TRANSFER TO RAVENSTHORPE & THORNHILL

Serious Railway Accidents (1)

During my time at Battyeford there were two very serious accidents on the railways. The first one is still very well remembered — the double collision at Harrow & Wealdstone on the West Coast main line at 8.19am on Wednesday 8 October 1952, in which 108 passengers and four railwaymen were killed. It was, and still is, the worst railway accident in peacetime in the whole of British railway history. Fog was involved and so was an Outer Home signal. The sequence of events leading up to the first collision was as follows: The 7.31am local passenger train from Tring to London Euston had been crossed from the Up Slow line to the Up Fast line on the approach to Harrow station, a regular move to give the train a non-stop run from Harrow to Euston. Approaching on the Up Fast line was the overnight sleeper from Perth to Euston, hauled by Pacific No 46242 *City of Glasgow*.

There had been intermittent fog, and fog working had been in operation, but shortly before 8.0am the fog cleared to the extent that the signalman's 'fog object' became visible and fog working was withdrawn. (A fog object was an easily recognisable structure, such as a signal, not more than 200 yards from the signalbox.) Withdrawing fog working meant that the signalman was now able to allow the Perth sleeper to approach as normal, which was fully in accordance with the Rules and Regulations. The local train was protected by a colour light distant signal, an Outer Home signal at Danger and an Inner Home signal at Danger. Unfortunately the driver of the Perth Sleeper failed to respond to any of the signals. This

was a classic lapse, seen many times over the years, and various systems of Automatic Train Control had been devised to counter such lapses, but they had not been installed on the West Coast main line, although a BR system was already being devised.

As so often happens in such circumstances, it was impossible to tell why the driver had failed to respond to the signals at Harrow, but there was a suggestion afterwards in railway circles that one of the injectors' handles had stuck and the fireman was trying to release it by hitting it with the coal hammer. His blow glanced off the handle and hit the gauge glass, breaking it and allowing scalding steam to escape into the cab, just as the train was approaching Harrow. This suggestion only came to light years afterwards, but came from an impeccable source — a Motive Power Officer who examined the driving cab controls immediately after the accident. The LM Region HQ saw no point in broadcasting this information, because it would have been of no practical value, and the solution to the problem — Automatic Train Control — was already in hand.

There was no great public uproar about this accident. Railway accidents were not uncommon, and this one happened to be worse because a Down express was approaching and only a few moments away. I can recall it well, but apart from being professionally interested it made no significant impact at the time. How different it would be today. TV programmes are still being made about railway accidents in which only a handful of people were killed. Perversely, this is because serious railway accidents are now so rare.

Serious Railway Accidents (2)

The second of these accidents occurred the following year on 15 August 1953 at Irk Valley Junction, Manchester, on the electrified line to Bury. A Down steam train, the 7.36am from Manchester Victoria to Bacup, was turning right at the junction and passing over the Up electrified line when the engine was struck a glancing blow by an Up electric train, the 7.20am from Bury, which had run past a signal at Danger. The front coach of the electric train careered over the viaduct and plunged into the valley below, killing nine passengers and the driver. The signalman had made an irresponsible and very serious error by allowing the Down steam train to foul the Up electric line when an Up electric train was approaching. The junction was within the quarter of a mile beyond the Home signal which the Signalling Regulations stated must not be fouled after it had been promised to another train. When inquiries were made into the accident it came to light that the standard of observance of the Signalling Regulations by some signalmen in the area was unacceptable, and poor supervision was blamed for this state of affairs. HQ took this very seriously, and instructions were issued setting out the frequency of visits to signalboxes by

Above: An undated view of Greetland station, with the line ahead leading to Sowerby Bridge, Rochdale and Manchester Victoria, and the line diverging to the right giving access to Halifax and Bradford Exchange. The latter is part of the route from Huddersfield via Bradley Junction to Halifax and Bradford. Both lines are still in use today for passenger trains. The station closed many years ago, but there is some local pressure for it to be reopened. *Real Photographs*

stationmasters, including regular visits out of normal working hours. Furthermore, an arrangement was introduced that periodically the Train Register Books of adjacent signalboxes were to be withdrawn and checked against each other to see whether they tallied. I have no idea how widespread this unsatisfactory situation was, but I was satisfied that it didn't apply in my parish, because I was always out and about and got to know my signalmen very well. I felt that I could trust them. But the visits and the checking had to be done, and a monthly return had to be submitted to District Office.

In-House Social and Educational Activities

I mentioned earlier that the railway companies tended to do as much as possible in-house. We even had our own semi-social activities in house. The District Signalmen's Inspector at Huddersfield ran what was generally known as a Mutual Improvement Class (MIC) for young stationmasters (of whom there were quite a lot in the Huddersfield area) and also for signalmen. We met once a week and discussed safety and signalling and the Rules and Regulations, and all manner of associated subjects, then had a beer afterwards and carried on talking. MICs were a thriving part of the railway in those days, and most engine sheds had one. Lord Cullen would have approved! We had a Railway Debating Society at Leeds that discussed various topics of railway interest. No topic was barred and you were encouraged to speak freely. We had quizzes and lectures at the Wakefield District Office. Many railwaymen took first aid courses and exams. There was a lot of enthusiasm in those days, and pride in the job.

Special residential courses were held periodically for young stationmasters, and my turn came towards the end of 1952. They lasted for six weeks and were held in the School of Transport College in Derby. This was a splendid purpose-built building, dating from 1938 when it was opened by the LMS, and its main feature was a large hall, around the sides of which ran a gauge 0 electric railway, fully signalled, with signalboxes every few yards. It was used not only to simulate normal working, when several trains ran to a predetermined timetable and all the 'signalboxes' were manned, but also to simulate accidents of various types, when small syndicates would discuss what action to take. It was all great fun and hugely interesting. In those days the railway was still a very diverse undertaking with huge amounts of freight traffic and employing well over half a million staff.

The Axe Falls

One morning in April 1953 I opened the morning correspondence (which came by train, of course) and out fell a letter from District Office stating that it was proposed to withdraw the Spen Valley line passenger service. This was pre-Beeching, but it was no surprise. The takings at the stations on the line hardly covered the porters' wages and the cost of running the stations. There was nothing left over for the train-running costs. The end came on Saturday 3 October 1953 and the last trains, the 10.40pm to Leeds and the 10.46pm to Huddersfield, departed to a thunder of detonator explosions. We had to get rid of them somehow! We also issued quite a few 'Last ticket to be issued at Battyeford' to enthusiasts, but we insisted on their being issued to different destinations so that everyone could claim to have a last ticket!

But how do you physically close a station? There were no more passenger trains, but the station offices were full of books, tickets and records of all descriptions. All the account books had to be made up to the end of the last day, the cash banked, and all the tickets bundled up and listed, and sent in to the Revenue Accountant. That was quite a job. Some of the signalmen had been transferred to Mirfield and some to Huddersfield, and the staff records, insurance and income tax cards etc had to be transferred, together with the correspondence files concerning the signalboxes. But we still had a great bonfire. Furniture and platform seats went to Central Stores in a van, whilst stationery and other stores, mainly cleaning, were sent to Mirfield, who moaned on about it. It took over a week, and I kept on one of the porters to assist me, even though he had been transferred to Mirfield. HQ seemed to have no idea that you couldn't just lock the station after the last train had gone, and walk away.

I become Stationmaster at Ravensthorpe & Thornhill

Not for the last time in my railway career I was redundant, but fortunately there was a vacancy for a stationmaster in my own grade at Ravensthorpe & Thornhill, on the Huddersfield to Leeds line via Mirfield. It was only a couple of miles away, within easy cycling distance. There was no station house, but as the Stationmaster's job at Battyeford had disappeared I was able to say in the house there. Freight and expresses continued to use the 'New Line' for some years, so I was still able to watch the 5.0pm Liverpool to Newcastle blast its way up the hill. And from my office at Ravensthorpe I was able to see not only the ex-LNWR line to Leeds but also the four-track Wakefield to Heaton Lodge Junction former L&Y main line. That was a bonus.

I now had only one signalbox to supervise, even though Thornhill LNWR Junction was on the doorstep, just a few yards away. This was on the L&Y Section, whilst the station was LNWR. That

distinction had disappeared 30 years previously but no one had thought to change it. My signalbox was on a different line — at Ravensthorpe L&Y, on the line from Thornhill to Heckmondwike and Low Moor. The passenger station had already closed, so all I had to do was to make a weekly visit to the signalbox, which I think was open on only two shifts. But that was not quite the only duty. The gas and water meters had to be read each Monday morning so that any leakage or exceptional use could be detected. A monthly return then had to be submitted to HQ, explaining any variation from the previous month or previous year. HQ paid the bills. Nothing on the railway was left to chance.

Ravensthorpe & Thornhill station was a typical LNWR wooden station, very similar to Battyeford, so I soon felt at home. There were two platforms and two porters, one on each shift. I now had 2½ years' experience as a stationmaster so felt quite confident in my new post, insisting that the porters wore their uniform hats when attending on trains. That didn't go down too well at first, but I pointed to the Rule, and the fact that they had signed an undertaking to obey the Rules. I could have said

Above: Six months prior to the date of this photograph, 12 September 1953, I had been told that the passenger service between Leeds and Huddersfield via the 'New Line' was to be withdrawn and that all the passenger stations would closed. It was no surprise — apart from a few commuters and shoppers to Leeds, there was little business, and there was a satisfactory alternative at Mirfield station, only about 10 minutes' walk away. The line had been built in the last decade of the 19th century to enable the LNWR to bypass the congested area on the L&Y around Mirfield, and to tap the substantial freight business in the Spen Valley. *Author's Collection*

that they either obeyed the Rule or resigned, but I didn't want to lose them, as replacements were hard to come by. The porters at Ravensthorpe & Thornhill were on a flat wage, but they had a pretty cushy job. There were not many passengers (the station was on the fringe of the town), and there was an excellent and cheap bus service. There was little parcels traffic, but there was a goods yard.

Above: I was in new territory now at Ravensthorpe & Thornhill. Therre was even less passenger business but more freight; in fact I was also the Goods Agent besides being Stationmaster. The express in the photograph, headed by a Farnley Junction Class 4-6-0 No 45063, has just passed through Mirfield and is taking the route through the station towards Leeds, but is not stopping. The line straight on leads to Wakefield Kirkgate. *Kenneth Field*

Below: Ravensthorpe station lies behind the smoke in this undated view. Top left is the goods yard and Thornhill power station, which received a full train load of coal each day. The express, headed by yet another grimy Class 5 4-6-0 No 45101 (26A — Newton Heath), is proceeding in the Mirfield direction. *Author's Collection/*

Above: The date of this photo is 18 October 1953; the place Garsdale. A Class 6P5F Horwich 'Mogul' No 42834, a Carlisle Kingmoor engine, passes through with a Skipton to Carlisle pick-up freight train for Carlisle, whilst in the back platform line a North Eastern 0-4-4T, No 67312, waits to return to Northallerton. This passenger service was also soon to be withdrawn, on 24 April 1954. These withdrawals preceded Beeching by almost 10 years. *J. W. Armstrong*

The Goods Yard

I was now officially Stationmaster and Goods Agent, but the main goods traffic was house coal. There was just one coal merchant, but we did have occasional goods traffic, often for the power station adjacent. Each day the trip working would arrive from the Wakefield area with a trainload of coal for the power station, which would be put off into their sidings. The engine would then collect the empties and depart to wherever Control had directed them, usually a colliery. These were not timetabled workings and some train crews liked to linger a while, having to be 'persuaded', gently or otherwise, to depart.

The wagon numbers were recorded both on arrival and departure, so that charges could be raised for undue detention. We didn't charge demurrage on an individual wagon basis, but on the number of 'Wagon Days', calculated on the number of loaded wagons received, minus the empties turned out. It needed a fair degree of accuracy and it wasn't unknown for arguments to break out with the Central Electricity Generating Board (CEGB). They incurred quite a charge because they accumulated loaded wagons during the week so that they had enough to see them over the weekend. They didn't like unloading the wagons currently,

into stock, and then feeding off the stock at the weekend, because this meant extra work. This annoyed me, especially when the collieries were crying out for empty wagons during the winter months, so I made sure they paid every penny.

Occasionally we received special loads such as transformers for the power station. They usually came on a Sunday by special train and were gently manoeuvred into the unloading area. This was always worth watching.

Whilst I was at Ravensthorpe we had an accident at a level crossing one Sunday morning. There was no 'On Call' arrangement at Ravensthorpe, but I was told about this accident, probably by a porter from Mirfield sent specially, so I cycled there to see what was what. A council refuse lorry had been crossing the Thornhill-Heckmondwike line at a private level crossing leading to the council tip, and had been hit by a passenger train, throwing the lorry to one side. The lorry driver was killed. In those days, trains were hauled by big heavy steam engines, whilst refuse lorries were still quite small. The train had suffered no damage and had gone on its way. By the time I got there the body had been removed to the mortuary and everyone had cleared off. It was all very low key, but there were lots of such run-of-the-mill accidents in those days (this was 1954). The Annual Ministry of Transport Accident Report for that year shows 251 people killed in the working of the railways, of whom 44 were passengers, 164 were railwaymen and 43 were 'other persons'. This excludes 83 trespassers and 156 suicides. (The results for 2010 were almost nil, excepting trespassers and suicides.) This accident kindled an interest in level crossings, which became one of my main concerns in later years, and indeed still is. A somewhat unusual interest, no doubt.

The Management Training Scheme

BR had instituted a management training scheme in 1950, and trainees were called 'Traffic Apprentices'. The scheme was based on one that the LNER had introduced in order to attract university graduates onto the railway and was very successful. The LNER was a very well-managed company, thanks to the North Eastern Railway

Below: I made a number of journeys from Bingley or Mirfield over the Midland to St Pancras, and was always impressed by the railway establishment at Wellingborough. As this photograph, taken on 26 August 1953, shows, it had a very large engine shed (15A), and a marshalling yard, known as Neilson's for some reason. Compound 4-4-0 No 41079 approaches the station on the Up main line with an express, overtaking '8F' 2-8-0 No 48350 with a train load of coal on the Up goods/slow line. No 41079 was a Millhouses (19B) (Sheffield) engine, whilst No 48350 belonged to Toton (18A). *T. B. Paisley*

heritage of scientific management. The LMS did not aspire to such a scheme and it was alleged that in order to get on you had to be well connected. There was certainly some truth in it and I came across several offspring of senior managers who generally were not as good as their fathers. Consequently, the LMS tended to be managed in a rather rough and ready way, rather than scientifically like the LNER, although Josiah Stamp (later Lord Stamp) did introduce several improvements. After nationalisation, several senior ex-LNER managers took more senior positions on the London Midland Region over the next 20 years.

The BR scheme was open to any member of staff of any grade under the age of 28, and there was a new intake each year, probably about a couple of dozen all told. If you wanted to be considered you put your name forward, and there was then a written examination to thin out the numbers. If you passed that examination you were then called for interview by a Regional panel of chief officers, a very daunting experience. Those who passed that hurdle then were called for interview at BR HQ. You were not told straight away at any of the three stages whether you had passed, so you spent a nerve-wracking two or three weeks at the interview stage before you heard whether you had been selected or not.

I decided to wait until I had had some experience of life as a stationmaster, which I fondly imagined might stand me in good stead at interview, and give me more time to build up a good service history. So, in February 1953, I took the step which had the potential to change my life. The purpose of the scheme was to provide accelerated promotion to senior positions for those who had gone through the three-year training course, a very valuable incentive to do well. I cannot recall the details of the written examination held in March, except that it was set by the Royal Society of Arts. Anyway, I passed, and then waited to be called for Regional interview. I attended for interview at York, the Regional HQ of the North Eastern Region, and although I can't remember many of the details, I do remember saying that Battyeford station didn't pay its way, because the staff costs were too high.

That must have gone down well because a few weeks later I received a letter from District Office to say that I had been selected for interview at BR HQ. Normally that would have followed a few weeks later, but it coincided with the demise of the Railway Executive under the Railways Act that year and it took months before anyone at the British Transport Commission realised that there were such things as interviews for Traffic Apprentices in the in-tray. However, they were arranged eventually, and I received a letter from Wakefield District Office, dated 26 February 1954 (just a year after I took the written exam), informing me to 'please arrange to attend at Room 27 British Transport Commission, 222 Marylebone Road, London N.W.1, at 10.30am on the morning of Tuesday, 2nd March, 1954, for interview by the Central Selection Committee'. I seem to recall a panel of four, who for some reason were very friendly indeed. Was that a good sign? Sometimes a panel is friendly because they are not going to appoint you so there is no point in giving you a grilling. Alternatively, they may have decided from my service history and the notes of the Regional interview, that I was OK, and that they were running late and wanted to get a move on. I didn't reason that out at the time, but speak from subsequent experience at both sides of the interviewing table.

Weeks of waiting followed, which stretched into months, until one Saturday morning at work the telephone rang and a secretary came on and said that Mr Barlow (the District Operating Superintendent at Wakefield and my boss) wanted to speak to me. He was a big, genial chap and without any preamble said, 'Congratulations'. I knew what it meant. It was truly a life-changing moment. My days at Ravensthorpe were over. It was the 8 May 1954.

Seven

SUMMER DAYS AT WINSTON

Winston, I hear you say. Where on earth was Winston and what was I doing there? In answer to the first question, Winston was a small wayside station on the line from Darlington to Barnard Castle, which wandered along for about 15 miles through the pleasant rolling countryside of the Tees valley. There were intermediate stations at North Road, Piercebridge, Gainford, Winston and Broomielaw, the latter serving a large military camp.

As for the second question, I mentioned in the previous chapter that I had been fortunate enough to have been selected for BR's management training scheme, which consisted of a three-year course covering all aspects of the commercial and operating railway and at all levels. This involved spending some time at small, medium and large passenger and goods stations, followed by marshalling yards and motive power depots, and concluding with spells in District and Headquarters offices. Everyone followed the same pattern, despite one's previous experience, and even though I had already been a stationmaster at a couple of small stations for three years, I had to conform to the timetable. Hence, on Thursday 27 May 1954, I stepped onto the platform at Winston out of the 10.5am from Darlington to Penrith, to start learning all about a small country station.

The first priority, however, was to find a bed for the night, and the Stationmaster recommended the Bridgewater Arms, a mile up a country lane in the village. I duly took my bags up there and booked a room for four nights a week, with full board, at what is now the unbelievable charge of £2 per week (or ten bob a day in 1954 vernacular). I was the only resident and was relieved to find that electricity had arrived in the village, although it hadn't reached the station. In common with many hundreds of small country stations, oil lighting was the rule, both at the station and even in the adjacent Stationmaster's house.

Winston station

Winston station was often used for training management trainees, so the Stationmaster wasn't at all surprised to see me. However, he was somewhat taken aback when I mentioned that I'd been a stationmaster myself (albeit on the London Midland Region), but I found that there was a lot to learn at Winston. My experience of small stations had been in the industrial West Riding, a world away from Winston which was little more than a hamlet, deep in an agricultural area. Not only was the station a mile from the village but the latter was also served by a frequent bus service between Darlington and Barnard Castle. It was not surprising, therefore, that the station saw few passengers.

The Passenger Train Service and the Signalling

The passenger train service consisted of three trains a day each way, calling at all stations between Darlington and Penrith, the main ones being Barnard Castle, Kirkby Stephen and Appleby. This was augmented by three trains a day each way from Darlington to Middleton-in-Teesdale. Departures from Winston on weekdays were as follows:

To Penrith at 6.44am, 10.31am and 4.41pm. To Middleton-in-Teesdale at 1.1pm, 5.56pm and

Above: The 10.15am train from Darlington to Penrith departs from Winston in June 1954 behind BR Standard Class 2 2-6-0 No 78018, a Kirkby Stephen engine. It was barely three months old when this photo was taken. *Author*

9.21pm. To Darlington at 7.1am, 8.17am, 12.30pm, 3.57pm, 5.37pm, 7.27pm and 10.15pm. There was also a late evening service to Kirkby Stephen at 11.6pm.

Former North Eastern Railway 'J21' 0-6-0s had been the mainstay of the Penrith trains for many years, but recently they had been replaced by newly-built BR Standard Class 2 2-6-0s. Kirkby Stephen (51H) had Nos 78016-9, built at Darlington. There were also quite a few of the former LMS-designed 2-6-0s in the area which had been built in the early 1950s. They were numbered 46471 to 46482 and were spread between Darlington (51A), West Auckland (51F) and Kirkby Stephen. They made a former LMS man feel quite at home, but no doubt the local traincrews regarded them with disfavour as foreigners. Shortly after I left Winston there was another major change in the motive power provided for the Penrith passenger trains. Four BR Class 3 2-6-2Ts came new from Swindon — Nos 82026/7 to Kirkby Stephen and Nos 82028/9 to Darlington. I wonder sometimes how the locomen reacted to those. At least the cabs would be nice and cosy over Stainmore.

The line between Darlington Hopetown Junction (where the Bishop Auckland line branched off) and Barnard Castle was double as far as Forcett Junction (Piercebridge), then single to Broomielaw, becoming double again to Barnard Castle. The double-line sections were worked by Absolute Block. There was a passing loop at Winston, and both the section from Forcett Junction to Winston (3m 418yd) and the section thence to Broomielaw (3m 1144yd) were worked by the electric token. I hadn't had much experience of this type of signalling in the West Riding since my trips from Keighley up the Oxenhope branch ten years earlier, so it proved to be a useful refresher. The timetable did not require any trains to cross at Winston, and as late running was unusual it didn't often happen.

Goods Traffic

There may not have been many passengers at Winston, but the goods side of the business was quite heavy. The station was served by the morning

Above: BR Standard 2-6-2T No 82029, a Darlington engine, waits to depart from Penrith for its return journey to Darlington with the 10.32am departure on 21 August 1956. The engine was built at Swindon in December 1954. *R. Leslie*

Below: The morning 'pick-up' goods train from Darlington calls at Winston in June 1954 to deliver inwards traffic and collect wagons for despatch. The engine is an ex-LMS design, Class 2 2-6-0 No 46472, one of a batch of 12 engines built for the North Eastern Region that were all allocated to sheds in the Darlington District. *Author*

trip, which brought in house coal, animal feeding stuffs and livestock and other traffics; indeed, it was sufficiently busy to require the employment of a clerk. Part of the warehouse was leased to some of the national animal feedstuff firms, and their representatives toured the surrounding farms seeking orders. These were then delivered by one of our motor lorries, and I can now reveal (being out of the clutches of the Training Committee) that I often whiled away the sunny days by going out with the lorry driver on his rounds. I got to know most of the feedstuff brands. They had funny names, such as 'sow weaner meal'.

I was also introduced to the arcane world of sack hire. I'd never heard of it before, but it used to be quite big business on former LNER lines in arable areas. Farmers could hire railway-owned grain sacks for a small rental, provided that they sent the grain by rail. The book-keeping involved was tortuous, to say the least. Every sack had to be recorded in a large ledger (the printing industry was kept afloat making large ledgers for the railway companies), showing the date on which it was hired and dispatched etc. If it was retained for too long, there were additional charges, but the real arguments started if a sack was never seen again or came back several weeks later (because the farmer had craftily sent it when full by road).

Now it so happened that I had taken my bicycle to Winston, and the Stationmaster (a wise old bird) innocently suggested to me one day that seeing I had my bike handy and the sun was shining, how would I like to visit some farmers whose sack hire accounts were overdue for payment? I fell for it, of course. The idea of spending a couple of sunny afternoons cycling around the pleasant countryside and having a chat with friendly farmers seemed quite attractive, but I soon learned that farmers hated parting with money and would make up all sorts of excuses for not doing so. They could be quite unfriendly, but they could sometimes be persuaded to part with a little on account (faced with an implied threat that if they didn't do so they might find, the next time they wanted some empty sacks, that our stock had somehow mysteriously just run out). Sack hire was enormously expensive in both clerical time and lost sacks, but whether the business was still viable by 1954 I have no idea. I never really mastered the process, which was Byzantine in its complexity even by railway standards.

Travelling Round the Area

I visited Barnard Castle quite often and discovered a line I knew nothing about. It came from Bishop Auckland via West Auckland and Evenwood, and whilst it could only boast two passenger trains a day each way, its main claim to fame was the coke trains which came from the yards at Shildon and St Helen's (West Auckland), destined for the ironworks of West Cumbria via Stainmore. Owing to the fragility of the iron trestle viaducts at Belah and Deepdale, between Barnard Castle and Kirkby Stephen, large locomotives were prohibited and much use was made of former LMS and BR Standard Class 2 2-6-0s, based at West Auckland shed, displacing the former NER Classes J21 and J25 0-6-0s which had worked the line for what seemed an eternity. However, the Route Availability grading over Stainmore was raised from RA2 (very low) to RA4, allowing double-heading and heavier locomotives, up to '4MT' 2-6-0s, both BR and former LMS. Whilst I was at Winston, new BR Class 3 2-6-0s, built at Swindon, were allocated to West Auckland, Nos 77000-04 and 77010/1, and shortly after I left, several Class 4MT 2-6-0s arrived in the area.

The Railway Observer magazine records that on 14 July a trial train was run from St Helen's Auckland to Tebay with a load equal to 22 loaded 21-ton hoppers. The locomotives concerned were Nos 77001 and 77002. However, when the Class 4MTs arrived, they were allowed to take 44 loaded 21-ton hoppers, with two engines at the front, and assisted at the rear from Barnard Castle to Stainmore.

The Bishop Auckland to Barnard Castle line had one other claim to fame, which many people will remember — the fortnightly express from Durham to Ulverston with a corresponding return working. It conveyed miners to and from the convalescent home there and ran via Kirkby Stephen and Tebay over Smardale viaduct (recently restored as a public footpath after many years of disuse), thence via the West Coast line to Hincaster Junction and across to Arnside via the Sandside line. The journey alone must have been a good tonic.

One of the finest sights and sounds around was that of a double-headed coke train making its laborious way up the steep gradient out of Barnard Castle to the summit several miles away, with a bit of assistance at the rear too. Great clouds of smoke and steam shot hundreds of feet into the air from

Above: Another BR Standard 2-6-2T, No 82027, leaves Barnard Castle with the 10.32am from Penrith to Darlington on 11 December 1954.
J. W. Armstrong Trust

Below: An elderly ex-North Eastern Railway Class J21 0-6-0, No 65103, departs from Barnard Castle with a train carrying holidaymakers home from Blackpool on 23 August 1952 . The class dates from 1886 but No 65103 dated originally from January 1892 and was subsequently rebuilt. It was allocated to Kirkby Stephen shed.
J. W. Armstrong Trust

Above: Another ex-North Eastern Railway veteran, Class J25 0-6-0 No 65695, trundles through the picturesque countryside near Gaisgill, between Kirkby Stephen (its home shed) and Tebay, with a mixed goods train on 30 May 1952. *E. D. Bruton*

Below: Three trains a day each way served the delightful rural station of Smardale, between Kirkby Stephen and Tebay. Passenger traffic was likely to be very light, but the Stationmaster had a splendid house (assuming it was his). Smardale is probably most famous for its two magnificent viaducts over Scandal Beck, one on this line and the other one on the ex-Midland Settle & Carlisle line. The trackbed of the NER Tebay branch was lifted many years ago but the viaduct has now been refurbished and is part of a nature trail, full of wild flowers, which extends for several miles. The Stationmaster's house is also still in existence. This scene was recorded in 1946. *W. Hubert Foster/courtesy John W. Holroyd*

Above: Two BR Standard Class 3MT 2-6-0s double-head a heavy eastbound passenger train over Stainmore on 17 August 1954. The pilot engine is No 77003 of West Auckland shed, which indicates that the train would proceed from Barnard Castle to Bishop Auckland, and thence to its final destination. Engines of this small class of 20 were built at Swindon in 1954. Ten were allocated to the North Eastern Region and 10 to Scotland. *J. W. Armstrong Trust*

Below: The lonely signalbox at Stainmore summit, and the famous sign announcing that it stands at 1,370 ft above sea level. *J. W. Armstrong Trust*

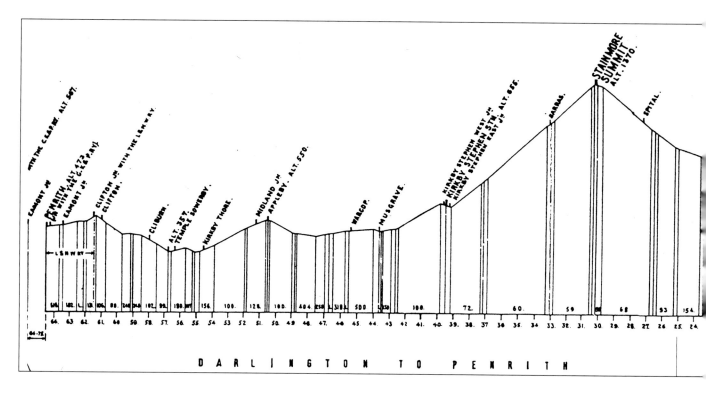

DARLINGTON TO PENRITH

A Railwayman's Odyssey

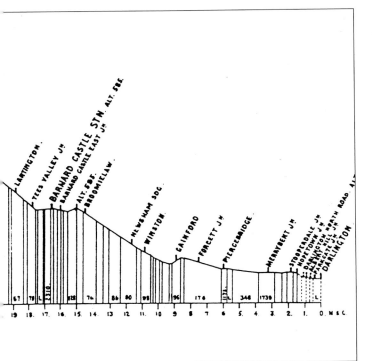

Below left: An eastbound train, headed by Class J21 No 65047, leaves Barras, six miles into the climb to Stainmore summit. *J. W. Armstrong Trust*

Below: The former NER station at Kirkby Stephen basks in the sun as Class 4MT 2-6-0 No 76048 prepares to leave with the 2.55pm Penrith to Darlington train on 25 June 1956. *T. G. Hepburn/Rail Archive Stephenson*

A Railwayman's Odyssey

A Railwayman's Odyssey

engines working flat out. The Stainmore line left the Middleton-in-Teesdale line at Tees Valley Junction and then described a complete half-circle to the left before swinging round again to the right, to ease the gradient. The noise of the engines working at their maximum tractive effort could be heard down in Barnard Castle for up to half an hour after they had left. The ruling gradient was 1 in 67 all the way up the 13 long miles to Stainmore Summit, a climb of no less than 785 feet.

Many must have been the heroic endeavours of drivers and firemen to reach the summit in bad weather, and many must have been the times when the signalman in his isolated and windswept signalbox peered out of the rattling windows wondering if the train was ever going to arrive. Stainmore was an inhospitable spot, surrounded by bleak, empty moorland as far as the eye could see. Not a place of beauty, unless you enjoyed wild, romantic vistas. The climb from Kirkby Stephen was almost as bad — 12 miles mostly at 1 in 59 to 1 in 72. Heavy snows were no stranger to the line, and the British Transport Film Unit produced one of its many excellent films *Snowdrift at Bleath Gill*, featuring the rescue of a goods train with No 78018 trapped in a snowdrift on the line in February 1955.

I took the opportunity one day to make a trip over the Stainmore line to Penrith on the 4.41pm from Winston, returning from Penrith on the 8.20pm. As it was a fine evening the views were outstanding. Mile after mile of sweeping moorland, interspersed with deep gullies, and over precarious and vertiginous viaducts, before dropping down into Kirkby Stephen; then, in complete contrast, a pleasant run along the fertile Eden valley to Penrith, joining the West Coast main line at Eden Valley Junction. Now I was back on home territory, and for good measure saw the Down 'Mid-day Scot', running 45 minutes late. North Eastern trains used the bay on the Down side.

Above left: In another busy scene at Kirkby Stephen, a BR 2-6-2T approaches Kirkby Stephen Junction signalbox with a passenger train on 20 May 1955. *J. W. Armstrong Trust*

Left: And now for a final view, taken on 29 April 1959, of Winston station, as seen through the front window of a DMU heading towards Barnard Castle. © *John Mallon Collection/NERA and Ken Hoole Study Centre Darlington*

Barnard Castle was quite a busy station serving four routes — Darlington, Kirkby Stephen, Middleton-in-Teesdale and Bishop Auckland. One by one they closed, and now you would be hard put to find any trace of a railway at Barnard Castle. At one time West Durham had a very extensive railway network, as the North Eastern Railway penetrated the length of every valley in search of coal and other minerals, but one after the other the branches began to languish as their staple goods traffic declined and eventually ceased. Passenger business was insufficient to keep them going once buses had taken away most of the traffic. Many stations and branches closed before Dr Beeching came along.

I also managed a trip over the Barnard Castle-Bishop Auckland line, continuing along to Durham via Brancepeth (the site of a large army camp) and returning via Darlington. Bishop Auckland was also a very busy railway junction serving several routes, including the Wearhead branch, part of which is today a preserved line, although it has recently been brought back into commercial use for moving coal. Other branches ran to Consett and Ferryhill. Today Bishop Auckland is at the end of a single line from Darlington, a pale shadow of its former importance, and served only by the awful 'Pacers'. The once commodious station has been rebuilt on a more modest scale, but there is a café outside displaying a remarkable selection of photographs and track layouts of the former glory days. So if you are ever tempted to visit the National Railway Museum's recently developed outpost at Shildon, known as 'Locomotion', a mile down the line but only three minutes from Shildon station, do pay Bishop Auckland station a visit.

All too soon my little 'holiday' was over, but I was determined to end it in style, so after saying my goodbyes I took my last trip over Stainmore to Appleby on the 4.41pm train. Alighting there I watched the tail lamp of my train disappear, feeling that I had really enjoyed my time at Winston and improved my railway geography quite considerably. Then I strolled gently down the hill to the Midland station, anticipating the pleasures ahead of a trip over the still busy Settle & Carlisle line in the evening sunshine. Eventually my train arrived, one of my favourite expresses, the long-lived 4.10pm from Glasgow St Enoch to Leeds, which I used to see almost every evening in summer for several years as it rushed through

Bingley headed by a 'Jubilee'. It also conveyed a 12-wheeled LMS dining car, a real beauty, attached at Dumfries where it had been detached from the morning Down express. I couldn't resist the luxury of dinner, and enjoyed one of life's finest experiences — a dinner in that splendid dining car with a glass of wine as the train wound its way up Mallerstang to Ais Gill, with the evening sun slanting across the valley and bathing the surrounding fells in a golden glow. It had been a vintage summer.

Eight

1957

—

HEATON MARSHALLING YARD BECKONS

Time to Get my Hands Dirty Again

During 1957, when I was coming to the end of my training, word filtered down that I should have some marshalling yard experience. I took this as meaning that the powers that be were having difficulty in filling a particular job, that of Assistant Yard Master (AYM) at Heaton, Newcastle, and were looking for likely takers. As it happened, I liked operating work and felt that my future lay in the Operating Department.

Heaton AYM was a three-shift job, and the reason for its unpopularity was the nature of the shifts. Instead of the conventional arrangement of early, late and nights, the shifts at Heaton were middle, late and nights, middle turn being 9.0am to 5.0pm. In shift work generally, the early turn is regarded as the most popular of the three shifts because shift changeover time is customarily 7.0am instead of 6.0am by agreement, which gives a short shift as well as an afternoon free all week.

In due course I was called for interview, which was conducted by the District Operating Superintendent, Mr Paton, and the Yard Master, Mr Slater. They were both very friendly, and I felt at home straight away. I learned that Arnold Slater had risen through the ranks from his beginnings as porter-signalman. He had great charm and tact, and was unflappable, and I felt instinctively that we would hit it off, which we did. In due course I was told that I had been appointed to the post, which was in Class 1, and I reported to Heaton on 3 July 1957.

I still lived at Mirfield with my wife, Val, and two-year old son, so it was necessary to go into lodgings. I was fortunate to find some at Monkseaton, on the North Tyneside electric line, which was very convenient for Heaton station, only a few minutes away from the yard. The landlady was accustomed to shift-workers, and in those days there were plenty of good lodgings around where you were well fed and looked after. I wonder if that's still the case? The local staff office usually had a list of them.

Finding a House – Top Priority

The next priority was to find a house. In 1957 the market for houses to either rent or buy was still very tight, but BR had a very large stock of houses to rent which they had inherited from the four mainline companies. When a house became empty, details were circularised, and one that particularly took my fancy was the Stationmaster's house at Stannington, on the main line just south of Morpeth. The Stationmaster's post had been abolished and supervision of the station had passed to the Stationmaster at Annitsford. The house was part of the station buildings (the station was still open for business), and had four bedrooms, a bathroom and electric light, rather unusual for country stations in those days. Oil lighting was still relatively common and bathrooms with running hot water might be considered a luxury. More about that later.

Back to Heaton. After a couple of weeks' familiarisation and learning the language, I was on my own. The yard was open from 6.0am Monday to 6.0am Sunday, so in most weeks we had a rest day. However, shortages of staff often meant that

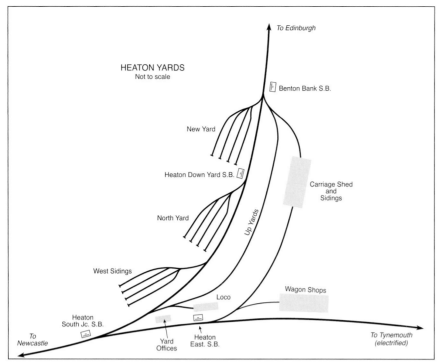

HEATON YARDS
Not to scale

To Edinburgh

Benton Bank S.B.

New Yard

Heaton Down Yard S.B.

Carriage Shed
and
Sidings

North Yard

Up Yards

West Sidings

Wagon Shops

Loco

Heaton
South Jc. S.B.

To
Newcastle

Yard
Offices

Heaton
East. S.B.

To Tynemouth
(electrified)

Below: A view in April 1966 of Heaton Yards looking north from Heaton Junction: at the top left are the West Yard Sorting Sidings; in the centre are the north main lines; in the top right corner is the departure road from the Up Yard Sorting Sidings and Heaton Locomotive Depot, whilst the two lines going off the picture at the right hand side are the electrified lines to Wallsend and the coast, and to the carriage sidings. This is a very congested layout. Class J27 0-6-0 No 65809 ambles across with three bnrakevans. *M. Dunnett*

we had to work our rest days, and even work extended hours to cover a colleague on leave or off sick. Within a couple of weeks I found myself working 9.0am to 8.0pm one week and 8.0pm to 7.0am the following week. And working rest days as well, but as I was in lodgings I didn't mind at all, and I knew that the extra money would come in useful for removal expenses. In later years you were paid a reasonable allowance to cover such expenses, but not in 1957.

When the Yard Master took his holidays, the AYM on middle turn stepped up. I was on middle turn that week, so within a few weeks of arriving at Heaton I was acting Yard Master. I enjoyed being

the boss, but the AYMs' jobs were equally interesting. Freight work may have lacked the glamour and prestige of passenger station work, but it was much more of a hands-on operation, with an infinite variety of problems large and small and much more scope for individual initiative. When I was a clerk, and learning how to be a stationmaster, I read a little book which said that the duties of a stationmaster were to see that the Rules and Regulations were strictly observed and that the working was strictly in accordance with the laid down instructions. Also that any infringements were to be immediately reported to the District Office. It also stressed that strict economy must be

observed in the use of stores and stationery. 'Strictness' was the buzzword. One felt that the most important duties of the day were to see that the toilets were clean and that the fire buckets were filled; these were the first things that visiting bigwigs inspected. Marshalling yard work was much nearer the real world.

Heaton Yards were on both sides of the north main line between Heaton South Junction signalbox, where the North Tyneside electric line branched off to Wallsend and Tynemouth, and Benton Bank signalbox. On the Down side, goods lines gave access to the West Sidings, the North Yard and the New Yard. On the Up side, the Up Yard lay in the angle between the north mainline and the North Tyneside electric line. This angle also contained the engine shed, the carriage sidings and shed, and the wagon shops.

Heaton South Junction signalbox was a very busy place. Apart from controlling the main lines and the junction, it also controlled access to all the Down yards, departures from the Up Yard and light engines from the shed. Halfway along towards Benton Bank there was a further signalbox, called

Above: A short distance along the electrified line to Wallsend, Class J27 0-6-0 No 65831 trundles towards the camera, whilst a Class V3 2-6-2T lurks in the background. The building on the extreme left is probably the Yard Master's office. *Author's Collection*

Right: An elderly Class J25 0-6-0, No 65110, shunts in the carriage sidings at Heaton East signalbox. *Author's Collection*

Heaton Down Yard signalbox, which dealt with departures from the West Sidings and the North Yard, and provided additional access from the Down main line to the New Yard receptions and Independent lines. Benton Bank signalbox controlled departures from the New Yard and gave access to the Up Yard, the carriage sidings and the engine shed. The main access to and from the carriage sidings was at Heaton East signalbox, which was situated on the North Tyneside electric line a short distance from Heaton South Junction. It was customary on night shift when making the rounds of the yards to call in at the signalboxes for a cup of tea and 'a bit crack'. The word 'crack' has since taken on a new connotation, unknown in those innocent days when it merely signified a bit of a chat. I was learning the language.

The 'Pleasures' of the Night Shift

One of the pleasures on the night shift during late spring and early summer, on fine mornings when

dawn broke not much after 3.0am, was to stroll along the line to visit the signalboxes at Little Benton North and South. They controlled a set of sidings which I was told had been put in during the war to ease the load at Heaton. They were still used to recess trains that could not immediately be accepted on to the receptions at Heaton. It was, of course, essential to avoid blocking the Up main line at Benton Bank by having trains standing there waiting acceptance into the yard.

Winter nights were a different kettle of fish, but the icy blast of a keen nor'easter straight from Siberia via the North Sea was tempered by the welcome warmth that radiated from the handlamp, oil-lit of course in those days. No one ever warmed their hands on a Bardic electric handlamp. In those days, too, an enormous amount of work was performed outside in all weathers during night hours in marshalling yards, engine sheds and carriage sidings.

Older readers will remember the "Starlight Specials' which were introduced about this time. They ran overnight from Scotland to London by various routes at a return fare of 70s and were extremely popular. There were a large number of trains using both the East Coast and the West Coast main lines. In addition we had the car-sleeper trains, another initiative which was very popular until BR tried to milk the market, and ultimately destroyed it, by increasing the fares beyond what the market would bear. The costing people said that the trains didn't pay, but costing of railway activities is not an exact science. I believe it to have been a very short-sighted approach. We also had convoys of Scottish seed potato trains during the season. They were exciting times, when the lines were full of all manner of trains. By comparison, it has to be said that today's railway scene is boring

Left: Tyne Commission Quay Docks were used for the Fred Olsen Line sailings to Norway, and there was a through service from King's Cross on certain days at 9.0am. The empty stock is seen being taken on 23 June 1962 to the carriage sidings, through Percy Main, by Class V3 2-6-2T No 67652. *M. Dunnett*

Right: A train of empty stock headed by Class V3 2-6-2T No 67656 takes the Jesmond line at Manors station on 21 May 1962. *M. Mensing*

A Closer Look at the Yards

The West Yard had 23 single-ended sidings and dealt with local traffic for the North Tyneside area. The North Yard had 15 single-ended sidings and dealt with 'rough' traffic for the Tyneside area and the north main line, and for former LNER depots in Scotland, both from the Tyneside area and from further south on the former LNER system. The term 'roughs' included traffic in unfitted wagons or otherwise unsuitable for conveyance on express freight trains: eg steel, bricks, minerals, scrap and empties. The New Yard dealt with 'premium' traffic, ie merchandise traffic mainly in fitted vehicles, for Scotland. It had six single-ended sidings and three double-ended reception sidings. A number of Anglo-Scottish express freight trains bypassed the yards, or stopped only for crew or engine change or to attach and detach portions. The well-known No 266, the 3.5pm Class C goods from King's Cross Goods to Edinburgh Niddrie Yard, called at the New Yard for wagon examination and water, and woe betide anyone who delayed it on the Down Independent. It was usually headed by an 'A4'. Class C trains were timed at an *average* speed

of 50mph, but often ran at 60, as they did when passing through Stannington. They were quite a sight then (and made quite a noise).

The Up Yard had 19 double-ended sidings and three receptions. It received traffic from the north main line and Scotland, re-sorted it and sent it forward. Some of the traffic was local for the Tyneside area, and some for further south. Quite a proportion of the traffic had to be transferred to the West Sidings, which entailed a lengthy and cumbersome crossing of the main lines and needed a substantial margin between trains at the South Junction.

The Down yards each had a shunting engine on three shifts, except the West Sidings, which did not have a night shift. The Up Yard had a three-shift shunting engine at both ends of the yard. In those days, the yards were open until 6.0am on Sunday mornings. The shunting engines were 350hp standard BR diesel-electrics, which had arrived the previous year (1956).

Marshalling yards were a source of mystery to most people, who just saw rows and rows of goods wagons standing in sidings, with little or no sign of

anything happening. However, it was all carefully planned and each siding was allocated to a different destination, either a goods depot or another marshalling yard. For example, in the Up Yard, sidings were allocated to local freight depots and to marshalling yards such as Middlesbrough (Newport), Darlington (Croft), York (York yards or Dringhouses) and Doncaster (Decoy). Local trips served the Tyneside freight depots and the Newcastle Control Office had 'as required' trip engines at its disposal for surges of traffic.

The mainline freight trains were based on an established plan in which the trains were timetabled in just the same way as passenger trains, and had connections to be made, just like passengers. Punctuality of Class C and D trains was important. However, the timetable could be adjusted on the day, depending on the flow of traffic. If there was too little traffic the train could be cancelled; if too much the Control would organise a special.

The Freight Train Classification Sysytem
Perhaps at this stage, an explanation to the freight train classification system would be appropriate:
Class C — covered a multitude of types of train and traffic, with the list commencing 'parcels, fish, fruit, livestock, meat, milk, etc' and continuing 'express freight pipe-fitted throughout, with the automatic brake operative on not less than half of the vehicles'.

Class D — express freight, livestock or perishable train, partly fitted with the automatic brake operative on not less than one third of the vehicles.
Class E — similar, but with not less than four braked vehicles connected by vacuum pipe to the engine, or a similar train with a limited load of vehicles NOT fitted with continuous brake.
Class F — express freight etc. NOT fitted with continuous brake.
Class H — unfitted freight
Class J — mineral or empty wagon train
Class K — local freight.

In general, the greater proportion of brake-fitted vehicles, the higher the speed. It's all about being able to stop if the signal is at Danger.

The main line departures from the Up Yard on the night shift were as follows:
271 10.25pm Class C Dringhouses
(6.35pm from Niddrie)
1283 12.10am Class H Stockton
1255 1.25am Class D York Up Yard
1209 3.50am Class H Darlington Croft Junction
1207 4.35am Class F Stockton
273 5.50am Class C King's Cross Goods
(1.0am from Inverkeithing)

Trains were identified by a number and were timetabled at the highest possible classification, but much depended on the availability of fitted

Below left: A empty train of North Tyneside DC electric multiple-units heads for Newcastle Central station on 1 May 1962. *M. Mensing*

Right: In an elevated view of the four-track main line from Newcastle Central station to Manors, a 'Q6' 0-8-0 plods along with a heavy load of coal on 31 August 1960. *Colin P. Walker*

Below: A stranger in the camp. On 11 August 1962, an ex-LMS 'Royal Scot' class 4-6-0 No 46109 *Royal Engineer* (home shed Holbeck — 55A) takes the long curve into Newcastle Central station with the 8.45am Saturdays Only train from Leeds City to Edinburgh Waverley. *J. M. Rayner*

vehicles. Some vehicles and some loads were not suitable for higher speeds, hence the need for trains in classes F and H. Both those classes required no vacuum-braked vehicles with the brake in use, but Class F trains were timed at a higher speed than Class H. Some wagons and loads were allowed only on Class H trains, eg some loaded tank wagons, salt wagons with grease axleboxes, crane wagons, wagons with a wheelbase less than 7ft 6in (eg single bolster wagons), loads overhanging by 4ft or more (eg sawn timber).

The yard staff were responsible for marshalling trains in the correct order. The guard was responsible for coupling up, calculating the load and taking a full load if available, depending on the class of engine, and for observing any length restriction on the route. Carriage & Wagon (C&W) examiners examined all vehicles arriving at the yards, but it was the guard's job to satisfy himself that all appeared to be in order with his train.

Marshalling yards usually had a few sidings set apart for C&W staff to repair 'cripples' which the examiners had red-carded on the receptions. A red card meant 'not to go' and signified that the wagon had a defect that rendered it unsafe for onward transit from the yard. The wagon could be either loaded or empty. If it were loaded, and if the wagon could not be repaired quickly, the load had to be transhipped into another wagon in the repair sidings. There was a rather elderly crane in the sidings to assist where necessary.

Hot Axleboxes and Shifted Loads

On one occasion we had a particular problem. Surplus warships were being broken up on one of the lochs off the Firth of Clyde, and 10-ton slabs of armour plating were being sent to steelworks in England. Whoever loaded them into ordinary goods wagons didn't appreciate the sort of knocks and bangs that unfitted wagons could receive during shunting and ordinary train-working, which caused the slabs to slide all over the place. This in turn led to uneven loading of the wagon, with the result that the axlebox at the corner of the wagon into which the slab had slid was bearing too much weight and could run hot. One of the first of such trains had to detach wagons with hot axleboxes at what appears to have been almost every siding between Edinburgh and Heaton. On arrival at the receptions, the entire train had to be transferred to the cripple/tranship sidings so that the slabs could be

repositioned in the wagons and secured against further movement with substantial timber packing. Moving a 10-ton slab in a wagon was quite a task.

Hot axleboxes were part and parcel of everyday railway life in those days, even though grease axleboxes were almost a thing of the past. Fortunately, it was a time when there were lineside signalboxes at frequent intervals all down the line, and when every wayside station had a few sidings into which crippled wagons could be detached. The signalmen's Regulation 17 'Stop and Examine Train' was in frequent use. A signalman could often identify a hotbox even whilst the train was approaching. A hotbox gave off a whitish smoke and a distinctive screech. It also had its own distinctive smell as it passed the signalbox. The signalman would then send the bell signal 'Stop and Examine Train' (seven beats on the bell) to his colleague at the next signalbox. The signalman there would put all his signals to danger for both directions, and when the train stopped he and the traincrew would go through the laborious process of detaching the defective wagon. Meanwhile, the main line would be blocked in both directions.

In later years, the problem arose of detecting hot axleboxes when all the lineside signalboxes had been closed and replaced by centralised power signalboxes. Fortunately, a couple of firms were able to supply hot axlebox detectors, which were installed about every 20/25 miles and sent an alarm to the controlling signalbox when a hot axlebox was detected. Overheating axleboxes had to run for quite a distance before the end of the axle would become red-hot and eventually break off, leading to almost certain derailment.

The detector counted the axles of a passing train and was able to indicate which wagon on the train was concerned, and also which side of the wagon. In the meantime, most of the wayside sidings had been closed, so comprehensive instructions had to be issued to traincrews and others setting out how they should deal with the wagon if an alarm was confirmed. Serious delay could be caused to other trains, and it is fortunate that the old short-wheelbase wagons were being phased out in favour of larger wagons with roller-bearing axleboxes. However, that was all in the future.

The most intensive, and most interesting, period of the day occurred in the New Yard during the afternoon and evening, when local trips were

Right: Having just passed over the King Edward Bridge connecting Newcastle with Gateshead, a King's Cross 'A4' No 60013 *Dominion of New Zealand* curves round towards the south with the 9.30am from Glasgow Queen Street to London King's Cross on 5 September 1960.
Colin P. Walker

bringing in traffic to be sorted for Scottish destinations. This work had to be completed for a whole series of departures, as follows:

9.0pm Class C Glasgow High Street
9.30pm Class C Portobello (Edinburgh)
9.45pm Fish Empties for Aberdeen (the 11.9am from King's Cross Goods)
10.0pm Class C Edinburgh Niddrie
10.55pm Class C Niddrie (12.18pm from Ferme Park, London)
11.30pm Class C Niddrie

11.55pm Niddrie (2.54pm from King's Cross)
542   12.15am Niddrie (6.0pm fruit from Whitemoor)

(These times are taken from the summer 1960 Timetable. By then, express freight trains had mostly been accelerated to Class C with the greater availability of vacuum brake-fitted vehicles.)

The Exitement of an Express freight yard
It was an exciting period, with light engines arriving at the New Yard from the shed to work

Right: Haymarket's 'A1' Pacific No 60159 *Bonnie Dundee* hurries up the East Coast main line towards Heaton and Newcastle on 1 September 1962. Haymarket (64B) had a reputation for maintaining its Pacifics in sparkling condition, but *Bonnie Dundee* looks remarkably dowdy. The line over the top carries the North Tyneside electric line between Backworth and Benton.
Ian S. Carr

forward, and being backed onto their respective trains, coupled up and brakes tested. It could be an anxious period too, if the engines were late in arriving, or if the brake test showed a failure. The wagons were coupled up and had their brakes tested by using the shunt engine before the train engine arrived. Any failures could then be dealt with by the C&W examiner, which might require a defective wagon to be shunted out of the train at the last minute. The procedure to be adopted if the train engine failed to create the required vacuum could be quite lengthy, and consisted of the C&W examiner testing the train in sections. If no fault could be found on the train the fault was assumed to lie with the engine, which had to be sent back to the shed and a replacement obtained. This could lead to further delays, as well as arguments with the shed master next morning. It was best avoided if at all possible.

However, the shunting staff were experts at the job, and delays were rare. It was very satisfying to see engines arriving one by one on time, big engines too, mainly Pacifics and 'V2s', and then to see these important trains with a full load of 50 vehicles departing on time, very gently at first as they pulled out of the sidings and snaked out on to the main line. The small, barely audible, puffs of steam from the loco chimney changed to a much more powerful bark as soon as the last vehicle cleared the points and the guard exchanged handsignals with the fireman to assure him that the train was complete. This was the very heart and soul of the railway, with each man playing his part to achieve success. It's now all history, and just a memory, but it could be quite a thrill to see it. Such magnificent engines, but those overnight express freight trains were important as customers wanted, and were entitled to expect, next day delivery of their goods.

The LNER had been very progressive in developing the operation of express freight trains. They often ran in several sections, some of which were dropped off en route. The Regulations allowed 15 vehicles to be conveyed behind the brake van on fully fitted trains, in order to expedite the detaching of sections intermediately.

The railway map of Edinburgh was extremely complex in those days, and names such as Portobello and Meadows meant nothing to me. I decided that the best way to find out was to pay a visit, so I arranged with our opposite number in Edinburgh to have a guided tour. It was most instructive. Niddrie was the main yard, just off the main line along the avoiding line. Portobello was a couple of miles south of Waverley, next to Craigentinny carriage sidings, and Leith Walk was one of the main goods depots. I also discovered Joppa (next to Portobello) and Meadows, whose location I cannot now recall. Who now remembers Wanton Walls Junction, or Lochend Junction, or Warriston Junction? The Caledonian had an equally impressive network too.

The AYMs had an office in a small single storey building at the south end of the Up Yard, the other half of which was occupied by the South End Yard foreman. Our window looked out directly on to the East Coast main line at Heaton Junction, a couple of tracks away. It was also situated just outside the engine shed, so that engines coming off shed passed directly in front of our office (and sometimes stood there for a few minutes waiting for the road and blocking out the light). For anyone interested in engines it was a dream. I have to say that my favourites were the later 'A2s' Nos 60525 to 60539. Haymarket had five of them and kept them in splendid condition, 60530 and 60534 to 37. If I had a particular favourite it would have to be No 60535 *Hornet's Beauty*, the very epitome of elegance, power and grace. Perhaps it was the 6ft 2in driving wheels that tipped the scales.

A Magic World for trainspotters

Nearly all the LNER Pacifics were winners in the beauty stakes, and I expect we all have our favourites. The 'A1s' and 'A3s' were equally splendid engines and really had no equals when King's Cross Top Shed and Haymarket turned them out in pristine condition, as they did regularly, and I say this with a vestige of envy as a former LMS man. It was always a source of mystery to me as to why some sheds turned out their engines as though they cared what they looked like, whilst others didn't bother. A clean engine *looked* more efficient and was a splendid advertisement. It gave railwaymen a pride in their work.

Heaton kept its top link engines in reasonably good condition and it had quite a large stud. When I went there it had 13 'A3s' — Nos 60051/2, 60069, 60072/3/7, 60080/2/3/5/6 and 60091/2. It had three 'A1s' — No 60116 *Hal o' the Wynd* (what a marvellous name for an engine!), No 60126 *Sir Vincent Raven* (very appropriate) and No 60127

Wilson Worsdell (an earlier North Eastern Railway locomotive engineer). Heaton also had two 'A2/3s' — No 60511 *Airborne* and No 60517 *Ocean Swell*, and one 'A2' No 60539 *Bronzino*. These were backed up by 15 'V2s', which were almost their equals in power, if not quite in grace. Heaton and Haymarket between them had more Pacifics than the entire LMS, but they were built for a different railway, a high speed racetrack. However, just to make me feel at home, Heaton had nine LMS Class 4 Ivatt 2-6-0s, the forerunners of the BR standard Class 4.

Above: Class V3 2-6-2T No 67651 waits awhile behind the single-storey Assistant Yard Master's office. Train-spotters would have loved it, as all the engines coming off Heaton shed passed the windows. *Author's collection*

Below: Hornet's Beauty, No 60535, a Peppercorn Class A2, stands in the sun as the acme of grace and beauty indeed. The photograph bears no indication of place or date, but it was a Haymarket (64B) engine and they normally kept their locomotives clean. Or it could be an ex-works photo when the engine was brand new. In any event, it frequently passed the AYM's office on an express to or from Edinburgh and it was always a pleasure to see it. *Hornet's Beauty* was certainly one of my favourite engines. *Ian Allan Library*

Above: Heaton shed (52B) has excelled itself with the preparation and cleanliness of its 'A3' Pacific No 60080 *Dick Turpin*, seen here leaving Newcastle Central station with an Edinburgh to King's Cross express on 9 April 1955. The magnificent signal gantry is also worthy of note. *Ian Allan Library*

Below: Top Link power for the 4.13pm train from Newcastle Central to Liverpool Lime Street via Sunderland on 9 April 1960 is provided by Class A3 4-6-2 No 60077 *The White Knight.* This was a Leeds Holbeck (55A) engine, and commendably clean. *Ian S. Carr*

We Get a House at Last – at a Station

A couple of weeks after applying for the house at Stannington I received a letter from the Estate Department stating that I had been allocated the tenancy. Priority was given to shift workers. In those days staff household removals were undertaken by Pickfords, which was quite appropriate as they were part of the British Transport Commission. They loaded all our worldly possessions into a household removal container at Mirfield, took the container to Mirfield goods depot and loaded it on to a conflat wagon. It then wended its merry way by goods train to Morpeth, involving several intermediate shunts, and was finally delivered from Morpeth goods depot by road. Household containers were wired on from yard to yard, and to the Control Office. I was on late turn when the container arrived at Heaton, and watched it with great care as it was shunted into a siding for the local trip to Morpeth the next morning. In fairness, it has to be said that the staff generally took care with household removal containers, and it arrived at our new home with its contents practically unscathed.

We moved in on 15 August 1957. There was another dwelling attached to the station buildings and it was occupied by one of the signalmen at Stannington station signalbox, Walter Clayden. We quickly made friends. Our bedroom was a huge affair and had a bay window overlooking the Up platform. The Up trains were about 12 feet away, and during the night there was a continuous procession of sleeping car expresses, parcels trains and fitted freight trains all roaring through at pretty high speed, followed by slower freight trains which came along rattling and clanking. Their imminent arrival was announced by the clanging of the great wooden level crossing gates being closed across the road. The first night we hardly slept a wink, but after that we never noticed the trains. It was strange.

Stannington station was about 12 miles by road from Heaton Yards, and initially I was quite happy to cycle to and from work, as I enjoyed cycling, but as autumn and dark nights approached I came to the conclusion that I must become motorised. I acquired a small 49cc motor cycle with a top speed of about 25/30mph which halved my journey time to work. On middle turn I went by train on the 7.27am from Alnwick, hauled in old-fashioned splendour by one of the last North Eastern Railway's mainline racers, Class D20 No 62395

(52D — Alnwick). It also worked the return service at 5.4pm from Newcastle, but it was finally withdrawn from service in November that year, the last survivor of the class. The 'D20s' were replaced by Class V1/V3 2-6-2Ts from Heaton. The Alnwick trains didn't usually produce exciting strangers at the front end, but on 20 August the 5.27pm from Alnwick to Newcastle produced a 'K1' 2-6-0 No 62019 bearing a 31B (March) shedplate. Another surprising stranger through Stannington was 'Director' Class D11 No 62690 *The Lady of the Lake* (64B — Haymarket) on the 7.40pm Newcastle to Berwick slow, usually a 'B1' turn, on 10 November. In April 1958 the reign of steam on the Alnwick trains came to an end when they were replaced by DMUs. At the time, it seemed an improvement, a superior form of travel.

Derailments Were Not Uncommon

Derailments in marshalling yards were commonplace; part and parcel of shunting wagons over hand points. The staff were generally adept at rerailing wagons by using portable metal ramps provided at various places in the yards. It was a question of skill in fixing the ramp in the correct position and providing timber packing for the wagon wheels to run on and guide them on to the ramp when pulled gently by the shunt engine. The timber packing was important — the local permanent-way inspector didn't take kindly to having chairs smashed by clumsy shunters and impetuous inspectors. There were naturally times when the derailment was too severe for ramps and packing, and then we had to call out the shed staff with their jacks. Beyond that, it was a job for the steam crane, as when No 60125 *Scottish Union* failed to stop at the exit signal on the Up goods line and ran off the trap points, finishing up ignominiously in the dirt. On another occasion No 60107 *Royal Lancer* came off the road at Heaton South End, but at least the steam crane didn't have far to travel.

Station House, Stannington, may have been a quite impressive address, but it was a very cold house too. Even as early as December in 1957 the temperature in our bedroom slumped to 36° F for several nights, but there was worse to come. It was a bad winter, with plenty of snow as well as sharp frosts. Several times in January 1958 the temperature in the bedroom went below freezing point, and the hard weather continued into

Left: There were just three of the well-known and popular 'D20s' left when No 62396 was caught on camera at Newcastle Central in October 1957, backing out of the station, probably after having brought in a train from Alnwick. The others were No 62381 and 62395. The 'D20s' were designed by William Worsdell, and the class of 60 engines was brought into service over a number of years at the turn of the century. *M. Dunnett*

February. I was on nights on 7 February, and when I dragged myself out of the warm sheets and scampered into the warm bathroom to get dressed I could hear the wind howling and snow beating on the windows. Going to work by road was out of the question, so I went up into the signalbox and asked the signalman what freights were coming on the Up road on which I could cadge a lift. I was in luck, 'Austerity' 2-8-0 No 90542 of 62C (Dundee Tay Bridge) was about half an hour away with a slow freight for Heaton Yard. Perfect! I had a warm ride to work, and was dropped off a few yards from the AYMs' office.

The Wind Blows and We Will Have Snow
It was a wild night and gradually the yards came to a halt as points became clogged by snow. The blizzard blew all night throughout the North East, but by daylight it had blown itself out and we were greeted by a clear blue sky and a hard frost. I left work about 8.0am, and set off to walk to the Great North Road, the A1, hoping that the snowploughs would have been at work and that I could get a lift home (people didn't mind giving lifts in those peaceful days). Actually, in other circumstances it would have been a wonderful walk, with the sun glinting off four-foot drifts in scenery resembling fairyland. I eventually arrived home just in time for lunch. One other item of interest that night was the presence of a Doncaster Class 9F 2-10-0 on Heaton shed, No 92169.

Motive Power Matters
Actually '9Fs' were starting to become quite common. On 30 July 1958, No 92058 from Wellingborough (15A) penetrated the North East fastness as far as Heaton, and a week later no fewer than nine 2-10-0s were to be seen at Heaton — Nos 92060/1/7/9, 92097, 92165, 92171/83 and 92190, mainly from Tyne Dock or the Eastern Region. The '9Fs' were splendid engines; what a pity that they hadn't been built earlier and didn't last longer. But

Right: Class A3 Pacific No 60065 *Knight of Thistle* looks to be in fine fettle as she pulls out of Newcastle Central, apparently at full throttle but possibly slipping, with the 'Heart of Midlothian' on 15 April 1960. *Ian S. Carr*

an ominous sign of the times occurred on 30 May when we were visited by No D8400, the first of a small class of 10 Type 1 Bo-Bo diesel-electrics en route from the North British Loco Works at Glasgow to the Eastern Region at Stratford. The whole class passed through Stannington in the next few months. An even more ominous event took place on 21 June 1958, when English Electric Type 4 diesel No D201 was to be seen at Newcastle at the head of the 5.5pm to King's Cross, having come off the Down 'Flying Scotsman'.

BR 'Clan' class Pacifics had been seen for a few months the previous winter. Nos 72000/2/5 were all seen within a few weeks after they were transferred to Haymarket from Polmadie in October 1957. However, they were back at Polmadie the following April. I never discovered whether they had been transferred temporarily to deal with additional traffic, or whether the Haymarket men didn't care much for them. Possibly the latter; the 'Clans' didn't have a very good reputation, although they were handsome machines.

I was passing through Newcastle Central station one day in April 1958 when I came across an astonishing sight — LMS Fowler 2-6-4T No 42411, a former Mirfield engine, on a local passenger train. It transpired that it had been transferred to Sunderland. The Fowler parallel-boiler 2-6-4Ts were very highly thought of on the LMS, but it wasn't likely that hard-nosed North Eastern locomen would look kindly on such an obvious foreign import. It was soon transferred back to the Leeds area.

Time to Move On

A couple of months later, news came that Mr Slater, our very popular boss, had been appointed Stationmaster at King's Cross, one of the cream jobs on the former LNER. We were all very pleased for him and knew that he was absolutely cut out for the job. I was deputed to arrange a leaving present for him, and a farewell 'do'. A collection was arranged and a barometer was duly purchased. Barometers were popular presents in those days. He had his last day at Heaton on 4 July 1958. Little did I know that three years later I would become his

deputy at the Cross. He was replaced by Mr Hamilton from Berwick, where he had been Stationmaster. We soon got to like him. Railwaymen seemed to be much more of a family in those days.

Stannington station closed to passengers on 13 September 1958, and I was beginning to reconcile myself to having to travel by road when on middle turn, as well as on the other two turns. However, a vacancy arose for Yard Master, Blaydon, which took my fancy. It was graded Special Class 'A'. I wanted to be my own boss, and

as luck would have it, my wish was granted. My last day at Heaton was Saturday 25 October 1958. There were some good railwaymen there whom I was sorry to leave, but I was looking forward to my new job, and every night in bed.

Below: No day trip to Edinburgh was complete without a visit to the Forth Bridge. A BR Standard Class 5 4-6-0, No 73106, makes its way through a tangle of girders with an Up express on 31 July 1958. A superb photo. *Author's Collection*

Nine

EXPLORING TYNESIDE 1958/59
I BECOME A YARD MASTER — MY OWN BOSS AGAIN

Introduction

A train journey from Newcastle to Carlisle today takes the traveller southwards across the River Tyne, with that magnificent view along the river on both sides, then down a deep cutting and underneath the East Coast main line, before the train swings west through Dunston to Blaydon and on to Carlisle. Approaching Blaydon (actually on the site of the old West Dunston Sidings at Derwenthaugh) the train calls at the Gateshead Metro Shopping Centre with its vast car park, but there is little to remind the traveller that 50 years ago the whole area was a vast network of lines and branches and sidings serving collieries, shipping staithes, gas works, electricity works and a variety of other industries. This whole region south of the Tyne can surely be called the birthplace of railways, called into being by the need to move coal from collieries, up in the hills, down to the river to be loaded into boats and shipped to London and other places. Railways and coal were the engines which drove the Industrial Revolution in Britain and were the foundation of our industrial and commercial success.

A Bit of History

I hope the reader doesn't mind a bit of history, but South Tyneside is steeped in it. One of the main events in the railway calendar was the opening of the Newcastle & Carlisle Railway (N&C) in 1838, which ran along the south bank of the Tyne from Blaydon to Redheugh, from which point a ferry took passengers (and goods) across the river to Newcastle. That operation didn't last long. The N&C built a bridge over the Tyne at Scotswood and extended its line along the north bank to Newcastle, eventually reaching the Central station in 1851. The south bank then concentrated on coal and goods traffic for over 100 years before the Scotswood Bridge was closed in 1982, causing the Newcastle to Carlisle trains to be diverted via today's route through Dunston and along the south bank to Blaydon.

A Journey from Blaydon to Redheugh in 1960 (on foot, of course)

Let's start at Blaydon station. Immediately we leave the station, the line divides at Blaydon Station signalbox (which also controls the level crossing gates). To the left the line proceeds through a complex of sidings to Scotswood Bridge and along the north bank of the Tyne to Newcastle. All the passenger trains go this way. We'll have a closer look at this area another day. To the right the line goes straight forward (the original N&C route), passing on the left a group of sidings known as Blaydon Mineral Sidings and, across a road, the loco depot (52C). This is the nerve centre for a number of traincrews who take empties to the collieries and then take coal to wherever it is required, using Blaydon's sturdy and reliable Class Q6 0-8-0s They do not work to a fixed schedule, but work to the orders of the Newcastle Mineral Leading Office. This merits a bit of explanation.

Coal does not flow in fixed quantities to the same destinations every day, therefore schedules have to be adjusted on a daily basis, based on forecasts of output and destinations provided by the Coal

Above: This is the view looking west through Blaydon station as it would have been in 1960. The line that curves away to the right behind the signalbox proceeds through a complex of sidings and over the Scotswood bridge across the Tyne, then along the north bank of the river to Newcastle. The line that comes straight to the bottom of the photograph continues to the industrial area south of the river, with access also to the East Coast main line southwards, and to Central station via Gateshead and the King Edward Bridge. The latter is today's route for the passenger trains between Carlisle and Newcastle since the Scotswood bridge was demolished. *Author's Collection*

Board. Much of the coal is shipping coal, to be loaded into vessels at Dunston Staithes, and it needs to be brought forward to coincide with the arrival of vessels at the staithes. The coal is said to be 'led forward', hence the name of the office. The Mineral Leading Office telephones its orders to the yard inspector at the Sidings, and he arranges for the appropriate traincrew to work each schedule. The traincrews operate under a bonus system, with handsome rewards if the work is performed quickly. Both sides benefit. The traincrews strive to complete their daily schedule and earn their bonus and an early finish. The company (now BR) gets the work done promptly and the engine is returned to shed in plenty of time for its next turn. These bonus schemes have been a long-established feature of the North East and have worked very well because they provide real incentives.

Immediately after leaving Blaydon Mineral Sidings, a line passes overhead which once took passenger trains from Newcastle to Blackhill (Consett) via Scotswood Bridge and the picturesque Derwent Valley, until the service was withdrawn a few years ago. There are a number of connections from that line to the Redheugh branch both at Blaydon Mineral Sidings and Blaydon Main Colliery signalbox a little further along our route. At the Colliery signalbox a line trails in from the right from Garesfield Sidings. This is the erstwhile Garesfield and Chopwell Colliery Sidings branch, which served a number of collieries but now I believe serves only an opencast site. This is followed by another line trailing in from the right, from the Swalwell opencast site, near Derwenthaugh signalbox, but it is the West Dunston staithes which catch our eye at this point. They too will close shortly, and the rundown of the area has already begun. There is a group of sidings here, known as West Dunston or Derwenthaugh Sidings, which serves the staithes and other local installations.

Above: The busy layout of Norwood Junction on 6 February 1966 sees Class Q6 0-8-0 No 63395 take the line to Dunston Staithes to pick up empty hoppers and return them to the Sunderland area. The 'Q6s' were powerful, efficient machines, ideal for coal traffic, and were designed by Vincent Raven, being introduced in 1913. There were 120 in the fleet. Behind the colour-light signal in the middle distance, the line on the left led to Gateshead and Newcastle, the line in the centre to Low Fell and the left hand line led to Norwood coke works. The busy signalbox stood on a gantry straddling the line to Dunston East, whilst the line on the right hand side of the photo led to Blaydon via Dunston. *A. R. Thompson)*

Below: Another 'Q6' leaves Low Fell yard with a trainload of empty hopper wagons for the West Durham coalfield. The East Coast main line runs along the far side. *J. W. Armstrong Trust*

Above: Norwood Junction on 6 February 1966. Class Q6 No 63436 takes empty hoppers from Dunston power station to the Sunderland area. *A. R. Thompson*

(Perhaps the author ought to point out here that the picture he paints is of a changing railway at an indeterminate date in the late 1950s.)

The tall chimneys and buildings of Dunston power station are the next features of note, busy as ever with trainloads of coal being delivered and empties being returned to the collieries. Here the line divides again. To the right there is a direct route to Gateshead and Newcastle, and to Darlington and York via Low Fell and the East Coast main line. Yes, it's a complicated area and reference to the layout plan is again required. But we will continue along the Redheugh branch, through a hive of industrial activity, past Dunston West signalbox, with major installations at Dunston Colliery and the CWS flour mill and soap works, followed by Dunston East signalbox straddling the tracks. This style of signalbox was a feature of the old North Eastern Railway, and there are several examples, eg at Norwood Junction and Wylam.

Norwood Junction is an important signalbox, which lies across the line from Dunston East at a point where it joins the direct line from Derwenthaugh to Newcastle and Low Fell. There is also a busy branch here which controls access to Norwood Sidings and the shipping staithes, with its endless procession of coal trains in and empties out.

Class J72 0-6-0Ts are in non-stop action here, pushing rakes of coal wagons from the sidings on to the staithes and bringing back empties. This is a new world for a railwayman, who finds himself dealing with shipping, as well as the NCB, the CEGB and a host of private siding owners. Truly, a railwayman had to be a jack-of-all-trades in those days. And dare I say it, today's railway looks like child's play by comparison and can hardly be said to have anything like the same absorbing interest. How glad I am to have lived through those days. But we'll call at the Inspector's office and maybe have a cup of tea. I made it a point never to refuse a cup of tea — you never knew when the next one was coming. Engine drivers were the same with water columns.

Whilst we are here we really ought to have a look at the staithes and walk along to the end. They are huge and can accommodate several coasters at each side. But imagine working up here in rough

Above: In this photo from 1965 'Q6' No 63395 appears again, having just left Low Fell sidings with a long train of large hoppers.
A. R. Thompson

weather with an icy east wind blowing straight up the river. This is the real world, the world of coal and ships and railways that made North Durham and South Tyneside prosperous. It's easy to forget now just how much work was performed out of doors in all weathers half a century ago, but also it's sad to relate that part of the staithes was recently set on fire by vandals, leaving a gap in the middle. The staithes are a valuable part of the North East's industrial heritage, and funding is being sought for repairs. However, back in the more peaceful times of 1958, reinvigorated by our bracing walk and a cup of tea we'll make our way to the end of the Redheugh branch. It's less than a mile now.

After passing Redheugh gas works we come to an historic spot — Redheugh Bank Foot, where the Tanfield branch trails in from the right. The Redheugh branch continues for a short way as a single line and ends in a simple set of buffer stops, but it's the Tanfield branch which attracts our attention. We ought to explore it whilst it's still there because although it's one of the oldest railway lines in the world, its future is uncertain. It runs for several miles to collieries in the Tanfield area and has to climb from sea level to 800ft, which requires it to be built with a number of rope-worked inclines, of which two still survive, at Fugar Bank and Lobley Hill. They are gravity worked. A rope is attached to a raft of loaded wagons waiting to be lowered down the incline, and then round a large pulley wheel at the bank top. The rope then runs all the way down the bank to be attached to a raft of empties at the bank foot. The weight of the loaded wagons descending the bank then pulls the empties to the top. Such arrangements were common at one time throughout the country but are now becoming rare. The collieries in the Tanfield area were already starting to close in the late 1950s and the branch itself closed in 1964. The southern end of the branch is now a preserved railway. In its early days the Tanfield branch crossed a well-known bridge — the Causey Arch. Here is real history. This stone bridge, which crosses a deep gorge, was erected in 1727, but the origins of the line date back even further to about 1632, when waggonways were built to carry coal to the Tyne, forming the basis of the Tanfield Railway.

Above: The extent of the steelworks plant at Consett can be judged from this photograph, taken at Consett North. *North Eastern Railway Association*

But now it's time to make our way back to Blaydon. Fortunately the whole district is well served by buses (one of the main reasons for the decline of local railways). Today we have been in a time warp. Almost everything we have seen — track, buildings, sidings, signalboxes, engines and wagons — is pure North Eastern Railway. Certainly the engines are — 'Q6' 0-8-0s, 'J27' 0-6-0s and 'J72' 0-6-0Ts — a testimony to the enduring engineering excellence of the north east. It was there for 300 years and vanished almost without trace in about ten. It's hard to believe. No more hustle and bustle. No more the clanking of wagons, the engines whistling on the staithes, ships' hooters sounding, signalbox bells ringing. Gone the big iron kettle simmering on the big iron stove; somewhere to warm your hands on a cold winter's morn. But today we've explored an area which few people really know much about, and which even fewer have ever visited. But it's the real railway. It was coal which provided the North Eastern Railway's profits. Passenger stations and express trains may be more glamorous, indeed are, but there is more depth and fascination, more to explore, in those dirty, dusty areas such as the Redheugh branch. Now we can only look back and be glad that we saw it whilst there was still time. But only just in time! Anyone fancy a trip to the Gateshead Metro Shopping Centre? You should see the queues

at weekends. I bet few of them would want to turn the clock back! But we might, if only in the mind's eye, as we continue our exploration and visit Blaydon Yards and Engine Shed, Scotswood Bridge Carriage Sidings and Addison Marshalling Yard.

I Become my Own Boss Again — as Yard Master, Blaydon

So far we have explored the Dunston area from Blaydon to Redheugh Bank Foot as it would have been in the late 1950s. I had gone there temporarily to cover the long-term absence of the Assistant Yard Master (nominally a middle turn job), but after a while a vacancy arose for Yard Master at Blaydon, which covered the adjacent area. If I got the job I would have to move home again, but at least I would no longer be working shifts and I could travel to work each day until I found a house. There were several railway houses available to rent and I chose one of these, an end-terrace up the hill from the town. The Stationmaster, Mr Dalby, lived opposite and gave my wife and I (and small child) a warm welcome. In fact, we were surrounded by railway families, mainly traincrews and signalmen. The office itself was at Addison Marshalling Yard, about a mile down the line towards Carlisle, somewhat remote from the extensive sidings at Blaydon, together with the carriage sidings at Scotswood Bridge, and the Engine Shed, which had its own shedmaster. So there were three of us looking after the area, the Shedmaster, the Stationmaster and me. The Stationmaster was located at Blaydon station and looked after the main line, the signalboxes and the goods depots.

A Tour of the Blaydon area as it would have been in 1960

The Engine Shed (52C)

The access from the main line to Blaydon shed was via a double running junction near Blaydon signalbox, and it was also possible to obtain access at the other end of the sidings at Scotswood signalbox. Such double accesses were always valuable, because it meant that any derailment or blockage of one access did not completely stop the job. My track layout plan shows the shed to have consisted of two turntables in tandem, each one providing standage for about 20 engines. One of the turntables gave direct access to the carriage sidings and to Scotswood signalbox, so it was quite a convenient layout. The engine shed was alongside and parallel to the Scotswood Road, and it looked as though it would have been quite easy to make unauthorised visits.

Blaydon had sub-sheds at Hexham and Alston for working the branches. The Shedmaster must have enjoyed his occasional trips to visit the far-flung parts of his empire. Whilst it would have been tempting to choose a warm sunny day for such visits, one had to avoid any temptation to behave like a Swiss clock 'and only come out on sunny days'. It was politic to make some visits on days when it teemed down endlessly!

In 1958 Blaydon's allocation, according to *The Railway Observer* supplement, a very useful little document issued by the Railway Correspondence & Travel Society, was:

Class B1 4-6-0	61019, 61100, 61238
Class J21 0-6-0	65033
Class J25 0-6-0	65675
Class J39 0-6-0	64812/14-16, 64842/9, 64858
Class J72 0-6-0T	69001, 69023-26
Class J94 0-6-0T	68010, 68035/6/8
Class K1 2-6-0	62002/6, 62010, 62021-30
Class Q6 0-8-0	63356, 63363, 63376/8, 63381/5, 63390/4/9, 63413, 63441, 63352, 63362
Class V3 2-6-2T	67634/6, 67653, 67682
BR Class 3 2-6-0	77011/14
Diesel shunters	D2049, D3673/4/8

Below: A commendably clean though somewhat elderly 'J72' 0-6-0T engine pauses for the photographer at Blaydon shed. The class, which ultimately totalled 113 engines, was introduced by W. Worsdell in 1898. The class was still intact after 60 years with additional examples being built by BR. *J. W. Armstrong Trust*

Above: Back at Blaydon engine shed (52C), Class K1 2-6-0 No 62023 coals up at the old-fashioned coaling stage in 1951. These engines were ideal for the Blaydon Yard/Addison Sidings to Carlisle freight service, and were introduced by Peppercorn in 1949, being based on a Thompson design. There were 70 engines in the class.
J. W. Armstrong Trust

The 'K1s' were used extensively on the Carlisle freight services, the 'V3s' on ECS workings, two of the 350hp diesel shunters worked at Addison Yard and one at Newcastle Forth Goods Depot. No 77011 worked on the Alston branch, which was the only steam-operated branch in the North Eastern Region at this time. But the main work was freight, with coal and empties predominating.

I mentioned that Sunday was a good day for visiting Blaydon shed. Not only were all the freight engines at home, but one might often see strangers from distant sheds which had worked into Newcastle on specials and taken their empty coaches (ECS) to Scotswood Bridge Carriage Sidings, eg Class D49 No 62763 *The Fitzwilliam* (50D — Starbeck) on 16 August 1959. Former LMS engines were also to be seen, eg 'Jubilee' No 45610 *Ghana* (17A) on 7 June 1959. Sunday 6 September 1959 was quite exciting, with Class 5 4-6-0s Nos 44851 (17A) and 45000 (5B), and BR Class 9F 2-10-0 No 92078 (18A). Unfortunately my records don't indicate how the latter two found their way to Tyneside.

Former LMS engines were not uncommon on passenger trains from Carlisle, although as far as I recall they were all rostered for engines from former LNER sheds. Carlisle Canal shed (68E) was rostered for some of the workings but borrowed from Kingmoor when there was an engine shortage. On 25 November 1958 Class 5 4-6-0 No 45138

(12A) worked the 2.0pm Carlisle to Newcastle and returned on the 5.20pm, whilst on 3 December 1958 'Jubilee' No 45721 *Impregnable* (5A) worked the 7.20am from Carlisle and the 12.20pm back. This was reported to be the first 'Jubilee' to have worked over the line.

Scotswood Bridge Carriage Sidings (SBS)

These consisted of 15 double-ended sidings in two groups lying between Scotswood Bridge signalbox and Blaydon signalbox. At one time they provided a lot of steam-hauled sets of coaches for branch and local lines in North Durham but some of these lines had closed and others had become worked by diesel multiple-units, which were stabled and serviced at South Gosforth. However, the Carlisle services were still steam-hauled and SBS also provided sets for some mainline workings to York, Sheffield and Birmingham, mainly FO and SO. In the late 1950s many relief and dated trains were run, so SBS could become quite busy. This is when the Yard Master put on his passenger hat to ensure that as far as possible all the ECS left the sidings on time. Fortunately I lived in Blaydon, so it was quite easy to pop down to the carriage sidings to have a chat with the Inspector there. The best access was via the engine shed yard, giving an opportunity for a quiet snoop around.

Blaydon Yard

There will probably be many readers who never travelled over the Newcastle-Carlisle line in steam days. It was not really a main trunk route so far as passengers were concerned, and the service was hourly or less. But it was an important freight route, and the area between the River Tyne at Scotswood Bridge and Blaydon signalbox, barely three-quarters of a mile, was a mass of sidings on both sides of the line. To the south lay the carriage sidings and the engine shed, whilst to the north lay Blaydon Yard. It had ceased to be a marshalling yard because this function had been transferred to a new yard at Addison, built so I understand during the Second World War to cope with increased traffic over this route.

However, Blaydon Yard was still used for recessing block trainloads. In its heyday it had consisted of two Down goods lines and two Up goods lines, presumably used as reception sidings, 10 single-ended sidings known as GN Sidings, 10 single-ended sidings known as Spike Sidings, and two sets of four single-ended sidings known as the Old Yard and Hexham Gullet. There were several shunting necks to allow shunting to be carried on simultanously in the old-fashioned way — draw back, push forwards, kick-off, stop, draw back, etc. It was slow, inefficient and labour intensive. I have been unable to discover when shunting ceased there, but in 1960 it was still quite busy handling block trainloads. There were six booked departures to Carlisle London Road, all Class H, at 12.35am, 2.0am, 5.20am, 10.50am, 1.35pm and 6.20pm, with a similar service in the opposite direction.

Between Blaydon Station and Addison Yard

Even in this short distance there are signs of one-time colliery activity, but the main development was the building of Stella South power station in the 1950s, lying on the south bank of the river and accessed from this line. The CEGB also built a sister power station on the north bank of the river, known as Stella North, with rail access being gained from the line that ran between Scotswood and North Wylam. Both power stations have now been demolished and the sites have been cleared.

Addison Yard

Addison was a new yard, all double-ended. It stretched from Addison Level Crossing signalbox, one mile west of Blaydon station, and Peth Lane signalbox, half a mile further along. It was a busy yard, with shunting taking place on three shifts at both ends of the yard, using 350hp diesel-electric shunting locomotives. It was a very pleasant location, almost out in the open country, even though there was a colliery on the opposite side of the line. Because it was a relatively compact yard it was a very friendly place, where everyone knew everyone else. In the office besides myself there was my middle turn assistant, George, a jolly and very capable chap who went on to become Stationmaster at Stranraer. He was very loyal and a great help, and I had no qualms at all about leaving him in charge whilst I was elsewhere. I also had a clerk, Mary, who acted as my secretary too. We were a very happy little family, with our own little empire.

The function of Addison was to receive traffic from the Newcastle area and the North East and sort it out for the various yards in Carlisle for onwards transmission to Cumberland and south-west Scotland. Mixed trains were marshalled (1) Carlisle London Road NE, (2) Carlisle Canal (NB), (3) Carlisle (Cal), (4) Carlisle (M&C) and (5) Carlisle (G&SW). There was a similar pattern of traffic in the reverse direction, and a number of express freights ran over the line bypassing Addison. The local freights were mostly handled by 'J39' 0-6-0s, but the Carlisle trains were handled by Blaydon's capable Class K1 2-6-0s, and part of my job was to see that the trains carried full loads and ran punctually. Each guard made out a journal showing the number of wagons carried and the equivalent load. He also recorded departure and arrival times, and passing times at reporting points. I could therefore follow up any delays, especially those elusive delays known as 'lost time in running', and I got to know the names of those drivers who were good runners, and also those who were not so good, much to the annoyance of the Shedmaster. Any delays shown as lost time in running had to be referred to him, and he would often come back and say that the driver reported

Above: Peth Lane signalbox and level crossing, looking towards Hexham. The signalbox controlled arrivals to, and departures from, Addison Yard. The yard had closed when this photograph was taken, as shown by the removal of the signal arm controlling movements to the yard, and also the crossover road for departures in the Carlisle direction. © *John Mallon Collection/NERA and Ken Hoole Study Centre, Darlington*

Below: Photographs of marshalling yards are rare, probably because access is difficult, and rows of wagons do not make a good picture. This group was photographed outside the Yard Master's office at Addison and shows my secretary, Mary Laidlaw, making a presentation to my assistant, George Johnson, to mark his promotion to Stationmaster at Stranraer Town. I am second from the left. George was a first-rate railwayman. *Author's Collection*

A Railwayman's Odyssey

having had the Distant on at such-and-such a box. That then had to be followed up with the local stationmaster. There were some 'interesting' telephone conversations!

I soon realised that I didn't know the Carlisle road very well so I did a number of brake van trips. It was really the only way of getting to know the guards, who were part of my establishment, as well as an excellent way of learning the road. Leaning over the rail in the brake van at the back of a freight

Above: Wylam station and level crossing, with the signalbox perched high on a gantry to give the signalman a good view. *Author*

Below: Blaydon's Class K1 2-6-0 No 62026 is seen here on an Addison Yard to Carlisle London Road freight passing Border Counties Junction signalbox and the junction for Reedsmouth and Riccarton Junction, in the early 1950s. The signal arm nearest the signalbox controlled the branch to Allendale. *J. W. Armstrong Trust*

train and watching the world go by on such a picturesque line as the Carlisle road was a very pleasant way of passing an afternoon, but it was also an important way of 'showing the flag' and letting the staff know that you were interested in them and their jobs. The summer of 1959 was one of the finest on record. Perfect for a brakevan trip, but January that year was reported to have been the coldest in the area for 40 years. The previous winter (1958) had also been very severe — long, cold and hard. Weather reports showed that signs of spring did not appear until 12 April, and that snow had fallen every day from 7 to 13 March and 19 to 22 March.

I was also keen to learn about the various Carlisle yards and their functions, and to see that we were helping them as much as possible, so I phoned the Yard Master and asked if I could have a visit. 'Certainly,' he said, 'I'll fix up a brake van tour and we'll go round together.' We agreed on the 22 July. He was as good as his word and I was quite surprised at the complexity of the goods lines, goods yards, depots and sidings around Carlisle. The whole area was long overdue for rationalisation and I learned of plans to build a huge new mechanised yard at Kingmoor, just north of Carlisle. Only with the help of hindsight did we realise that Carlisle New Yard should never have been built, and that as far as possible trains from England should have gone straight through to Mossend (near Glasgow) or Millerhill (near Edinburgh) without intermediate shunting at Carlisle.

The new yard at Kingmoor never repaid its investment. Within less than 20 years it had become a white elephant. However, we were not to know that. Predicting the future so far as railways are concerned is extraordinarily difficult, especially when politicians and the government become involved. The Yard Master and I had a long chat, mulling over ideas of how we could help each other by changes to the pattern and timing of trains, and the marshalling arrangements. On the way back to Addison, leaning over the brake van rail, I recalled how in the school holidays I had visited Carlisle station and was disappointed to find that there were no freight trains. Now I knew why. They all use the goods avoiding lines.

Being Yard Master at Blaydon was a very happy experience and I enjoyed being my own boss. However, it was clear that the writing was on the wall for Addison Yard. There were plans to build a huge new marshalling yard on the East Coast main line just south of Low Fell, to be known as Tyne Yard, and it would take in all the work currently being done by the various yards around Tyneside. A vacancy then arose for Yard Master at the New England Yards, Peterborough, so it looked like a good time to move on. My last day at Addison was 28 November 1959 and as I said my goodbyes I knew that I was leaving a first-rate set of railwaymen. But New England beckoned and I knew that there would be bigger challenges. Would the GN men turn out to be as good as the Geordies? And would there be time for brake van trips through the rolling Lincolnshire countryside?

As a postscript, the whole area occupied by Addison Yard is now covered with the inevitable industrial units, and one looks in vain for any indication at all that there was ever a thriving marshalling yard here.

Below: On the Allendale branch itself, Class J21 0-6-0 No 65082 makes light work of three wagons and two brakevans between Langley and Staward. *Neville Stead*

Ten

GOOD TIMES AT PETERBOROUGH AND NEW ENGLAND 1959/61

Introduction

On a day like any other, if there is such a thing in that strange and mysterious world of railway life, I was sitting in my office at Addison Marshalling Yard minding my own business, when the phone rang and the female voice at the other end said, 'Mr Purnell wishes to speak to you.' Now, Mr Purnell was the Assistant District Operating Superintendent at Newcastle, a position of some importance, and naturally I was curious as to why he wanted to speak to me. He came on the phone and his voice was warm and friendly. 'You're wanted at New England as Yard Master as soon as possible,' he said, 'so tidy up the loose ends at Addison and get ready to move. They [meaning the Eastern Region] want you to start on Monday 30 November [1959]. I'll see you before you leave.'

News of promotions always brings mixed emotions to start with. Naturally you're glad to be promoted. It means more money and a wider sphere of responsibility, but I was very happy at Addison and got on well with the staff. There were some very good railwaymen in the North East and I liked the people there, but we lived in a railway house with an outside toilet and a tin bath. The idea of being able to afford to buy a house with all mod cons was certainly very appealing, especially to my wife, with one child and another on the way.

On the following Monday I took one of my Compensation Days and travelled to Peterborough to organise some lodgings. Compensation Days were one of the many peculiar features of railway life: they were the days off that you earned if you worked on a Bank Holiday, which I had done on a number of occasions. I met Mr Coates, the Stationmaster at Peterborough North station, and he suggested that I might try the residential staff hostel at Spital Bridge shed, just a short distance away. This sounded like an excellent idea, so I called to see the boss there, who agreed to give me a room for a limited period.

These staff hostels had been provided at a number of places after the war, mainly to accommodate traincrews who had transferred from elsewhere to fill vacancies, and they provided meals throughout the day. It also meant that I could have a look round Spital Bridge shed before breakfast to see what was about. In those days Spital Bridge hosted engines from both the Midland line and the North Western line, so as a former LMS man, I felt very much at home next to a shed full of Midland '4F' 0-6-0s, LNWR 0-8-0s and LMS Class 5 4-6-0s. The first night I was somewhat restless, being woken every few minutes by engines whistling, trains rattling past, and even detonators exploding (it was very foggy and the fogsignalmen were being kept busy).

The next important item was to find a house to buy, so I visited a number of estate agents. There was a very nice semi available in Cambridge Avenue for £2,275, 10 minutes' walk from my new office, so I clinched the deal the following week and we moved in five weeks later. I've never done it so quickly since. In those days, Peterborough was still a quiet market town, with a pace of life to match. It was still a railway town too, with several thousand of its inhabitants employed on the railway in the Traffic, Motive Power and Civil Engineering Departments. There was also a Carriage & Wagon

Above: Peterborough — my new home for a while. Class B1 4-6-0 No 61079 runs into North station under the 'Crescent' Bridge with a King's Cross to Skegness train on 19 July 1958.
Dennis Ovenden

Below: The ex-LMS Class 4F 0-6-0s were sufficiently versatile to be used on stopping passenger and excursion trains. No 44519, of Leicester (15C), runs into Peterborough North station with a local train from Peterborough East to Leicester London. Road in July 1961.
John C. Baker

Above: A BR standard Class 4MT 4-6-0, No 75043, leaves Peterborough East with a local for Leicester London Road via North station, in September 1960. *John C. Baker*

workshop, a large General Stores Dept, a Revenue Accountant's Department and a District Commercial Office. Railway officers were still persons of some importance in the town, and one of my own goods guards was Mayor of Peterborough at the time, so I found myself being invited, together with my wife, to mayoral functions.

Mention of the Revenue Accountant's Department reminds me of a week which I had spent there a couple of years previously studying the accountancy processes. It was interesting, but made me glad that I was an operator and not an accountant. During the light evenings I had arranged for a conducted tour of New England and Spital Bridge sheds to examine the workings, because I knew little of the Eastern Region and one never knew when such experience might come in useful. I was escorted round the premises by the Running Foreman. Quite a contrast to being escorted off them in earlier days!

All the routes which converged on Peterborough were still in use, except for the M&GN (Midland & Great Northern), which had closed at midnight a few months earlier, on 28 February 1959. Fortunately I had managed to find time the previous year to travel over that beloved but impecunious railway on my way back north from London via a very circuitous route from Liverpool Street to

Yarmouth, and on to Peterborough by the 12.56 train. It was a truly delightful journey which transported one back half a century.

There were two other equally delightful cross-country routes which were still open: to Rugby via Seaton and Market Harborough, and to Northampton via Wellingborough London Road. They were both former LNWR routes, through lovely rolling countryside, with their little wayside country stations whose colourful and well-tended gardens spoke of a former glory, but the passenger service of no more than half a dozen trains each way per day told its own story. They lingered on for a few more years before inevitable closure, although the Rugby route was well used by freight trains.

The decade of the 1960s was one of profound change on the railways. It was not all negative. The new goods depot at Peterborough had just opened on 13 July 1959 to absorb traffic from the surrounding area, with the intention of providing an improved and more economical service. It was

Above: Wansford was on the ex-LNWR line from Peterborough East to Northampton. An ex-LMS parallel-boilered 2-6-4 tank engine, No 42353, heads for home (2E) with a three-coach local train on 4 October 1960. Strictly speaking, LNWR property did not begin until 28 chains from East station, which had belonged to the Great Eastern Railway. The line between Wansford and Peterborough now belongs to the Nene Valley Railway. *Author's Collection*

Below: A beautifully-clean ex-LMS Compound 4-4-0, No 41095, brings a local train into Peterborough North station. *Eric Blakey*

A Railwayman's Odyssey

Above: Just north of Werrington Junction, where the line to Grimsby branches off, Pacific Class A2/3 No 60521 *Watling Street* (Gateshead — 52A) heads a King's Cross to Newcastle express on 22 July 1959. *D. C. Ovenden*

located alongside the old GN Spital Yard and provided each evening a large number of fitted loaded vans for a wide range of destinations, which were mainly taken to Westwood Yard to be attached to Down express freight trains. Mr Simpson was the Goods Agent.

This was to be merely the beginning of the modernisation of the railways in Peterborough. A month after the new goods depot opened, proposals were made public of the intention to rebuild completely the cramped North station on a larger scale, allowing the closure of the East station and the elimination of the very restrictive 20mph speed restriction on the main lines through the station. However, much more interesting from my point of view was the proposal to build a completely new marshalling yard in Peterborough, north of Westwood Bridge and partly on the site of the now disused Wisbech Sidings. New marshalling yards were an important feature of the 1955 Modernisation Plan, and several were already being planned and built. The planning of the Peterborough new yards was already quite advanced and I attended my first meeting of the planning group during my first week in the job. Thereafter, detailed planning meetings followed each other thick and fast, and it was exciting to be involved in the venture.

It is interesting to recall that a little booklet produced by the LNER in 1946 for 4d (that's four old pence), setting out details of the LNER's postwar Development Programme, foreshadowed the construction at Peterborough of a new Central station, a new centralised goods depot and new marshalling yards. Plus alterations to existing running lines, a new flyover junction, the modernisation of New England locomotive depot and new District Offices. All for £1,682,000! Well, we got part of it — the station, the goods depot and the engine shed.

I Start my New Job

I took over the job on Monday 30 November 1959 and met Harry Goodchild, who had been covering the job meanwhile. Harry was one of the three Assistant Yard Masters (AYMs) who worked round the clock. He was a splendid railwayman, and a great help and support. He was utterly reliable, and knew the job from A to Z. The AYMs had an office

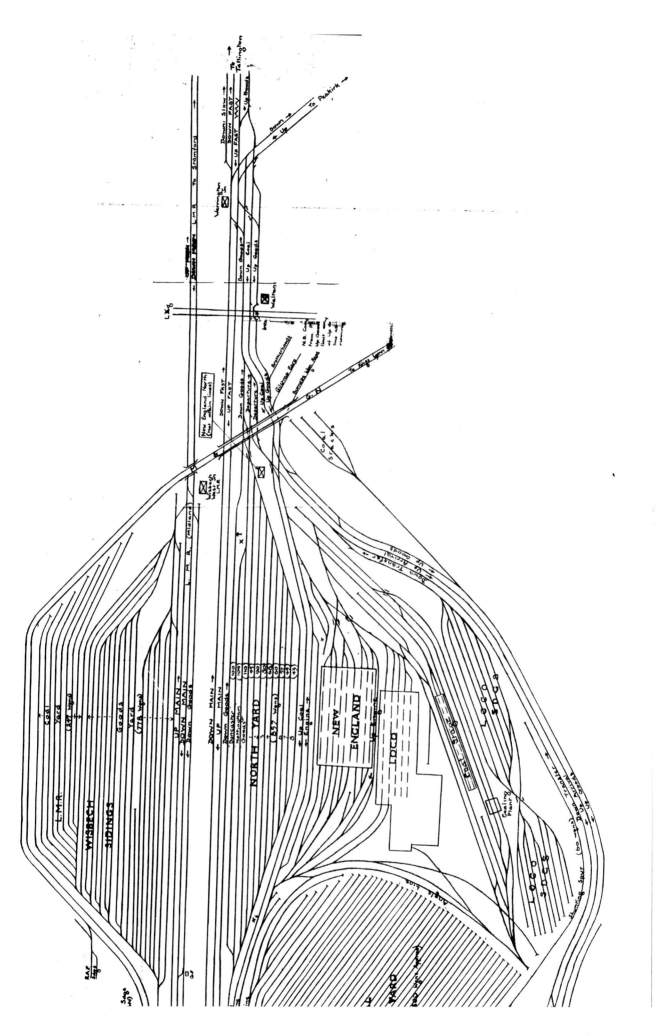

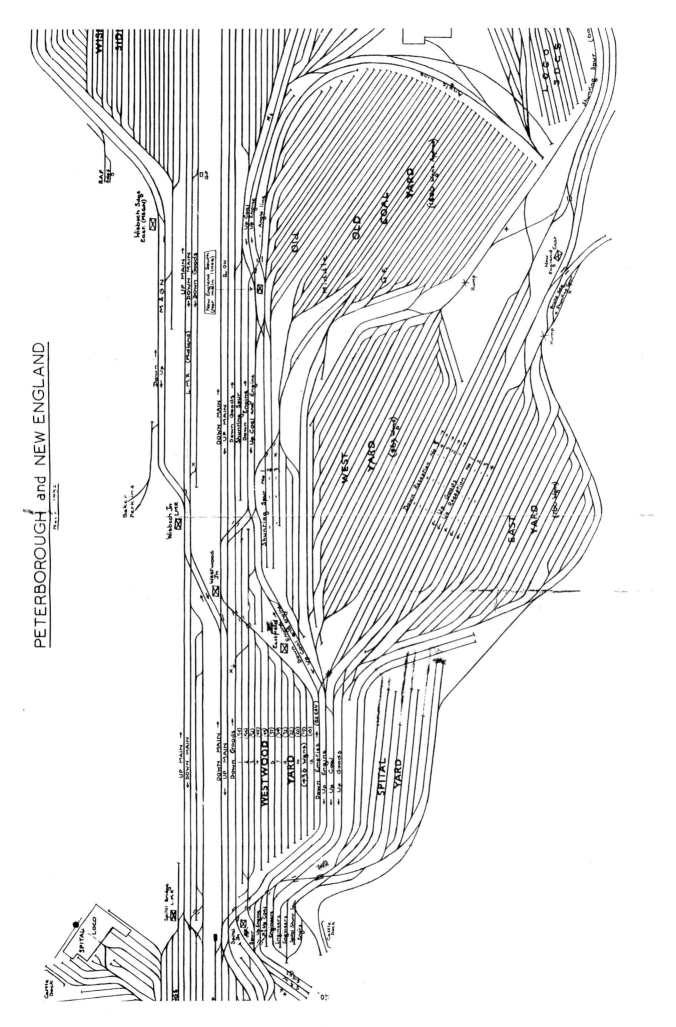

PETERBOROUGH and NEW ENGLAND

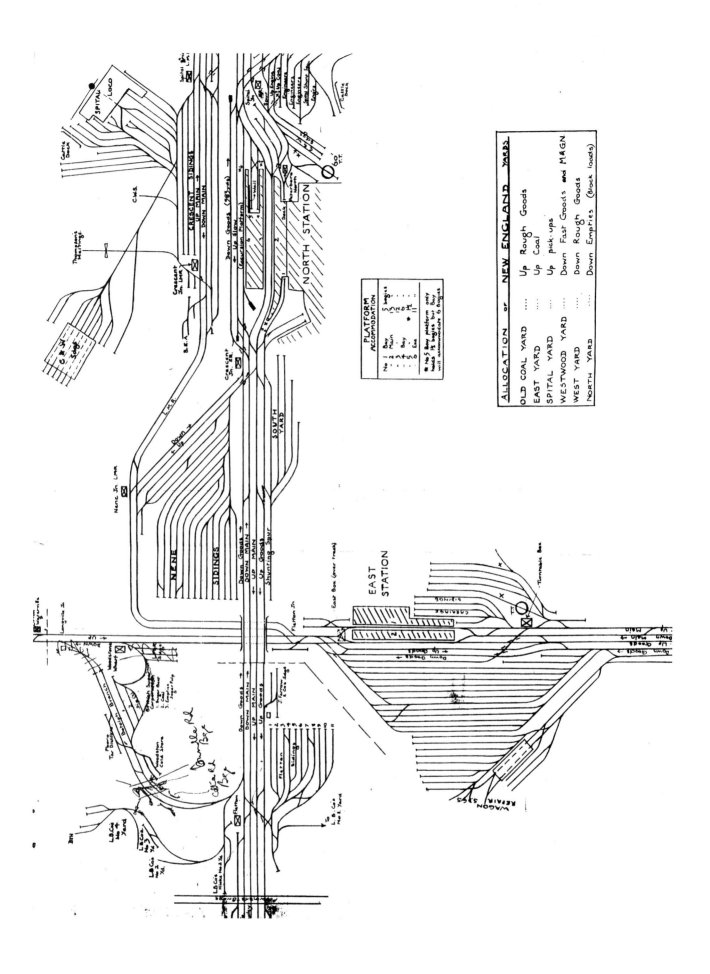

Above: Passing through Essendine at over 100mph today, one would never know that there was ever a railway installation of any sort there. Yet, there was a substantial layout, with branches at both sides to Stamford and Bourne respectively. *Sir Nigel Gresley* No 60007 departs with the 1.30pm service to Grantham on 11 October 1958. Less than a year later, Essendine station and both branches were closed. *P. H. Wells*

in a block adjacent to mine, so I could always keep in touch. They were mainly concerned with the current working of the yards, and of keeping the traffic flowing as efficiently as possible. My job in simple terms was to see that the yards were run as effectively and economically as possible. It was a challenge that I was glad to accept. In those happy days of the grown-up railway you were given a fair degree of freedom of action and were expected to get on with the job with the minimum of interference. If you saw something that needed doing you just dealt with it, applying common sense and the fruits of experience. This, of course, was in the carefree days before the invasion of the management freaks, and long before the nightmare days of the SRA (Strategic Rail Authority, now defunct), the ORR (the Rail Regulator, now replaced by an office-load of them), the HSE, etc, etc.

My area of responsibility covered all the freight yards and sidings on the GN line at Peterborough, plus the main line from Westwood Junction to Walton Crossing and Werrington Junction signalboxes. At the north end of the parish I worked to the Stationmasters at Essendine on the main line, and Peakirk on the Grimsby line. The Stationmaster at Peterborough North was responsible for the passenger station and the carriage sidings, and for the main line south of Westwood Junction. He was very good to work with and we got on well. The Midland side still belonged to the LM Region, but it was transferred to the Eastern Region on 1 February 1960, only a few weeks after I started at New England, and I suddenly acquired several miles of the Midland line, much to my surprise and delight, plus several signalboxes and sidings, and the recently closed and extensive marshalling yard known as Wisbech Sidings. That made me feel really at home! However, Spital Bridge shed closed on the same day and the majority of its engines were transferred to March, apart from some which were returned to the LM Region. The shed was demolished shortly afterwards and is now the site of the power-operated signalbox. The coaling plant was demolished by explosives one Sunday morning (20 March 1960), witnessed by quite a crowd stationed at a discreet distance, and disappeared in a huge cloud of dust.

Above: On 19 August 1961, a month after I left New England for King's Cross, Class A1 Pacific No 60125 *Scottish Union* heads north with a train for York. The lines in the centre of the photograph lead directly to and from the main New England yards, whilst on the skyline right of centre stands the new Goods Depot. *P. H. Wells*

Below: A fine viewpoint of the East Coast main line, on which a 'V2' 2-6-2, No 60887, is approaching Peterborough North station with a Class E freight on 23 June 1954. The lines in the centre lead to and from the extensive yards at New England. At extreme left are the Midland lines to and from Stamford and Leicester. *R. E. Vincent/Transport Treasury*

A Railwayman's Odyssey

Harry Goodchild stayed on middle turn for a few days so that he could show me round the area and introduce me to all the staff. I had a small office staff, consisting of Mr Cole, the Chief Clerk, three clerks — Mrs Preston, Neville and Nick — and a typist Wendy. It was a very happy little team. The remainder of the staff at the yard consisted of the three AYMs, about 15 yard inspectors, 50 shunters, 120 goods guards, 50 signalmen and some ancillary staff. It was going to take some time to get to know them all.

The yards were very extensive and had grown like Topsy over the years to deal with increases in traffic. The plan will help the reader to understand the layout. Westwood Yard dealt mainly with northbound express freight traffic, the North Yard (the Down yard) was used for staging through loads, mainly empties, whilst the other yards were used for shunting and sorting the general run of freight traffic other than express freight, known as 'roughs'. Much of it was coal and empties. The East Yard and the West Yard were relatively modern and were double-ended. There were four Up reception roads and five Down reception roads. Both yards were laid out for hump shunting. The Old Coal Yard was well named. It consisted of three separate sections with a total of 43 single-ended sidings, originally used for sorting loaded coal wagons for a very wide range of destinations and consignees, and could be used by three shunting engines simultaneously. Southbound through express freight trains calling to attach and detach were dealt with here.

The main flows of traffic were as follows:
On the Up: From Colwick, Doncaster and the North
On the Down: From Ferme Park (London) and intermediate stations
Transfer trips from Peterborough East.

The coal traffic was very heavy, mainly from the Nottinghamshire and South Yorkshire coalfields, and nearly all in unfitted (unbraked) wagons.

New England Loco Depot
In the middle of all this lay the important loco depot of New England, formerly 35A, but now 34E under King's Cross. The Shedmaster was Mr Woffindin, very capable, very thoughtful, very helpful, and unflappable. Necessary attributes for such a post. We got on well, although his eyebrows sometimes went up a little at some of my more extreme ideas. He was a steadying influence. Under his control were 128 steam engines and 17 350hp 0-6-0 diesel-electric shunters. There were no mainline diesels. All the freights were steam-hauled, except for the occasional diesel on one of the fitteds. New England and the freight workings were still the traditional railway. The Shedmaster probably had a staff approaching 1,000.

The allocation in May 1960 was as follows:

'A2' Pacifics	60500/4/6/8, 60513/4 (6)
'V2' 2-6-2	60820/1/9, 60832, 60845, 60853, 60867/9, 60874, 60893/7, 60906, 60914, 60924, 60966 (15)
'B1' 4-6-0	61060, 61070/3/4, 61113, 61207, 61210, 61272, 61282, 61302, 61331, 61391 (12)
'K2' 2-6-0	61763 (1)
'K3' 2-6-0	61805, 61830, 61864, 61978/9 (5)
'J6' 0-6-0	64177, 64196, 64223, 64240, 64251/3, 64265 (7)
'N2' and 'N5' 0-6-2T	69266, 69274, 69293, 69506, 69513, 69521, 69540, 69571, 69582 (9)
Ex-LMS Class 4 2-6-0	43067, 43081/2/4/6/8, 43127, 43150/1 (9)
BR Class 9F 2-10-0	92034-38, 92040-42/44, 92140-49, 92178-84/7/8 (28)
'Austerity' 2-8-0	(36)

The Class 9Fs were invaluable for working heavy freights to Ferme Park at a reasonable speed, using just one set of men working out and home, and a great improvement on what had gone before. Coal trains had always trundled along at about 25mph, into and out of goods lines waiting for paths on to the main line. It had sufficed, but it was uneconomical in the use of traincrews and locomotives. The '9Fs' really showed what could be done, and the GN Section was quick to take advantage, as indeed was the GC Section between Annesley and Woodford. Southbound Class H freight trains used to take 4½ hours from New England to Ferme Park with 'Austerities', but the '9Fs', running in accelerated Class E unbraked timings, could do it in less that three hours.

Above: A fine shot of an 'Austerity' 2-8-0, No 90223, on a Class H freight running gently through Peterborough North station before diverging on to the Up goods line, in July 1961. *John C. Baker*

Below: One of New England's large fleet of BR Standard Class 9F 2-10-0s, No 92183, sets off from New England with a Class E freight train in July 1961. *John C. Baker*

A Railwayman's Odyssey

Above: Class A3 Pacific No 60100 *Spearmint* winds its way carefully through the 20mph curves just beyond Peterborough North station with a Down express on 19 August 1961. A tender-first 'Austerity' is standing on the Down goods line (the notorious 'Golden Mile'), waiting for an opportunity to cross the Up and Down main lines to gain access to the New England yards.
P. H. Wells

The absence of 2-8-0s in Classes O1, O2 and O4, with their many variants, is noteworthy, but they were daily visitors on trains from Colwick and Doncaster. Colwick had the 'O1s' and the 'O4s', whilst Doncaster had the 'O2s'. 'Austerities', of course, were everywhere, and they had displaced the LNER 2-8-0s at New England. The existence of a solitary 'K2' at New England was somewhat intriguing, but it was used as a stationary steam boiler.

Another startling event, and a sign of the times, occurred simultaneously with my arrival on the scene. That event was the withdrawal of the first two 'A2' Pacifics, Nos 60503 *Lord President* and 60505 *Thane of Fife*. It will be remembered that these had been built originally as part of a batch of six numbered 2001-06 by Nigel Gresley in 1934-36 as 2-8-2s for working heavy express passenger trains on the Edinburgh–Aberdeen route, but rumour has it that they caused such grief to the civil engineer owing to their long coupled wheelbase that they were converted to 4-6-2s as soon as their designer had passed on. Whether that is true or not, his successor, Edward Thompson, lost no time in rebuilding them and earning himself a large amount of obloquy from Gresley fans. However, the rebuilding appears to have been no more successful

and the top express passenger sheds turned up their noses at them. As a result, they were dumped on York and New England.

Even more horrifying to East Coast fans was the shock withdrawal of the first of Gresley's Pacifics. In December 1959 came the news of the condemnation of No 60104 *Solario*, accompanied by feelings of horror that reverberated throughout the railway world. However, it became known that No 60104 had suffered severely cracked and broken frames, and the cost of replacement could not be justified, especially in view of the fairly imminent arrival of the 'Deltics'. But it was a sad event nonetheless. Gresley's Pacifics had been part and parcel of the East Coast main line for almost 40 years. No 60104 itself had appeared in March 1923, and can truly be said to have defrayed its

Above: A rather grubby B1 4-6-0, No 61348, is just about to pass under the Great Northern main line bridge with the 12.52pm from Leicester London Road to Peterborough East on 31 July 1959. This train remained on the Midland line through Peterborough and did not cross to the North station. The engine's home shed was the former Midland depot at Spital Bridge (31F), which would be closed within a few months.
P. H. Groom

initial cost many times over. The 'A3s' were never surpassed for grace and beauty, and for their efficiency and turn of speed.

Signalboxes

When I first arrived at New England, the Yard Master had seven signalboxes under his control. On the main line north of Peterborough there were Westwood Junction, Walton Crossing and Werrington Junction, whilst in and around the yards there were New England North, New England East, New England South and Eastfield. When the Midland side was transferred to the Eastern Region on 1 February 1960 my empire expanded quite a bit. New England then acquired Nene Junction, Crescent, Spital Bridge, Wisbech Junction and

Wisbech West Junction signalboxes, which brought the total to twelve. This list is compiled almost from memory, so may not be entirely accurate. The level crossing at Marholm, about half a mile north of Werrington Junction and worked by a resident crossing keeper, marked the last outpost. It was very much out in the flat country, miles from anywhere.

It was always a pleasure to spend an hour or so at Werrington Junction, where the Grimsby line turned off, and watch the crack expresses racing by. It was an important regulating box and the signalmen had their work cut out, but they were expert at it. There was a constant procession of freight trains, both on the main line and the Grimsby line, ranging from the important fish trains and the overnight fully fitteds, to the more humble (but possibly more profitable) slower freight and coal trains, and empties. The Grimsby line was used by a lot of the coal trains and empties as far as Woodhall Junction, where they turned off towards Lincoln and Pyewipe Junction, to avoid cluttering up the East Coast main line.

I felt entirely at home in my newly acquired Midland signalboxes, because I had learned the trade in Midland boxes in my spare time years earlier, but GN signalboxes were different, and even the Signalling Regulations were not entirely standard until later that year, even though it was 12 years after nationalisation. So I had to climb a learning curve. It was politic, and probably wise too, not to flaunt my Midland upbringing in the heartland of the GN, but as I had come to New England from the North East, part of the old LNER, I was readily accepted.

I found folks in Peterborough to be generally quite relaxed and easy-going, appropriate for what was still largely a market town in the heart of a prosperous agricultural area, although the town did have some important engineering works. How it has changed in the last 40 years! I have been there many times during that period and witnessed those changes with the decline of its industries, especially the railway industry, and its rise as an overspill town. More recently still has been its emergence as a dormitory town for London commuters, a development made possible by the acceleration of train services on the GN main line and the provision of a frequent train service. In 1960, daily commuting from Peterborough to London hardly existed. Now there is a very sizeable army of commuters, with five expresses at their disposal between 07.00 and 08.11 (as at 24 June 2012), all doing the journey in under an hour, and filling the East Coast's coffers, supported by several First Capital Connect outer-suburban EMUs taking just over an hour and doing it somewhat more cheaply but in correspondingly less comfort.

The supervision of signalboxes was carried out according to a laid down pattern. Those near the operating centre had to be visited daily; others once a week. In addition, visits had to be made out of normal working hours at least once a month. The AYMs were responsible for supervising the signalboxes around the yards, whilst the Yard Master did the others. Visiting signalboxes was certainly one of the more enjoyable parts of the job, and an excellent way of keeping an eye on the workings. It was also a good excuse for getting out of the office if one were needed. The Midland boxes, which were not too far away, were visited

Below: Occasionally a railway enthusiasts' group would penetrate the fastnesses of New England yard. This group came from Leicester one weekend, and we took them all round the yards in brake vans. I'm on the extreme left.
Author's Collection

on foot, but Walton and beyond were usually visited by bicycle, ridden down the side of the track. A very pleasant way of spending a sunny afternoon or evening, but it also had to be done in winter and in darkness, and on the night shift. Visits in darkness would usually commence at the AYMs' office, and more often than not would include visits to various parts of the yard. An oil-lit handlamp lit the way. And I had long ago been taught by a wise old stationmaster that a farmer's boot is the best manure.

Walton level crossing had an unusual layout, because the GN main line and the Midland line to Stamford and Leicester ran parallel, and each had its own signalbox. Road users had to cross seven running lines — the Midland had Up and Down main lines, whilst the GN, in addition to the two main lines, had a Down goods line, an Up coal line and an Up goods line. Long, heavy goods and coal trains crawled unendingly along the latter two. Delays to road traffic were often extensive, and the signalmen in those boxes needed thick skins. Road users could be very bad-tempered, but I had constantly to remind the signalmen that it was the railway that paid their wages and not the car driver. There was one particularly notable feature at Walton Crossing — a lineside pick-up apparatus for mailbags. I can't recall which trains were used, but it was always interesting to see it in action. Now, like so much to do with railways, it's all part of our history along with the travelling post offices.

Visits to Colleagues in Other Yards

WHITEMOOR
It was obviously useful to be on easy terms with one's colleagues in the marshalling yards to which we worked, so that a good working relationship could be established. My first 'excursion' was to Whitemoor with Inspector Baines. Whitemoor was a huge marshalling facility, which had been modernised by the LNER in 1929 and 1933 when two new yards, one Up and one Down, had been built on modern principles, consisting of double-ended hump yards using hydraulic rail brakes. The yards were vast, with over 40 sidings each, and there was a large engine shed alongside. The potential throughput was said to be 8,000 wagons daily, and its importance arose from its strategic position at the north-west corner of East Anglia, where it received traffic not only from Colwick,

Doncaster and beyond but also from the LM Region, both Midland and Western Sections, via Peterborough. There was also a huge flow northwards and westwards of agricultural produce, but it was on the wane. Road haulage was biting into the traffic.

I also used these visits as a means of exploring 'new' territory, and had a very enjoyable trip to Cambridge and back, outwards via Ely and back via St Ives and Huntingdon. The rapid dieselisation of the GE Section was apparent by the fact that I saw more diesel than steam locos that day. One of the notable steam engines I saw was 'Britannia' Class 4-6-2 No 70013 *Oliver Cromwell* (32A — Norwich), now active in preservation.

FERME PARK
As it was Easter 1960, and the yards were very quiet, I took the opportunity to have another 'excursion', this time to Ferme Park. It was a fine morning and I was up in time to catch the 5.55am from Peterborough to King's Cross, then along to Euston, where Pacific No 46212 *Duchess of Kent* was simmering on the buffers. I was immediately transported back in my mind's eye to a lovely prewar evening at Penrith, when I was standing on the castle mound and saw this engine speeding through on an express, my first 'Princess'.

But quickly reverting to reality, I made my way to Harringay West via Highbury and Finsbury Park, where I met the Yard Master, Mr Evans. It's difficult now to tell that there was ever a marshalling yard there, as the whole area is covered by carriage sidings and sheds, but it had an important role in making up trains for yards and depots in the other Regions in the London area, particularly for the various yards on the Southern, such as Battersea and Hither Green via the intriguingly named 'Widened Lines' and Blackfriars. I resolved to have a brake van trip through King's Cross one day. After lunch we visited Clarence Yard and King's Cross East Goods, where there were plenty of Pacifics of all types to be seen. It was a very interesting day indeed, and a good introduction to an area that I did not know well. I came home from St Pancras via Leicester and Stamford, and once more I noted that diesel locos and diesel multiple-units were becoming very widespread.

Just by way of digression, and having been bitten by the branch line bug, I took a day off a few days

Above: A transfer trip from Whitemoor Yard to New England passes through Peterborough East in the charge of Class O2 2-8-0 No 63956 in September 1960. *John C. Baker*

later and had a marathon excursion, starting with the 7.5am from Peterborough North to Sandy, thence to Bletchley along the line from Cambridge (noting that the flyover was almost complete and that ex-LNWR 0-8-0s were in evidence). Next, along to Oxford via Verney Junction and Bicester London Road and on to the old Great Western, but promising myself a trip over the Verney Junction-Buckingham-Banbury branch one day soon before it closed. Oxford was busy both with freights and expresses and plenty of steam, and I had the pleasure of being conveyed in true Great Western style through Banbury to Leamington Spa General, noting the agreeable prewar architecture of the station. The former LNWR station, Leamington Spa Avenue, across the road, was very much a poor relation. I then travelled on to Nuneaton via Kenilworth and Coventry, a line which in those days had an hourly service, for a quick dash to Crewe and a sandwich. Ivatt 2-6-2T No 41204 (89A — Oswestry) was simmering quietly in a bay. After 'inspecting' the electrification works, which appeared to be complete, I travelled home via Stoke, Derby, Leicester, Market Harborough and Seaton, arriving at Peterborough East about

11.0pm. Quite a long day, but it illustrates how easy it was to travel round Britain by train in those days before closures really began to take effect.

COLWICK

It was as easy to get to Colwick by goods train (and much more interesting) as it was by passenger train, so one morning in May 1960 I travelled there by goods train in the brake van with one of my guards. I could have gone on the engine of course, an 'Austerity', but I always found that a third man on the footplate is one too many. For a start, you had to be very careful to keep out of the way of the fireman when he was swinging his shovel (and avoid at all costs any invitation to have a go, which was likely to result in the firehole door being missed completely and coal being spread all over the footplate, to the disgust of the driver and the delight of the fireman). Secondly, if the engine was

Above: An ex-GN 0-6-0 of Class J6, No 64175, is seen here in delightful surroundings near Hadley Wood with an engineer's train. The loco was allocated to Hitchin (34D). *Derek Cross*

a rough rider you were too busy hanging on for dear life to worry about anything else, and thirdly it was too noisy for any form of civilised conversation. It only became enjoyable when you were stopped for signals; then you could relax.

I once travelled from Hull Fish Docks to Leeds on a 'K3' 2-6-0. Those fish trains really hopped along (and I think I mean that literally, or at least that's how it felt). Naturally, the enginemen assured me that it was a normal ride and didn't seem in the least perturbed, but it took weeks for the bruises to disappear. Shortly afterwards I went on an 'Austerity' along the old Hull & Barnsley from Springhead Yard to Brodsworth Colliery, in the Doncaster area. It was a beautiful spring morning, the countryside was looking at its best, we had a full trainload of empties and we gently meandered along. Even the engine behaved itself, so it was a joy. Coming back with a 'full digger' of shipping coal (how did that expression originate?) the 'Austerity' had to work hard on the fluctuating gradients, and again it was an enjoyable ride. Now

it's all ancient history — the H&B, 'Austerities', shipping coal, Springhead Yard. All have gone, apart from our memories.

But back to the Colwick train. I was met en route by an old friend, Ken Appleby, who was, I think, Chief Controller at Lincoln District Operating Office. Once again, I was impressed by the sheer size and scale of the yard, which was in effect two main yards, one Up and one Down, with a large loco depot alongside. Colwick's traffic was mainly coal from the Nottinghamshire coalfield, but the GN's tentacles had spread way beyond, to Burton (for the lucrative beer traffic), and to Derby, Uttoxeter and Stafford. Almost everywhere, it had been in competition with the Midland but the latter had been there first and had bagged the best routes, leaving the GN with hills and gradients. I wanted to travel through the colliery country, so Ken took me up the Leen Valley from Nottingham to Mansfield and on to Worksop (via the Midland route, there being no suitable GN passenger route). LMS Standard taper boiler 2-6-2Ts were the mainstay of the passenger service on that route, and we saw No 40115 at Kirkby-in-Ashfield and No 40073 at Worksop, both 16B — Kirkby. A few years later I would be back in the area with the job of closing the GN lines and Colwick Yard, but that's a story for another episode.

Eleven

MORE GOOD TIMES AT PETERBOROUGH

Some Locomotive Jottings

The local football club, Peterborough United (known as 'The Posh') were doing well in the FA Cup and on Saturday 30 January 1960 they were playing Sheffield Wednesday away (they lost). There was considerable support for the team, and 13 special trains were required. The engines used were Nos 60054 (34F — Grantham), 60105 (34F), 60111 (34F), 60500 (34E), 60504 (34E), 60506 (34E), 60508 (34E), 60513 (34E), 60826 (36A — Doncaster), 60867 (34E), 60874 (34E), 60875 (36A) and 60908 (36A). It seems remarkable now that the GN was able to rustle up 13 front rank engines and 13 sets of coaches in addition to all its other commitments that day. In the evening I went out to Werrington Junction signalbox to see them

all come back (or at least most of them — there are limits!). Nos 60504/6/8 were all withdrawn the following year.

Some interesting sightings recorded that year (1960) were:
- 'V2' 2-6-2 No 60882 (64A — St Margaret's) on New England shed on 5 April;

Below: An 'A4' streamliner, No 60034 *Lord Faringdon,* makes a stately approach to Peterborough North station through the speed-restricted curves, with an express from Leeds Central to King's Cross on 14 October 1961. 'Top Shed' (34A) was renowned for the cleanliness of its engines. *P. H. Wells*

- BR 2-10-0 No 92196 (40B — Immingham) on 22 April;
- BR 4-6-0s Nos 75047/8 (27A — Bank Hall) working through to March on holiday trains from the Leicester direction on 20 August;
- LMS Class 8F 2-8-0 No 48397 (41D — Canklow) on the 5.45pm Doncaster-New England on 30 August.

Engines mainly ex-Doncaster Works provided some interesting and unusual sightings during 1960:
- A shiny BR 2-6-0 No 76045 (51F — West Auckland) on New England shed on 28 May, and a few days earlier the scoop of the year green BR Class 5 4-6-0 No 73023 (86C — Cardiff Canton);
- 'K3' 2-6-0 No 61952 (52D — Tweedmouth) at New England on 21 August;
- 'A3' Pacific No 60097 *Humorist* (64B — Haymarket) arrived at New England on a freight train on 7 September;
- 'A2' Pacific No 60532 *Blue Peter* (61B — Aberdeen Ferryhill) arrived at New England on the 5.24am Class H freight from Doncaster on 13 October;
- 'A4' Pacific No 60015 *Quicksilver* (34A — King's Cross) arrived at New England on the 2.40am Class F from Newport on 15 October;
- 'K1' 2-6-0 No 62010 (52C — Blaydon) on New England shed on 28 October;
- 'A4' Pacific No 60011 *Empire of India* (64B — Haymarket) arrived on a coal train on 10 November.

The reason for the sudden influx of ex-works Pacifics from Doncaster is unknown, but they were obviously being 'run-in' on a slow train before being returned to their home, I am indebted to the columns of *The Railway Observer* for some of this information. At the end of 1960 there were still 13,321 steam locomotives on the operating stock, and so far as New England shed and yards were concerned it was still a steam railway, apart from the diesel shunters. But new mainline diesels kept appearing ominously past New England on their way from the manufacturers to the south. Brush Type 2s became commonplace, but on 10 March D8220, was seen on the Midland side. And during July Deltic high-speed trials took place between King's Cross and Grantham.

Other items of interest that year (1960) included the following:
- (Actually in 1959) on 14 December, I was travelling from the north to Peterborough and recorded 100mph and slightly over for five consecutive miles coming down Stoke Bank, the only time I have recorded 100mph on a steam train. I congratulated the driver on arrival at Peterborough but forgot to record the engine number.
- On 20 and 26 April there were Ian Allan specials from King's Cross to Doncaster hauled by GWR 4-4-0 No 3440 *City of Truro* piloting Midland Compound No 1000 (20th) and No 1000 piloting 'B12' 4-6-0 No 61572 (26th).

Royal Trains were not at all uncommon, and I went to Walton Crossing on 26 May to see 'A4' Pacific No 60032 *Gannet* pass, taking HM The Queen and the Duke of Edinburgh to Horden (Co Durham). The Rules regarding Royal Trains required the stationmaster (or other person in charge) to be on duty for the passage of the train. Normally the AYM on duty would deputise, but I would always be on duty for HM The Queen. Royal Trains had a habit of passing through Peterborough at somewhat inconvenient hours: the Down trains about midnight and the Up trains in the early hours of the morning.

The Working of the Marshalling Yard

Miners' 'Bull Weeks'
I arrived at New England on 30 November 1959 at the very beginning of the heaviest and most difficult month for traffic working. It wasn't helped by the prevalence of fog for the first few days, and it is difficult nowadays to recall the pea-souper fogs that we used to have in the days before the Clean Air Act removed the scourge of rows and rows of smoky house-chimneys. Hump shunting was particularly affected, and there are relatively few hours of daylight in December. New England's humps did not have the luxury of rail brakes, as at Whitemoor and Toton for example, and wagons running down the humps had to be controlled by handbrake by the shunters running alongside. Not a happy occupation in a thick fog, or even on a sunny afternoon for that matter. Looking back, I can't help wondering how we got people to do it, but it was a different world then.

Above: Another 'Top Shed' streamiler, No 60021 *Wild Swan,* threads its way cautiously through Peterborough North station with the Down *Elizabethan* on 19 July 1958. Generations of schoolboys (and some older men too) would have given their eye-teeth to have been at the regulator. *D. C. Ovenden*

Below: But it was coal, muck and grime that brought in the profits. Class O2 2-8-0 No 63956 makes a return visit to our pages at the head of a heavy unfitted coal train, seen just leaving the New England yards and approaching the station in April 1961. Handling a train weighing over a thousand tons with just the engine and tender brake needed special skills. *John C. Baker*

The next problem was the sheer volume of traffic. New England's main traffic was coal, and it was always believed that miners worked harder in December in order to pay for all their Christmas treats. As a result, coal came flooding out of the pitshafts and into wagons at an exceptional rate. The marshalling yards that served those collieries could hardly keep pace, and a backlog of traffic built up as the week progressed, which could be cleared only by resorting to expensive weekend working. The yards were normally closed on Sundays, but had to be opened specially, and a huge special train programme was organised to work traffic forward and bring back empties. There was nothing unusual in this; it happened every year and not only in December. Most weekends in winter saw a special train programme.

Yard staff and traincrews alike were very happy to work on Sundays because it meant extra pay at enhanced hours, Sunday rate for yard staff being at time and three-quarters. The train working programme was relatively simple — loaded coal

Above: Yet another 'Top Shed' streamliner, No 60010 *Dominion of Canada,* at the head of the Down *Tees-Tyne Pullman* approaches Walton Crossing, about a mile north of Peterborough. The Pullmans were very popular, and lent a touch of elegance to railway travel. It was sad to see them go, and both the railways and their passengers have been the poorer for it. The white cabin at the side of the train marks another piece of history. Mailbags were picked up at this point for the north. *D. C. Ovenden*

trains would come in from the north and the east and return with empties. The yard would sort the loaded wagons into their respective destinations, then New England men would work loaded trains forward, mainly to Ferme Park Marshalling Yard (London) and return with empties. The aim was to ensure that the yards started 'clean' on Monday morning, with no backlog, and that the collieries had plenty of empties. These Sunday specials were worked by volunteers. The Shedmaster would post a notice asking for volunteers to work on Sunday, and that would govern how many trains could be run. But at least there was no shortage of engines.

Marshalling Yard Congestion

This was a perennial problem. The booked freight timetable pattern was based on the number of trains required to move the expected level of traffic, and at times of extra traffic it was the practice to run additional trains. Or at least it would have been if

engines and men and guards had been available, which was often not the case. In practice it often happened that insufficient engines and men and guards were available to run the *booked* service. The number of engines allocated to a shed was based on the timetable, plus spares to cover servicing, repairs and periodical exams, etc. So why were trains sometimes cancelled — 'no engine'? A telephone call from the yard to the shed would be met with the response: 'If you give me back my engines on time after their previous working I will ensure that you have the engine on time for its next working.' I often had a stroll down to the shed to have a chat with the Shedmaster, and he used to emphasise the importance of this, not only for traffic working purposes but also so that he could plan boiler washouts, exams, etc with confidence.

The problem was twofold — delays to trains en route, and delays to trains waiting acceptance into the yard. I couldn't do much about the first item, but I was determined to do something about the second. It was important to do so, because if outbound trains from the Up Yard were cancelled

Below: Another 'Top Shed' engine, Class B1 4-6-0 No 61364, drags a long rake of empty 16-ton mineral wagons from the Down goods line on to the Down main line in March 1961. It will then cross the Up main line to access New England yards. Trainloads such as this went straight to the North Down Yard to await being worked forward, rather than into the Down Hump yard. The lines on the extreme right form the Midland line to Peterborough East. *G. D. King*

the yard became congested, resulting in delays to other trains waiting acceptance into the yard from the north, with the possible loss of their back working. Men on long hours would put their engine on shed and go home 'on the cushions'. I now learned about the 'Golden Mile'.

This was the Down goods line behind Peterborough North station, where freight trains for the yard would queue up waiting for one of the reception sidings to become free, and if they had to queue long enough, and if they were already late, outward trains would be cancelled because their allocated engines were still standing on the Golden Mile. Moreover, there was a risk that the enginemen would miss their turn the following day, leading to another train being cancelled. It was a problem that arose mainly on the late turn owing to the flow of traffic.

Something had to be done to break the vicious circle so we introduced a procedure whereby if a train could not be accepted into the yard from the Golden Mile it had to be run forward and put off in the Down Empties Yard, where there was usually spare accommodation. It could then be drawn out and transferred to the appropriate yard next morning, when traffic was quieter. It had the desired effect. Fewer outbound freight trains were cancelled — 'no engine', and congestion in the yards was reduced, but there was a certain amount of grumbling. It wasn't called the 'Golden Mile' for nothing. Traincrews standing on it were earning nice little amounts of overtime. But Harry Goodchild, the senior AYM, supported the idea all the way and the yard staff respected his judgement.

Shortages of Guards and Equipment

There were about 125 posts for goods guards at New England, but the actual number on the books was rarely much above 100 owing to the difficulties in recruitment. The deficiency was mainly met by what was known as rest day working. When weekly hours were reduced after the war from 48 to 44, the daily hours remained at eight, which resulted in an eleven-day fortnight. The 12th day was taken as a Rest Day, and the rosters were organised so that the Rest Days rotated through all the days of the week but were not rostered on night turns. Most guards were quite happy to work Monday to Friday Rest Days because there was extra pay, and in those old-fashioned days they didn't like to be at home during the week twiddling their thumbs and getting under their wives' feet. So the arrangement was popular for both management and staff. And some guards were happy to work overtime to cover half of a vacancy on local traffic working. So we managed to scrape through but it was a perennial worry, and sometimes a train had to be cancelled because we just couldn't provide a guard. It was a problem common to all marshalling yards.

However, trains were sometimes cancelled for what can only be described as silly reasons. Sometimes there was no brake van available. The Region was supposed to move brake vans around from areas of surplus to areas of shortage, but it was very hit and miss because yards were unwilling to declare a surplus. They liked to keep a few 'up their

Below: Unusual power for a local train from Leicester London Road to Peterborough East: a Stanier taper-boilered '5P6F' 2-6-0, No 42953, brings its five-coach train under the East Coast mainline bridge in September 1960. The engine was allocated to Crewe South (5B).
John C. Baker

sleeve'. Periodically, the Region would hold a brake van census on a nominated Sunday, in which Regional Inspectors would participate, and the holes and corners in which brake vans would be found was astonishing. Orders would be issued next morning for surplus brake vans to be moved from one yard to another, but it was neither well organised nor effectively monitored. If a train arrived at New England with more than one brake van, no one asked Control who the spare one was destined for. It was quietly squirrelled away. The railway worked on the basis that charity began at home and always had done, and I had already developed Nelson's 'blind eye'.

So, we had a brake van. But a brake van needed a tail lamp and two side lamps and a shunting pole and a brakestick. Sometimes they were in short supply too. So periodically we would have a tail lamp etc collection day in the yard. Several staff would be brought on duty on a Sunday to scour the sidings for equipment left lying about, and it was amazing just how much they discovered. Most of it was damaged and had to be sent away for repair. The Stores Department should have sent us replacements immediately, but we didn't hold our breath. It didn't happen. Acrimonious letters and phonecalls followed. Appeals to HQ for help were ineffective. It was not a good way to run a railway.

In fact it infuriated me, having to cancel a freight train because we hadn't enough side lamps (especially when I knew it was partly our own fault).

The Cripple Problem

'Cripples' were empty wagons that needed repairs before being loaded again, and they were labelled by C&W examiners with a green 'For Repairs' card. They were then retained on hand in the yard until the C&W staff received orders from their HQ for the wagon to be sent to a particular wagon shops or private wagon repairer (of which there were several). They were then over-labelled with the destination label and sent forward. So far, so good. We firmly believed that the first priority of the C&W Department was to ensure that they always had plenty of work in the pipeline, so that they were never in a position of having men idle waiting for work. You can't blame them for that, but it resulted in lots of cripples hanging about all over the system and clogging up the yards. So, on the principle that charity began at home, marshalling yards took steps to unclog themselves by sending a dribble of 'For Repairs' cripples on outgoing trains to other yards. The receiving yard had its own problems and merely sent them forward to the next yard. And so on.

I examined a few incoming trains and was rather taken aback by the extent of the problem. Most rough trains seemed to have up to five cripples in their consist, which was a waste of train capacity and shunting time. Some cripples may have spent their entire lives just shuttling up and down the East Coast main line. Appeals to the C&W Department to do something about the problem fell on deaf ears so, being a bit cross about it (and headstrong as well), I resolved to bring matters to a head. It was

Below: An 'Austerity' 2-8-0 goods engine, No 90180, heads a Class F freight along the Up main line near Stevenage on 20 May 1961. It was a New England engine and the headcode would indicate that the wagons were loaded, most probably with coal, heading for Ferme Park yards (Hornsey). *D. Trevor Rowe*

summertime and the yards were quiet, and I had a lovely empty marshalling yard just across the line, the old Midland Wisbech Sidings, unused for a year or so. Aided and abetted by the ever-stalwart Harry Goodchild, instructions were issued that all green-carded cripples received on inwards trains were to be put on one side and taken across in trainloads to Wisbech Sidings. Even I was astonished by the result. Very quickly we had several hundred wagons in Wisbech Sidings and the C&W staff were not amused. 'What the hell do you think you are playing at?' was one of the milder expressions used. Our retorts were equally colourful. Put politely, we said that they could not expect us to store green-carded wagons in the marshalling yards indefinitely and that they must speed up their procedures. Eventually it worked. We had shamed them into it.

The Surplus Wagon Problem

From time to time, certain types of wagon would

Above: This fine Midland Railway signal gantry, recorded in 1960, stood at Wisbech Junction, just north of Peterborough North station.
The two lines on the left lead to the M&GN, the two lines beneath the gantry are the main lines to Leicester, and the next line is the goods line.
Author

be surplus to immediate requirements. The freight rolling stock (FRS) distribution arrangements were based on daily returns from all goods depots and sidings, setting out their requirements for loading, and details of surplus wagons. Instruction would then be issued in the afternoon regarding the destinations of surplus wagons. If those wagons were not required elsewhere, they were usually sent to the nearest marshalling yard to be held for further orders. Marshalling yards would receive orders in the evening setting out where to send surplus empties, or alternatively to hold them waiting further instructions. However, during surplus

Left: Stanier 8F 2-8-0 No 48195 inches forward as it tightens the couplings on a loose-coupled coal train at Wisbech Junction in 1960. The engine is allocated to Toton (18A) and the train is probably heading for Whitemoor.
Author

A Railwayman's Odyssey

periods, such further instructions tended not to come, and the cripple problem was repeated. Rough trains then tended to carry a nice selection of surplus types of empty wagon.

The same solution. Across to Wisbech Sidings with them. Wisbech Sidings had capacity for more than 1,000 wagons and they were beginning to need it, but fortunately the FRS people were extremely co-operative and ordered away trainloads of wagons of specific types. But then there was a snag. One morning the District Engineer entered my office with that stern expression which civil engineers tended to assume when faced with something that annoys them, especially when it's their pet hate, the Operating Department. He said something to the effect of 'What the hell do you think you're doing using Wisbech Sidings? I haven't been maintaining them since they were closed.' I was used by now to people storming into my office and exclaiming 'What the hell etc', but I put on my most ingratiating expression and explained what I was trying to do. 'I can't

guarantee that you won't have derailments,' he said, reluctantly, 'But I'll see what I can do.' We won. We didn't have any. And the yards stayed fluid.

The Fitted Yard

The fitted yard at New England was called Westwood, and it was where the northbound crack express freight trains (the fitteds) were dealt with. They were known as Class C trains. The term 'fitted' merely indicates a wagon or van equipped with the vacuum brake and OK to run in an express freight train. Railways had a mania for complicating things, and we also had semi-fitteds, known as Class D, on which perhaps the front half of the train was composed of fitted wagons, allowing us to provide an express transit for unfitted vehicles containing goods which required an express service and were marshalled in the rear.

The railway also had a mania for publishing booklets covering every possible activity, and there was one which set out how many vehicles could be conveyed over each section of line by each class of engine on each class of train. At one time these express freights ran at speeds of up to 60mph or more, but a string of derailments resulted in a series of reductions in the maximum speed allowed, which had the unhappy effect of lengthening transits and making the old firm less competitive with road haulage.

The freight Working Timetable itself was a fascinating document. It contained detailed timings of all freight trains, with passing times at the more important signalboxes and junctions; plus route availability details of all locomotives, hours of duty and locations of C&W examiners, lists of signalboxes and hours of opening, details of additional running lines, point to point running

Below: One of the many fully-fitted freight trains in which the GN line excelled is seen heading north near Potters Bar behind 'V2' No 60855 on 14 May 1960; it may well call at New England fitted yard (Westwood) to attach and detach portions. Class V2 2-6-2s were specially designed by Nigel Gresley, the CME, for this type of traffic in the 1930s; the class eventually numbered 184, providing first the LNER, and then the Eastern and North Eastern Regions, with an ample supply of excellent, powerful locomotives, equally at home on express passenger trains. *K. L. Cook*

Above: An 'A2/3' class Pacific, No 60516 *Hycilla*, is seen in Peterborough North station in July 1961, having come light engine from New England shed to take over a Down express. The locomotive's home shed is York (50A), which could not rival 'Top Shed' (34A) or Haymarket (64B) for the cleanliness of its engines. *John C. Baker*

Below right: One of New England's many Class 9F 2-10-0s, No 92040, deputises for a diesel on the Uddingston (Glasgow) to Cliffe (Kent) cement empties on 25 May 1963.
Ian Allan Library

times for all classes of train, details and hours of all pilot, trip and shunt engines, and probably other things which I have forgotten. A veritable mine of information. New England had four local trip, shunt and yard to yard transfer pilot engines.

Nationally, there was a vast network of overnight express freight trains which dovetailed into each other. It was a miracle of planning but depended on a high degree of punctuality. Peterborough produced quite a lot of loaded fitted vehicles each day, especially the regular daily vans from the new goods depot, but not in every case enough to provide full train loads except to London. Vans for the Down direction were mainly attached to Down express freights which started from King's Cross Goods.

Most of these trains were formed into sections to be detached at various yards en route and we had to attach ours in the appropriate sections. It was a work of art to watch it in operation, and I would often stroll down to the yard in the evening to do so. The train engine (often a Pacific, and even a streamliner) would work at one end of the train and the local pilot at the other end. The staff could attach and detach to and from half-a-dozen sections and get a train away in 25 minutes. It was brilliant, and it was always a thrill to see the train put

together again, the brake created, the right-away given, then the big engine start to move, slowly as it gathered its train, and then gradually accelerate as it snaked its long train of 50 vehicles out of the sidings on to the main line. Once clear, the driver would open up and the sharp beats of the exhaust would begin to reverberate from the surrounding buildings. Even the memory of it still thrills. It thrilled me at Heaton, and it never ceased to be a thrill as long as we had express freight trains hauled by a big shiny steam engine. Management geeks

New England Freight Train Timetable 1960

Down Train Departures

Boston	1.45am, 6.35am, 1.45pm, 3.20pm
Colwick	1.12am, 6.8am, 6.50am, 8.32am, 9.35am, 11.2pm.
Doncaster Belmont	3.36am, 12.20pm, 11.8pm
Doncaster Decoy	2.55am, 4.52am, 4.35pm, 10.50pm
Frodingham	10.48am, 11.50pm
Mansfield Con Sdgs	3.50am, 9.27am, 10.0pm, 11.25pm (all via Spalding)
New Clee (Grimsby)	2.2pm
Ranskill	4.26am (cripples)
Scrooby	9.35pm (empties)
Stamford	6.0am
Warsop Jnc	5.45am, 8.10am (both via Spalding)
Worksop	2.34am, 7.28am
York	7.58am, 12.2pm

Many of the trains conveyed block loads of mineral empties. Trains via Spalding went on via Boston, Woodhall Jnc, Bardney and Lincoln Pyewipe Jnc.

Down Trains dealt with at Westwood Yard	**Time at Westwood**
534 11.58pm Class C Ferme Park to Heaton	1.58am to 2.25am
11.14am Fish Empties Class C King's Cross to Aberdeen	2.0pm to 2.10pm (Loco)
262 12.22pm Class C Ferme Park to Niddrie	3.20pm to 3.42pm
714 4.28pm Class C King's Cross Goods to Dringhouses	6.55pm to 7.22pm
9.12pm Class C Westwood to Manchester Ducie Street	
9.56pm Class C Westwood to Doncaster Belmont	
524 8.32pm Class C King's Cross Goods to Park Lane	10.30pm to 10.58pm
9.15pm Class C King's Cross Goods to Sheffield	11.7pm to 11.34pm
9.45pm Class C Clarence Yard to Doncaster Belmont	11.54pm to 12.20am

Most of these trains were marshalled in sections. A Peterborough section was detached at Westwood, and forwarded wagons were attached in the appropriate sections. It needed quite a slick operation to maintain a punctual departure.

Down Terminating Arrivals

From Ashburton Grove	one train (empties)
Clarence Yard	two trains
Ferme Park	17 trains
Goldington CEA	one train (empties)
Hertford North	one train
Highbury Vale	one train (empties)
Hitchin	two trains
Holme	one train
King's Cross Goods	four trains
Letchworth	one train
Little Barford CEA	one train (empties)
New Southgate	one train
Peterborough East	five trains
Welwyn Garden City	one train
	Total 39 trains

Up Departures (starting at New England)

Ferme Park	3.42am, 6.50am, 6.55am, 7.3am, 7.30am, 9.4am, 2.8pm, 2.16pm, 2.24pm, 4.18pm, 4.24pm, 6.6pm, 7.37pm, 8.30pm, 8.43pm, 9.8pm,11.4pm
Goldington CEA	10.24am
Hatfield	1.37am
Highbury Vale	7.58am
Hitchin	11.20am, 9.32pm
Holme	12.16pm
Letchworth	4.28am
Little Barford CEA	9.47am
Peterborough Eas	2.10am, 4.30pm, 8.0pm (fish), 11.20pm
Welwyn Garden City	6.20am
Whitemoor	10.12pm
Wood Green	7.35am

Up Through Trains

8.50pm Class D Grimsby to King's Cross
8.5pm Class C Leeds to King's Cross Goods
1.45pm Class C Fish Aberdeen to King's Cross Goods
6.5pm Class C Niddrie to King's Cross Goods
7.25pm Class C Park Lane to King's Cross Goods
11.45pm Class C Dringhouses to King's Cross Goods
12.55am Class C Inverkeithing to King's Cross Goods
5.30pm Class C Fish New Clee to King's Cross Goods
7.19pm Class C Fish Grimsby to King's Cross Goods
 Class D Boston to Ferme Park
9.0pm Class D Boston to Ferme Park
7.23pm Class C Mansfield CS to Ferme Park
9.50pm Class C Boston to South Wales

Time at New England

12.5am to 1.4am
12.46am to 12.54am (Water)
1.14am to 1.34am (Loco)
1.38am to 1.50am
2.36am to 2.54am
3.8am to 3.38am
1.14pm to 2.2pm
8.2pm to 8.22pm (Water)
9.26pm to 9.45pm
9.20pm to 10.7pm
10.43pm to 11.0pm
10.57pm to 11.32pm
11.20pm to 12.10am

Up Arrivals

Boston	two trains	Mansfield CS	three trains (via Spalding)
Colwick	eight trains	Newport	one train
Dewsnap	one train	Ollerton Colly Jnc	one train
Doncaster Decoy	three trains	Retford	one train
Doncaster	one train	Sheffield B Rd	one train
Dringhouses	one train	Stamford	one train
Grantham	one train	Warsop Jnc	one train (via Spalding)
Hexthorpe	two trains (via Spalding)	Worksop	one train
Loversall Carr	one train		*Total 32 trains*

Twelve

LIFE AT KING'S CROSS IN THE EARLY SIXTIES

How I came to be there

I became Deputy Station Master (DSM) at King's Cross not particularly by choice, but because there had been a reorganisation and the DSM's post had been created. It had been advertised on the Vacancy List in the usual way but I had let it pass by, as I felt that my next career move ought to be in Divisional operating management. However, fate decreed otherwise. My boss at Heaton when I was a shift assistant there had been Arnold Slater, one of the nicest chaps you could ever hope to meet, and

we got along together very well. He had gone from Heaton to be Stationmaster at King's Cross and we all felt that he was a perfect choice for the job. He was tall and impressive in appearance, totally

Below: A view of the smoke-blackened frontage of King's Cross station shortly after the Second World War. Much of the area in front of the station is occupied by the London Underground system. *National Railway Museum*

A recent view of the frontage of Kings Cross, which affords an interesting comparison with the photograph of 80 years ago reproduced in the October issue

Above: A view of the King's Cross 'throat': in the centre stands the signalbox and the three double-track tunnels; to the left is the locomotive depot; the platform on the right is the suburban platform known as York Road. Trains using that platform then proceed to Moorgate via the 'Widened Lines' which run parallel to the Metropolitan underground lines. *D. W. Hawkins*

unflappable and with that gift of being able to get on with anyone, from the highest in the land to the lowest member of staff (quite literally).

However, I was 'persuaded' that it would be in my best interests to apply for the vacancy and, being able to take a hint, I did so and was called for interview. It was a very friendly affair and a week or two later I was told that I had been appointed. I often wondered later if I had been a 'blocking' candidate to keep someone else out who might have thought he should have been appointed. Anyway, to cut a long story short, I arrived at King's Cross on Monday, 19 June 1961, to take up my new duties as DSM, working once more for my old boss. As was customary in those days, there was no job specification, and when I asked Arnold what I was supposed to do he was quite vague. I don't think he knew himself really.

It was an archetypal 'one-over-one' situation, rightly abhorred by management organisation planners, but Arnold said that HQ had wanted there to be a senior presence on the platforms much more frequently, not to take part in any activity, but just to be there to be seen by the public so that they could be reassured that there was 'someone in charge here'. Just imagine, walking up and down the trainside reassuring passengers before the departure of important trains, and trying to look important too. I had a uniform hat so heavily laden with gold braid that I rather resembled an admiral

of the fleet, but at least it lent an air of authority to the wearer. So HQ was pleased with the result. It was also indicated to me that when not wearing my uniform hat it would not be appropriate for me to go bare-headed when on duty and I was given the choice of a bowler or a homburg to wear on those occasions when I needed to be incognito. I chose a homburg, rather fancying myself as Herbert Lom. Bowlers were for undertakers or Loco Inspectors.

The organisational chart below the Stationmaster and me was a Commercial Manager, who looked after the booking and enquiry offices and similar commercial staff, and a Parcels Agent, who looked after all the parcels traffic. There were also three Assistant Stationmasters who covered the three shifts and ran the operating side of the station on their shift, but they were not sufficiently senior to have applied successfully for the DSM's post. This rankled with them and they still wanted to have direct access to the Stationmaster, which I was tactful enough to accept. However, it was quite

different with the Parcels Agent. It was a big job and he needed guidance. More about that later.

The previous week Gerry Fiennes, who I think was GN Line Manager at the time, had sent for me. Quite rightly he wanted to be sure that I would be OK in such a high profile job. It was a genial interview. Gerry Fiennes was a big man in all senses of the word and he was a railwayman's railwayman — very popular with the staff, who thought highly of him. However, he was not quite so popular with the Board when he spoke out about

its shortcomings. He hadn't taken to heart the lesson that you don't speak out in public. It was fine within the industry and there were several thriving debating societies. There was also a periodic journal to which staff were encouraged to contribute on any topic they chose, a useful safety valve.

My first day at King's Cross turned out to be a long day and a fairly exciting one, as the Royal Train arrived in the evening at 7.53pm bringing HM The Queen back to London. I watched the Stationmaster carefully to see just what he did in case I had to deputise for him in the future. There was no such thing as training on the job in those days. You were expected to know what to do or find out. I don't know whether job descriptions existed then, but there certainly wasn't one for my job. You looked to see what needed doing and then got on with it. They were robust days, before the importation of high-flown management theory from the USA.

Above: One could well argue that Gresley's 'A4' streamliners were Britain's most popular and well-loved locomotives. They certainly attracted a lot of attention. Sports jackets are well in evidence as an admiring crowd takes photographs. A beautifully clean 'A4' of 'Top Shed', No 60022, the world-famous record holder *Mallard*, is waiting to depart with an SLS and RCTS Joint Tours Committee Special — the 'Aberdeen Flyer' on Saturday, 2 June 1962. *Eric Oldham*

Below: 'Britannias' were regular performers on the Cleethorpes to King's Cross service. They were impressive-looking machines. No 70039 *Sir Christopher Wren* waits impatiently for the 'right-away' with the 4.10pm departure on 26 April 1961. Immingham shed (40B) had three of the class, Nos 70039-41. *G. A. Richardson*

King's Cross was 76 miles from Peterborough and too far for daily commuting, so it was necessary to find digs (yet again). Fortunately a colleague of mine who had, I think, been Yard Master at Tinsley, had just moved to a job in London and he asked me if I would like to stay at his digs, which were in Harringay, just a couple of stops up the line. He could recommend them, he said, and no wonder. It was just an ordinary terrace house but the husband worked at Smithfield market and the evening meal tended to consist of either a big fat steak, or a big lump of beef, or several chops, or half a roast, etc. We lived like fighting cocks and the location was handy for early mornings or late evenings at the Cross, as I had learned to call it, on VIP duties. The hosts' summer holiday consisted of taking the car to the north coast of Scotland, where they went every year. There were no motorways in those days, other than a bit of the M1, and just getting there and back must have occupied most of the fortnight.

Motive Power Changes

King's Cross in 1961 hadn't really changed much since prewar years. Steam was still almost supreme, and whilst some of the 'A2 'variants had been withdrawn, the remainder of the LNER Pacifics were almost untouched. There were still the original 34 'A4' streamliners, 71 of the prewar 'A3s', some of them almost 40 years old but still in fine fettle, and 50 'A1s', postwar locomotives of superb design. There were also 30 A2s. The East Coast main line could still boast the finest stock of powerful racehorses in the country, and I say that with some envy as a former LMS man.

'V2s' were still to be seen, together with 'B1s', whilst 'Britannias' appeared on the Cleethorpes trains. Diesels made what might be described as sporadic appearances and were very unreliable at first. Every day, diesel diagrams were worked by steam locos. Every day, diesels failed en route and had to be replaced by standby steam locos. It is fortunate indeed that the Eastern Region had had the wit to retain a good supply of the old faithful Pacifics.

The sight of one of these old faithfuls slowly and effortlessly easing a heavy train out of the station and into Gas Works tunnels, with the coupling rods of the motion gently rotating, short bursts of exhaust steam erupting from the chimney, then the gleaming carriages slowing passing by (yes, we cleaned our trains), was one to stir the heartstrings to their very depths, even though it was a scene to be repeated many times daily. It was the mixture of sight, sound and that indescribably nostalgic smell of hot oil and sulphur that excited the senses in a way that diesels and electrics cannot. Who cares that steam engines were dirty, smelly, grossly inefficient beasts, needing to be fed and watered at every opportunity? They were magnificent and never ceased to thrill. And even at the trainside there was a palpable atmosphere. There were comings and goings. Sad goodbyes and cheerful hellos. Most long distance journeys by express train were something out of the ordinary. People's senses were heightened. In those days passengers could lean out of the door windows for the last few words and maybe a hug and a kiss, and a reluctance to leave go as the train began to move.

However, sentiment apart, from an operating point of view the diesels won hands down, at least when they could be relied on. They didn't need to visit Top Shed as King's Cross shed (34A) was universally known, cluttering up the station throat. They didn't need to be turned. They were capable of a higher and more predictable power output, and fortunately the Eastern Region had had the foresight to order 'Deltics' of 3300hp. No D9007 was delivered in June 1961 and the last of the 22, No D9021, put in an appearance on 10 May 1962. But they were noisy beasts, especially when they were standing on the buffers. Pleas to the Motive Power Department to get the drivers to shut the engines down were met with the excuse, 'If we shut them down we may not be able to start them up again.' We didn't really believe it, but we dare not take the risk of having a dead diesel on the buffers and losing it for its outward working.

The 'Deltic's were Gerry Fiennes' idea and he tried to persuade the Board to order 23 of them, to replace 55 steam locos. He wanted more power than the 'Peaks' and the EE Type 4s, and even the Brush 2750hp. He also wanted 100mph capability. He had great foresight. He should have been Chairman of the BRB and we might have got somewhere. The 'Deltic' saga went back to the mid-1950s, when English Electric recognised a need for a more powerful diesel-electric locomotive than those proposed in the 1955 Modernisation Plan. English Electric proposed to use two 'Deltic' diesel engines to manufacture a powerful and

relatively lightweight locomotive producing 3,300hp. It was a private venture by English Electric, and the London Midland Region saw no long-term use for it in view of the planned electrification of the West Coast main line. Eastern Region management was lukewarm at first to Gerry's plans, but Sir George Nelson, who was Chairman of English Electric, approached Sir Brian Robertson, Chairman of the British Transport Commission, personally and the BTC authorised the building of 22 'Deltics'.

Above: 'A3' No 60046 *Diamond Jubilee* waits to be released to go to 'Top Shed', after bringing in an express in July 1961. She was a Grantham (34F) engine. *A. W. Flowers*

Below: A sign of the new order: the 'Deltics' had arrived — 22 of them — specially to work East coast expresses. No 9005 appears to be backing out of the platform, having just brought in train No 1A07 in May 1973. *I. J. Hodson*

Above: Gresley's versatile 'V2' 2-6-2s were also at home on express passenger trains. No 60902 (34A) powers away with the 10.25am to Peterborough on 12 March 1962 and clears Hadley Wood North tunnel. *M. Edwards*

Type 4 diesels came in a flood from 1961 onwards, but even by late 1963 there were still 135 Pacifics on the books, spending most of their time, or so it seemed, deputising for failed diesels. A lineside census at Easter 1963 counted 62 trains hauled by steam locos, including 50 Pacifics, compared with 58 diesels.

Domestic Affairs

Finding a house was priority number one, but house prices in the London area were far higher, even in those days, than they were in Peterborough. And even though I had secured a significant improvement in grade, my take home pay had not increased because I was now in the 'management' grade and you weren't paid for overtime or Sunday duty. It was supposed to be reflected in the actual salary levels, but it wasn't. According to my income tax returns for 1960/61 and 1961/62, my annual earnings had increased by a measly £12, which wasn't going to make finding a house any easier. However, there was another consideration. For historical reasons I still possessed my old LMS travel concessions which gave me 20 miles' free residential travel on former LMS routes, ie based on Euston or St Pancras. They were not transferable to former LNER routes, which meant that I could only obtain eight miles free, based on King's Cross or 12 miles if I transferred my entitlements to the BR standard, which were inferior to those of the LMS.

In any case, there was nothing within reasonable range of King's Cross that was in my price range for a house, so I began to look around the Watford area. Arnold Slater was as good as gold and let me have an afternoon off anytime. I came across a very likely house at Abbots Langley, just north of Watford, which actually backed on to the main line from Euston. What could be nicer? I put in an offer almost as soon as I started at the Cross, it was accepted, and I sat back and waited. It seemed to be too good to be true, and it was. Nothing happened, and when I pressed the estate agent he eventually told me that the owners hadn't found anywhere to go yet. I couldn't wait any longer and withdrew my offer.

In the meantime I began to survey the Midland main line. There was nothing within my price range until beyond Harpenden, but then came Luton, which was a distinct possibility and where houses were both plentiful and cheaper because it was 30 miles from London. There was a good train service, using the Rolls-Royce-engined DMUs, and we quickly found a very nice modern semi about a mile from the station. So we sold our house in Peterborough quickly and moved to Luton on 17 October 1961. We had no car, but I was quite happy to use my bicycle and leave it at Luton station. In the mornings I sometimes caught the Edinburgh sleeper which was non-stop to St Pancras, and travel in comfort (yes, third class). Otherwise it was the DMUs, which used to have a fair turn of speed with their Rolls-Royce engines. On the Up, we seemed to go helter-skelter through Cricklewood and Kentish Town at about 85mph and I could feel the buffers at St Pancras coming ominously near. However, the driver always managed to stop, but in those days they often entered terminal stations at quite high speed (no AWS or TPWS to slow them down and you went in on green signals).

Below: A historic day and a sad one for lovers of the steam engine. 'A3' Pacific No 60103 *Flying Scotsman,* absolutely spotless and burnished to the nth degree, waits to leave King's Cross, surely its ancestral home, for the last time (or so it was thought then) on its way to Doncaster, on 14 January 1963. I was somewhere among the crowd. *British Rail*

A Famous Engine Bows Out

The world's most famous steam engine, *Flying Scotsman*, No 60103, went out in a burst of glory on 14 January 1963, on its last journey from the Cross at the head of the 1.15pm Leeds/Bradford. Alan Pegler, its new owner, was on the footplate, and there was great excitement among the huge crowd of railway enthusiasts and photographers who spilled over onto the tracks. Fortunately the British Transport Police were far more lenient in those days and recognised that here was history in the making. Even the local railway staff, not renowned for being over-sentimental, were impressed. It was the end of an era, and a portent of things to come. That was particularly the case for those grizzled old railwaymen who could look back to the dying days of the Great Northern Railway when *Flying Scotsman* backed down into the station to proudly take its first Anglo-Scottish express on its way. A lot had happened in those 40 years whilst *Flying Scotsman* swept up and down the main line with hardly a care in the world, or so it seemed.

The Coldest Winter for 250 Years

It was the coldest January in London since 1838, and the entire country was blanketed by frozen snow. Frost every night for over two months and the coldest temperature I have ever recorded, when

all the mercury went into the bulb — 0°F. Overnight sleepers arrived hours late caked in ice and snow. On 6 February 1963 the Up 'Royal Scot' was diverted via Newcastle and the ECML, on one of the rare occasions that Shap was blocked by snow. A 'Duchess' would have been a treat, but we had to be satisfied with No D300. However, we did have a 'Duchess' one day (or a 'Princess Coronation' to give it its Sunday name) when No 46245 *City of London* worked an enthusiasts' special to Doncaster on 9 June 1963. Even more unusual was the sight of a 'Jubilee' the previous day, a great rarity, when one of Holbeck's favourites, No 45597 *Barbados,* worked up from Bradford with a special train for the Provident Clothing Company. Was this the first-ever visit of a 'Jubilee' to Kings Cross? And what was the Provident Clothing Company?

The Finale for Steam

But steam engines were becoming rare, and the summer timetable for 1963 marked the end of diagrammed steam workings to King's Cross. My log for Thursday 27 June 1963 records that I hadn't seen a steam engine at King's Cross all that week, and they became an increasing rarity from then onwards, although even as late as September, steam could still be seen, deputising for failed diesels. However, July also marked the demise of the very unreliable 'Baby Deltics', which usually left the station hidden from view behind a thick cloud of exhaust smoke.

In 1960 Top Shed (34A) had 18 'A4s' and 12 'A3s', but by late 1963 it had closed and a new diesel maintenance depot had been opened at Clarence Yard, referred to as Finsbury Park 34G. By this time 34G had acquired a stud of 29 Brush Type 4s, numbered in the range D1500 onwards, as well as eight 'Deltics'. 'Peak's and English Electric Type 4s worked in from Gateshead, Haymarket and Leeds. 'Deltics' worked in from Gateshead and Haymarket. These four ECML depots had 142 big diesels at their disposal, although some worked on other routes.

Train Services

These have changed out of all recognition. In 1961 there were far fewer mainline trains than today, they were slower, the service started later in the morning and finished earlier in the evening, but they served a wider range of destinations. The daytime ECML service was as follows:

• Anglo-Scottish — seven trains. Average journey time to Edinburgh over seven hours. Fastest train the summer-only 'Elizabethan' in 6hr 35min non-stop. In 2012 there are 19 trains with an average journey time to Edinburgh of about 4hr 20min.

• Leeds/Bradford — nine trains, of which eight conveyed a Bradford portion. Average journey time approaching four hours. Fastest train the 'Queen of Scots' Pullman non-stop to Leeds in 3hr 30min. In 2011, thanks to the redoubtable Christopher Garnett of GNER fame, there were 33 trains with an average journey time of about 2hr 20min. By contrast, there is now just one through train to Bradford Forster Square.

Below: A 'Baby Deltic' arrives at King's Cross. Only 10, Nos D5900-09, were built, and they were not a success. All 10 were allocated to 34B. When accelerating out of the station, they produced more smoke than a steam engine. *Ian Allan Library*

• There were also four trains to Newcastle, which was also served by the Anglo-Scottish trains. There were two through trains to Hull, two to Cleethorpes, two to Sheffield and one to Teesside.

The East Coast main line partners always had a policy of looking after the passenger, dating back into the 19th century, and was the basis of their commercial success. This was exemplified by the number of through carriages which were run. The 10.20am to Leeds had through carriages to Harrogate, Ripon, Hull and Bradford. The 5.20pm 'Yorkshire Pullman' had portions for Leeds, Bradford, Harrogate and Hull, and the 6.12pm Leeds had portions for Bradford, Halifax and Hull. Scarborough had through coaches on the 12.30pm Newcastle, Sunderland via the coast on the 3.10pm Newcastle and Saltburn on the 5.35pm Newcastle. Fixed formation trains put paid to all that. Hull and Harrogate have particularly suffered. One of the main reasons for the increase in the number of trains to Scotland and the West Riding is that the service starts much earlier in the morning and ends much later in the evening. That is the product of a much accelerated service, but it has reacted on the extensive sleeper service which operated in the early 1960s — there is no longer the demand that there was.

The Pullman Trains

The mention of Pullman trains brings to mind the splendid service that they offered, and for which the later so-called Pullmans were a very poor substitute. Pullmans gave standards of comfort and service which have never been surpassed, and the small supplement required was worth every penny. The trains were the 'Master Cutler' (7.20pm Sheffield), the unnamed 11.20am Sheffield, the 'Queen of Scots' (11.50am Glasgow via Leeds), the 'Tees-Tyne Pullman' (4.50pm Newcastle) and the 'Yorkshire Pullman' (5.20pm Harrogate). Pullman trains gave the station an air of dignity even amongst the usual smoke, grime and general clutter of the terminus in those days. And I can't help wondering if there isn't scope today for some Pullman trains for people who like a bit of service with flair, instead of today's mediocre offerings. A sort of four star hotel on wheels. Perhaps one day an entrepreneur will come along and do it. A speed of 100mph would be fast enough for a Pullman train for a smoother ride, but then such a train would get in the way of all those businessmen nattering into their mobile phones and playing with their laptops.

Below: 'Britannia' class Pacific No 70039 *Sir Christopher Wren* emerges from Wood Green tunnels with the 4.10 pm King's Cross to Cleethorpes service on 15 June 1962
P. H. Groom

Train labelling

These multi-portion trains needed careful labelling, and the most effective method was the simplest — a small paper label stuck on the window of one of the compartments of the coach. That reassured passengers more than any word of mouth could. Talking of compartments reminds me that all the regular mainline trains were composed almost entirely of compartment stock, apart from the dining vehicles, and it was very noticeable that when open coaches were included in the formation as strengthening vehicles or in dated and relief trains, passengers always went for the compartments first, in preference to open coaches. I wonder what would happen today if East Coast were to introduce compartments on its trains?

Train labelling brings to mind the vexed question of roof boards. Nothing looked smarter than a train that was fully roof-boarded from end to end, particularly if it was a named train and had the additional boards. However, it needed constant supervision to ensure that trains had a reasonable number of boards and it was almost an impossibility to equip fully a train, except perhaps for the most prestigious. Roof-boards had a mysterious habit of disappearing, and though we kept ordering more, the delivery took months and we never caught up with the deficiencies. There is probably to this day a room down in the cellars at King's Cross that has not been opened for years and is full of roof boards secreted away by the staff to lighten their workload.

Changing roof boards or reversing them was quite easy on the platform side of the train but much more difficult on the other side where staff had to lean out of windows and manipulate the long boards as best they could. Roof-boarding sounds a simple operation but the logistics were complex. It was much better for it to be done in the carriage sidings before the empty stock worked into the station, but ladders were needed for both sides. This was one of the items that Philip Shirley, the Batchelors Peas man and BR Deputy Chairman or something similar, commented upon, but we never found a suitable answer, and it took many years for one to be found.

In 1961 it was still possible to identify certain trains as sufficiently important to carry a name, and the timetable was full of them. We can all remember the 'Elizabethan', the 'Flying Scotsman' and probably the 'Talisman', but who remembers the 'Northumbrian' (the 12.30pm Newcastle), the 'Tees-Thames' (the 2.0pm Saltburn) and the 'Heart of Midlothian' (the 1.0pm Edinburgh)? However, the practice gave a note of distinction, even though the trains concerned were often no better than other trains to the same destination.

The Losers

It will be seen from this review of the train services from King's Cross in 1961 that many provincial towns and cities are badly served today by comparison. Harrogate, Ripon, Scarborough, Teesside, Wearside and Halifax have all lost their through service, whilst Bradford has only a meagre service and Hull has only one (although a different firm provides several). Sad to say, this perhaps

Below: Memories of the good old days of luxury Pullman travel behind a Gresley 'A3'. This was the 'Yorkshire Pullman' with No 60062 *Minoru,* disfigured by smoke deflectors, at speed near New Barnet on 2 August 1961. *R. S. Greenwood*

reflects in part the reduced commercial importance of at least some of these places. It is also an inevitable consequence of fixed formation trains such as HSTs, and of electrification. And it has to be said that through carriages were expensive to operate. But they gave a service to passengers, which was the fundamental belief, almost a religion, of the East Coast companies and their successors. Going back years before, to the pre-grouping companies, the range of through carriages which they operated was quite astonishing, and a blessing to the elderly or passengers encumbered with luggage.

Above: Another ceremonial occasion at King's Cross — billed as the last-ever 'A4' streamliner to leave King's Cross. On 24 October 1964, No 60009 *Union of South Africa* stands at the head of a special train to Newcastle and back, organised by the Stephenson Locomotive Society and the Railway Correspondence & Travel Society. By now, No 60009 had been transferred to Aberdeen Ferryhill shed for working the Glasgow services, but had been lovingly prepared for this journey. Fortunately, we can still see 'A4s' today as there are several in preservation. *M. Pope*

The Sleepers

Finally, we must remember that station activities did not cease after the departure of the early evening series of expresses. Mails, parcels post, parcels and newspapers were big business, building up to a peak from mid-afternoon onwards. And of course there were the sleepers, a whole series of them, starting with the 'Aberdonian' at 7.30pm, followed by the 10.15pm Aberdeen, the 10.30pm Dundee, the 11.20pm and the 11.35pm (the 'Night Scotsman') to Edinburgh and the 1.0am (the 'Tyneside') to Newcastle. Sleepers at King's Cross are now only a distant memory, the victim of an improved and faster daytime service spread over many more hours. But those who used them might still feel that a night in a sleeper was far preferable to getting up in the middle of the night to catch the 5.5am from Leeds to Kings Cross or the 4.50am from Newcastle. Pullmans and sleepers and comfortable seats that matched the window spacing, and restaurant cars that were so popular that two sittings were needed to meet the demand, are but distant memories of a bygone age. But they tell us that that is progress.

Thirteen

MORE TALES FROM 'THE CROSS'

The Daily Routine

I liked to arrive at about 8.15am to see how the morning commuter services were performing. There was little I could do about it because the traffic was almost entirely inwards, but if trains were delayed it was thought to be important that I should make an appearance as a recognisable authority to whom complaints could be directed. It was much better to defuse them in this way, and even if I could do no more than offer an apology, passengers were generally satisfied that someone in authority had listened to their complaints. Perhaps this is one of today's problems. Where do you find someone to complain to on any station, large or small? How do passengers recognise someone in authority?

The next job was to satisfy myself that the empty stock for the morning departures was ready in the sidings or on its way into the terminus, and then have a gentle stroll round the station. It was called 'being on parade', and in those days it was considered important to be seen. It was thought that passengers liked to see someone in authority on the premises and felt reassured.

The Daily Ritual of 'Morning Prayers'

'Morning prayers' came next. These took place in the Stationmaster's inner sanctum, and in addition to the two of us there were the Passenger Commercial Officer and the Chief Clerk. Coffee

Below: A double-headed suburban train to Hertford North seen near Finsbury Park on 22 April 1958, headed by Class N2 0-6-2Ts Nos 69541 and 69592. Both engines are commendably clean, as one had come to expect with 'Top Shed' engines. *Brian Morrison*

and biscuits were brought up from the Refreshment Rooms below on a silver salver with starched linen napkins. The Refreshment Room staff obviously thought that it was a good idea to keep well in with the stationmaster. The morning's correspondence was dealt with, then we usually had a good chat about wider issues before the Stationmaster or I went off to attend to the departure of the 'Flying Scotsman'. We met again in the afternoon for a general round-up, and for tea and pieces of fruit cake. Older rail travellers will remember those slices of dark fruit cake, served in practically every Refreshment Room throughout the country. We also had editions of the evening papers and mulled over the headlines. Railways were never out of the news then, as now. It was the Beeching era.

We were never short of morning papers. They were collected from incoming trains and the cleanest, neatest copies were delivered to the Stationmaster's office. Copies of evening papers were dispatched from King's Cross to a variety of local destinations, and a bundle was left for the staff. Newspaper traffic by train was big business in those days. It was thought to have been thrown away because the newspaper proprietors were fed up with their business being disrupted by strikes and threats of strikes by ASLEF and/or the NUR.

Were the Trade Union bosses dismayed at this turn of events? If they were, they never showed it. Did Trade Union members tell their Head Office what was happening? If they did, it obviously cut no ice.

The 'Wind of Change' Blows on the Railways Too — the Litter Bin Saga

Harold Macmillan's famous phrase about the 'Wind of Change' was affecting us too. Dr Richard Beeching had become Chairman of the Railways Board and had brought in new blood at the top, something almost unheard of. Grizzled old railwaymen might have looked down their noses, but these new brooms soon made their presence felt. London termini were generally felt to be scruffy and untidy, which in general terms they were. For a start there were still plenty of steam locos about, accompanied by the usual clouds of smoke, steam and soot. Parcels and mails traffic produced its own clutter and litter (and sometimes its own smells of fish, pigeons, milk, etc). But there were no litter bins at the Cross. People deposited their cups, bottles and cigarette packets in all sorts of holes and corners. And this was before the days of everything being pre-packed!

The edict went out from on high — King's Cross must have litter bins. The staff were appalled.

A Railwayman's Odyssey

Below left: A beautifully cleaned 'A4' No 60028 *Walter K Whigham* waits at Belle Isle to back down to King's Cross for the 'Elizabethan' on 6 July 1961. I often witnessed the departure of this prestige train after 'morning prayers'.
Eric Treacy

Right: The following month, on 14 August 1961, the 'A4' No 60009 *Union of South Africa* was in action on the 'Elizabethan'. Here the locomotive is seen bursting out of Copenhagen Tunnel. No 60009 has only another 392 miles to go, non-stop, but this Haymarket (64B) engine looks in fine fettle.
Colin P. Walker

It was one thing to sweep the platforms and stir up clouds of dust. That had always been done. But empty litter bins? That was degrading. However, the litter bins came, in dozens, to be fixed to walls and railings and any other suitable vertical surface. And the staff had to be persuaded to empty them. But persuading the British public to use them was a different matter. In 1960 it was felt to be the God-given right of every free-born Englishman (and the Scots and the Welsh and the Irish?) to deposit his litter wherever he happened to be standing. I use the male gender advisedly — women were much tidier.

But persuasion had to be applied somehow. We were visited periodically by representatives from on high to see how the great 'Clean up the London stations' campaign was going on. Fortunately, we were usually tipped off by a kindly secretary when such a visit was imminent and we all scampered around picking up any bits of litter that we could find. We always left a cigarette packet in a fairly prominent place (an old soldier's trick) so that it could be pounced upon triumphantly by the inspection party. This gave them great satisfaction because they thought that they had caught us out; it also terminated the inspection and they repaired to the stationmaster's office for tea and cake. It was not unknown for one of the inspection party to examine the packet to see if it was empty. This caused great glee all round and lightened the mood. The staff at the Cross could be very devious when occasion demanded.

Another Revolution — the Turnround Train

I have mentioned Philip Shirley before. He was one of Beeching's new appointments to the Board and he came into King's Cross each Monday morning on the Sheffield Pullman, to be met by the top-hatted Stationmaster. He used the Stationmaster as a sounding board, firing off innocent-sounding questions such as what happened to the coaches of trains after they arrived from the north. He wasn't at all impressed to be told that some sets were worked out to the carriage sidings to be cleaned and serviced and then brought back into the station later, but he didn't say anything at the time. However, he had obviously pursued the question with HQ because we were asked to see which trains

Above: A train of empty stock from King's Cross passes Holloway South signalbox on its way to the carriage sidings with Class L1 2-6-4T No 67773 in charge. *Brian Morrison*

Below: King's Cross wasn't all glamour. The inner-suburban services were very workaday indeed. King's Cross shed (34A) had a large stock of these strong and reliable 0-6-2 tank engines, some equipped with condensing apparatus for working on the 'Widened Lines'. They dated from 1925. Class N2/2 N. 69528 is seen at Aldersgate, en route from Moorgate to New Barnet, and will soon arrive at the so-called 'Rathole' platform at King's Cross.
D. C. Ovenden

could be cleaned, serviced and turned round in the station.

This may seem a reasonable request in the year 2012, when nearly all trains are turn-rounds and it works perfectly well. No one would think of sending them ECS (empty coaching stock) to the carriage sidings, but in 1961 it was a revolutionary idea. The staff were appalled (again). It was a tradition bordering on a religion that East Coast main line trains started their journeys clean. It was a matter of pride. The idea of passengers having to join a dirty train at the Cross quite rightly horrified them. We did our best to wash the windows, but it had to be done whilst passengers were joining the train, and it made a mess on the platform (and in the train, with wet footmarks). In those days before the station frontage was rebuilt there wasn't room to queue passengers in the circulating area.

The main issue, from an operating point of view, was the fixing of a minimum turn-round time, to allow for loading and unloading, cleaning and servicing, watering toilets and catering vehicles and carrying out reservations. And add a margin for late running — a very fine judgement. The turn-round time then determined the timetable, because it was important that a train should depart as soon as

possible after the end of that time, in order to liberate the platform for other trains and release the incoming engine. However, it worked reasonably well, because East Coast main line punctuality was pretty good. In fact, my notes show that on Saturday 12 July 1963, at the height of the summer season with lots of additional trains, all trains departed on time. Nor was that unusual.

A Press Campaign About Too Many Staff

The next attack, which had been whipped up by the London newspapers, came over the question of knots of untidy-looking porters hanging around at the station front waiting for passengers with luggage alighting from taxis, and hoping to earn a couple of bob (to use the vernacular of the time) by carrying the said luggage to the train. Now this was big business, and it was very important to the running of the station that lower-paid members of staff should be able to supplement their earnings in this way. Despite the overheated labour market at the time, there was never any staff shortage at the Cross.

This was a jungle. It was called weaseling, and apart from ensuring that all vacancies were filled it enabled a service to be given to passengers without staff having to be employed specifically for that purpose. The pattern of work at the station was governed by the train service and there were peaks and troughs. In the troughs the staff went weaseling. They served both arrivals and departures and there were unwritten codes of practice among

Below: The is the 'Rathole' platform at King's Cross, used by inner-suburban trains from Moorgate. Now part of history.
Author's Collection

the men, which had become established since the war, to ensure that they all had a reasonable share of the business. Before the war there had been men known as badge porters who were allowed to be on the station purely for the business of carrying passengers' luggage, and who were unpaid, or may even have had to pay for the privilege. Something similar was tried recently.

The edict came from on high. There must not be more than six men at the station front and they must stand in a neat line. Any others must be hidden from passengers' view. So a rather smart little waiting room was built for the surplus and we had to employ a supervisor to maintain discipline. A weaseling Rule Book was produced, setting down standards of conduct, and agreed beforehand with the staff representatives. We never knew how much the staff earned, but during the summer months it was substantial. It was a time when plenty of people carried lots of heavy luggage. However, the system worked. The staff were satisfied; so were the passengers; and so were we.

Dukes and Duchesses and Slightly Lesser Mortals

Talking of VIPs, each morning the station Reservations Office supplied us with a list for that day. Each office on the ECML telegraphed these details to other offices, so that we knew both outward and inward VIP comings and goings. This was a swanky part of the job, because press and television were usually interested in the higher-up VIPs. Harold Macmillan, the Prime Minister, often travelled to and from King's Cross. He was completely at his ease in dealing with both the public and the media and he would stop and have a chat with the engine driver. VIPs did that sort of thing!

Below: One Saturday afternoon I had to smarten up to meet Harold Macmillan off the train and escort him to his car. He was perfectly at ease and waved at passengers as we walked down the platform. In typical Macmillan style he paused to have a word with the locomen, who look most interested in what he was saying. He was a great actor, and was unaccompanied, apart from his private secretary. I was the only security. Sadly, that peaceful, postwar period was coming to an end. *Author's Collection*

A Railwayman's Odyssey

His successor, Sir Alec Douglas-Home, was a little more diffident. When he succeeded to the Conservative Party leadership he was at home in Scotland and came hot-foot on the overnight sleeper to present his credentials to HM The Queen. There was a larger than usual gathering of the media but as a matter of courtesy he didn't want to meet them until he had seen Her Majesty. We had been tipped the wink about this on the railway grapevine, so we arranged for his car to be secreted away in the old carriage drive next to platform 1, and for the train to run into that platform. He was very relieved when we ushered him straight across to his car, but the media were not at all amused. We made ourselves scarce pronto. It didn't do to offend the press, but we normally gave them good facilities. In those days VIPs did not include footballers or pop stars, but I wouldn't have minded the odd film star (of the female variety, of course).

Problems with the 'Talisman'

When the 'Talisman', 4.0pm to Edinburgh, was introduced to give a later service to the Scottish capital, it was restricted to a limited load of nine coaches so that it could run in accelerated timings. It had 68 first class and 222 second class seats, and HQ had decided as a policy that they were all reservable. Standing was not allowed. This caused problems only at busy periods, but especially on Friday evenings when people would turn up without reservations, claiming not to know about the all-seats-reserved arrangement. In those days, as now, not all reserved seats were claimed, so the platform staff had the delicate task of assessing shortly before departure how many spare seats there would be and indicating to the barrier staff how many unreserved passengers might be allowed through. It was the last day-service to Edinburgh and there were plenty of heated arguments, but the staff were pretty adept at dealing with the situation in a professional manner. It would have caused less aggro to have one coach unreserved and treat the train like any other.

Below: In early BR days Class B2 4-6-0 No 61671 *Royal Sovereign* is seen in the station locomotive yard at King's Cross. It may have worked a service from its home depot at Cambridge (31A), but it was also a Royal train engine, which perhaps accounts for its cleanliness. *Eric Treacy*

The evening 'Talisman' was formed off the 4.0pm from Edinburgh the previous day, which was rather inefficient utilisation, but it was not an isolated example. The 12.30pm 'Northumbrian' was formed off the corresponding Up train the previous day, as were, if I remember correctly, all the Anglo-Scottish services.

Train Announcing — Yet Another Problem

We had three train announcers who were all excellent speakers with good clear voices. Train announcing was regarded as a woman's job because it was thought that their voices carried better than men's against the noisy station background. They were very resourceful, too, when they had to depart from the normal script. East Coast main line trains were good runners, but when an Up train arrived late it had become customary to say sorry and try to give some sort of explanation. This could be difficult if an express were delayed by a slow running freight train up in the north somewhere, or if a signalman had let one run with a tight margin somewhere up north and it had lost its path. If the Control Office couldn't help with the reason for the delay, the train announcer would refer to 'operating difficulties', or if she was desperate 'to circumstances outside our control'. However, the new brooms didn't like this. They said that circumstances should always be within our control and it gave a bad image to indicate otherwise. And we wouldn't have operating difficulties if we ran the service efficiently (Sounds like someone we know — it must have been his father.) Very true,

but it was a counsel of perfection and we lived in an imperfect world.

One day, the Chief Civil Engineer, a very big nob who had his office in the East Side Suite at the station, heard the announcer explain the cause of a delay as 'defective track'. He was mightily affronted and told the stationmaster not to use that phrase as it might cause the passengers great concern about their safety. Of course, he was quite right, although we felt like telling him to mind his own damn business. However, the Stationmaster was always the soul of discretion and was very adept at handling such situations.

Actually 'a defective signal' or a 'track-circuit failure' might well have had the same effect, but it would have taken too long to explain to the passengers the technical causes of such failures, and how they were not unsafe because they automatically switched signals to Danger. However, it had become an issue that would not go away, so we took the announcers into our confidence, and jointly we worked out a series of explanations to suit most situations. We then produced a little booklet and sent it to HQ so that they would know what we had done. We heard no more. We perhaps didn't realise it at the time, but

Below: During off-peak hours, freight trains used the York Road platform line at King's Cross to gain access to the 'Widened Lines', en route to the Southern Region via Blackfriars. They returned via the 'Rathole'. *Author's Collection*

the old rule-of-thumb railway where people used their own common sense, experience and resourcefulness was giving way to a new, regulated and more highly organised operation, relying less on people using their initiative and native wit and more on pre-prepared guidelines and instructions. The management revolution had arrived.

One word we never used in announcements was 'accident'. They were passed off lightly as incidents. We didn't want to worry people, and certainly didn't want to make them accident-conscious. In those days, passengers considered the railways very safe and no one ever voiced any safety concerns to me. And another great advantage was that we had a very sensible and level-headed Railway Inspectorate.

Industrial Disputes
The railways had more than their fair share of industrial disputes, although we generally managed to avoid generating any locally, thanks to Arnold Slater, the Stationmaster, who was held in great esteem by the staff representatives, known as the Local Departmental Committees, or LDCs for

Above: King's Cross freight depot was a major establishment, and during the late afternoon and evening a whole stream of fully-fitted and semi-fitted express freight trains left the depot for destinations as far north as Aberdeen and to Sheffield, Manchester and Glasgow. They were generally hauled by Pacifics and 'V2s', but 'B1s' were also used for the nearer destinations. One of the latter is seen here — No 61200 (34A) — near Hornsey in 1963. *N. Gascoine*

Below: These were still the old-fashioned days when large firms would hire a whole train to take their employees and families to London for a day out. On this occasion, Saturday 31 August 1963, 160 employees of Crosse & Blackwell's Peterhead factory in Aberdeenshire were having a day out in London to attend a Gala Sports Day, and I was there to greet them. I was having a busy day. I had an early morning appointment to meet HRH Princess Margaret off the Up 'Aberdonian', then later in the day the Prime Minister came off the 'Yorkshire Pullman' (both pictured elsewhere in this chapter). The latter was to be seen on TV in the evening, to my wife's great pleasure. *F. H. Radford Ltd*

short. A strong LDC was a great asset to us, because it helped to prevent sporadic disputes from breaking out. One day we discovered that a group of staff were regularly claiming overtime which they hadn't worked. The LDC Chairman heard about this and came to see the Stationmaster to see what he intended to do. The upshot was that the Stationmaster very tactfully and cleverly agreed to let the LDC Chairman handle it himself, because he was a toughie and we knew that he would deal with the staff concerned in such a way that they would not dare to transgress again. It would also act as a warning to any other staff who might be thinking of trying it on. It was dealt with effectively without creating any anti-management feelings, but I doubt if such a procedure will be found in today's industrial relations primers.

One-day strikes when the whole railway was shut down provided an excellent opportunity to walk through the tunnels at both ends of the station — Gas Works and Copenhagen tunnels at the north end, and the Widened Lines tunnels to King's Cross (Met) at the other end. The latter were used by inner-suburban trains to and from Moorgate, which called at the York Road platform on the inwards journey, and at platform 17 on the return. York Road was inconveniently located, and platform 17 was a smoky slum. The trains themselves were little better, being formed usually of two of Gresley's close-coupled articulated four-car sets, the Quad Arts, hauled by the elderly but still capable 'N2' tanks. It is hard to remember now that outside the peak hours the Widened Lines were used extensively by freight trips from Ferme Park yards near Hornsey to depots and yards on the Southern. The traffic was mainly coal going south and empties coming back. In those days we needed those six lines and three tunnels north of King's Cross.

We did have a home-made dispute on one occasion. The staff who travelled out to the carriage sidings to put reservation labels on seats had become disgruntled for some reason and decided that they would quietly fail to reserve one of the busiest trains on a busy Friday evening. They told no one and we knew nothing until we were tipped off when the empty stock was already on its way into the station. The station announcer quickly asked all passengers with reserved seats to proceed to the far end of the platform, and as the empty stock slowly drew down the crowded platform the staff swiftly locked the doors of the last few coaches until the train stopped, then opened them to allow passengers with reserved seat tickets to join. One understandably angry lady demanded to be provided with the seat she had paid for and wouldn't listen to any excuses. She was so worked up that I thought she was going to hit me, but I was saved by the guard blowing his whistle. It was the only time during my stay at the Cross that I felt in physical danger. King's Cross station is not in one of the capital's most salubrious areas, but one could walk in the surrounding streets quite safely and alone at any time. How times have changed. Staff assaults were very rare in those days.

I had now spent three summers at the Cross. It had been a real education in human nature, as well as pretty high profile, but it was time to move on. I could not have chosen a better time. The Board had decided that the Regions should be reorganised on a traffic division basis, bringing together the formerly separate operating and commercial districts. The London Midland Region had just finished planning its reorganisation and reshuffling the staff, and as a consequence there were a number of unfilled posts. One of them particularly interested me — Assistant Movements Superintendent in the Barrow Division. I sent in my application, waited on tenterhooks, and on Saturday morning, 5 October 1963, Mr Slater walked into my office with his hand outstretched and told me I'd got the job. I was getting out just in time; the following week the *Consumer Report on London Stations* was published! And so, on Monday 21 October 1963, I travelled to Barrow on the 7.50am from Euston and a new chapter in my railway career opened.

Fourteen

KING'S CROSS TO THE BARROW DIVISION — A WHOLE NEW WORLD OPENS UP

After three summers at King's Cross I felt I ought to be moving on. My time there had been full of interest and had given me an excellent insight into the working of a large passenger terminus. I had also learned a lot about human nature, about what made people tick, which was to stand me in good stead in the future. It had not been time wasted.

Owing to one of the many reorganisations which plagued the London Midland Region in its endless search for a more efficient and less expensive organisation, a vacancy had arisen for the Assistant Movements Superintendent in the Barrow-in-Furness Division. I had a yearning to be back on the lines of my old company, the LMSR, which I had left back in 1954, and when I heard that the Division included not only the lines around the coast from Carnforth to Carlisle, together with all the branches, of which there were a fair few at that time, but also the West Coast main line from Carnforth to Gretna and, glory of glories, the Settle & Carlisle line from Settle northwards, I became very keen to get the job. A couple of weeks later I was told that I'd got the Barrow job at a salary of £1,600, which sounded a lot then.

I was overjoyed. I'd always loved the Lake District, and to have it on my doorstep, and plumb in the middle of the Division, was like a dream. My friends were less than impressed. 'What have you done wrong? Sounds like more of a demotion to us.' And I could never persuade my mother otherwise, who thought that being DSM at King's Cross was only two steps away from being Chairman of the British Railways Board.

As usual I had a week in which to tidy my desk and get ready for the move, and I immediately started looking through my archives to find out all I could about the Barrow Division. My last week at the Cross started as my first had done — with a Royal duty. HM The Queen eame back from Balmoral on the Up 'Aberdonian', rather than the Royal Train. It was a lot cheaper for the Royal Household, being a private, and not a State, journey. Not to be outdone, I was on duty early the following morning to attend to the departure of an all first class special to Sheffield for the English Steel Corporation. But that was the end of the glamour (and the uniform, although the black mac came in useful for quite a few more years and I had a couple of spares).

Off to Barrow

Barrow was a long way from Luton, where I lived. On Monday 21 October 1963, I caught the first bus into the town, then the 6.35am to St Pancras. With a degree of some pleasurable anticipation I caught the 7.50am from Euston, changing at Crewe into the 6.45am from Euston, which we had overtaken. The 6.45am stopped at all intermediate stations of any importance and didn't get to Crewe until 11.17am, 4½ hours later. I thought, 'Typical LNWR!' The 6.45 went through to the station called Workington Main, arriving there at 4.49pm, over 10 hours from Euston, but a train-spotter's dream! It also conveyed through coaches for Windermere. I got to Barrow at 2.45pm, the train having called even at Hest Bank and Bolton-le-Sands. The Barrow people probably thought I was

Above: A fine shot of 'Jubilee' 4-6-0 No 45592 *Indore* crossing the River Lune on the viaduct just north of Lancaster Castle station, at which it has called on its way to Windermere. The train is the 5.10pm from Manchester Exchange, a businessmen's train with a long history. Carnforth (24L) is now the engine's home shed, but for many years it was a Camden (1B) engine. Diesel-electrics have taken over its work there. *Ron Herbert*

Below: My train from Euston even called at Hest Bank (between Lancaster and Carnforth)! Hest Bank was a favourite place for watching trains in my schooldays, and 20 years later in 1962 schoolboys were still train-spotting there. They are closely observing unrebuilt 'Patriot' No 45510, which was unnamed. It was a Lancaster (24J) engine. *Author*

never coming. There was no restaurant car on the train and I hope I remembered to take a flask and sandwiches. Quite possibly there had been a train running in similar timings, a 'Parliamentary Train', since Edward VII was on the throne and I could feel the ghost of Sir Richard Moon (autocratic Chairman of the LNWR) all around. He thought 40mph was quite fast enough for an express passenger train.

I Arrive at Barrow at last

I wasn't a total stranger to Barrow but I hadn't been there for some years. My first job was to find the Divisional Office, which was about a mile from the station. The Divisional Manager (DM) Bill Grainger welcomed me warmly and introduced me to my immediate boss, the Divisional Movements

Above: A Sunday afternoon Glasgow/Edinburgh to Liverpool express has just passed through Hest Bank station, hauled by 'Britannia' class Pacific No 70052 *Firth of Tay* on 18 June 1961. Its home shed was Polmadie (66A).
N. A. Machell

Superintendent, Bob Butter, and some of the staff. They were all very friendly and even a bit laid back, but then this wasn't London. The first priority was to find somewhere to lay my head and it was suggested that I try the Sun Hotel in Ulverston. A

Below: The home of the Barrow Divisional Office, at St George's Square, Barrow, in 1963.
Author's collection

telephone call sufficed, and the DM sent me off in his car. I thought, 'I'm going to like it here.' The financial arrangements on transfer paid for a hotel for the first fortnight, then a lodging allowance. In those days there was no shortage of good digs, and a couple of days later one of my senior staff recommended a place where he himself had stayed, and it turned out to be very good.

Railway Organisation

Before the current reorganisation, there had been five organisational layers on the London Midland Region — (1) station or depot, (2) district office, (3) divisional office, (4) line office (operations only), (5) regional HQ. In the current organisation (2) and (3) were merged. Carlisle and Barrow District Offices disappeared into the new Barrow Divisional Office, located at Barrow. The Line Office was at Manchester. The organisation was still top-heavy, and only a couple of years later the Barrow Office was closed and merged with Preston, which later was itself merged with Manchester. The three Line Offices were then merged at Crewe. In the later 1960s all the stationmasters' posts were abolished and replaced by a much smaller number of Station Managers and Area Managers. A much leaner and more effective organisation evolved, but we diluted that important local supervision, and we are still suffering for it.

However, modernisation and rationalisation (apart from Carlisle New Yard about which more later) had so far bypassed the Barrow Division and it still had 68 stations, about 60 Stationmasters and Goods Agents, and nearly 200 manual signalboxes, of which about 30 were in the Carlisle area (the LNWR had Nos 1 to 13 at Carlisle, the manning costs of which were quite considerable).

Moving from a station as important as King's Cross to a seemingly remote Divisional Office was still a major culture change, or would have been if I had not had the benefit of three years' management training, which encompassed all levels of a Region. At station and depot level your job was to apply the laid down Rules and Regulations and the various Books of Instructions several inches thick, and see that your staff did the same. Punctuality, safety, economy were the order of the day, and at passenger stations there was little room for individual initiative. There was a bit more room for manoeuvre at marshalling yards, but at Divisional level you had a much bigger canvas to paint upon and lots of scope. And I found that there was a lot in the offing.

Most Divisions were based around one large central area, but Barrow was different. It was dispersed over many miles of beautiful countryside and coastline. The most important centres were Barrow and Carlisle, but there were several others of importance, such as Workington and Whitehaven. From Carnforth to the Regional boundary south of Gretna Junction was 70 miles. Settle to Carlisle was 72 miles. Carnforth to Carlisle via the coast was 114 miles. Penrith to Workington was 30. Plus all the branches and freight-only lines. It was a big parish and keeping a watchful eye on it all and showing the flag was very time-consuming, but important too. Barrow to Carlisle by train took three hours via Carnforth or Lancaster. By road it was less than two, straight through the heart of the Lake District. And visiting almost anywhere on the S&C (Settle & Carlisle line) by train was impracticable owing to the lengthy journey times involved. The Engineer's Saloon was invaluable, as we shall see.

Back to Learning the Road

On my third day, Mr Butter picked me up in his car and we went to a meeting at Whitehaven, over the fells, followed by lunch in a hotel and a glass of wine. Those were the days when a bottle of Blue Nun was really living it up. I thought for the second time 'I'm going to like it here.' We should have gone by train, but Mr Butter found the car more convenient. He used a Ford Anglia and he was a terrible driver, quite mad. I made my excuses and came back to Barrow by train. The following Monday I went to Carlisle on the 10.25am Leeds-Glasgow, having spent the night at my mother's in Bingley (yes, Val and the family were there too). This was late October and a lovely sunny day. The countryside was in its finest autumn colours and it was beautiful, especially when viewed from the dining car. For the third time, etc etc.

I went on to Workington to meet the District Controller there, Frank Upton, and we became great friends. He had been a District Signalman's Inspector at Skipton at one time and was originally

Below left: A Barrow shipyard workers' train crosses the Bascule Bridge, in the docks. The train engine is a parallel-boilered 2-6-4T. Barrow shed, formerly 11B, renumbered 12E, had eight of them at one time. *Dr M. J. Andrews*

Right: An 'Austerity', 2-8-0 No 90592, approaches Carnforth station, sporting a stopping passenger train headcode and with what appears to be a single coach. An unusual occurrence (early 1960s). This photograph is notable for its illustration of Carnforth Junction No 2 signalbox. *John A. Phillips*

Below: Corkickle station was in Whitehaven at one end of a very troublesome tunnel. At the other end was Whitehaven Bransty station. The train appears to be a short pick-up goods, and is headed by a Class 2MT 2-6-0 No 46432. *Dr M. J. Andrews*

a signalman on the LNWR main line near Norton Bridge. He had a lot of interesting tales to tell. Workington was quite a busy area in those days, with its steelworks, collieries and mineral branches. It had been an area of intense railway development towards the end of the 19th century and some of those lines were still being used for freight. I came back to Barrow on the 6.28pm train (through coaches to London St Pancras) but the 5.8pm departure had sleeping cars as well. One of the trains also conveyed a TPO vehicle (Travelling Post Office), which gives some indication of the commercial importance of this area in times past. I went back the following day to see the

Above: An Ivatt Class 4 2-6-0, No 43006, at Workington station with five brake vans on 7 May 1966. The class was introduced in 1947 and a number of the first 10 came to West Cumbria just as the LMS was being nationalised. The class eventually extended to No 43161, but the great majority went to the Eastern and North Eastern Regions. The LMS design was incorporated in the later BR version, the 76xxx series, which first appeared in December 1952. *David Percival*

Below: A Stanier Pacific, No 46241 *City of Edinburgh*, waits for the right-away with an Up express at Carlisle on 11 July 1964. *Author*

Above: An Ivatt Class 2 2-6-0, No 46455, crosses the Etterby Viaduct at Carlisle with a short (and expensive) transfer trip from Upperby Sidings to Kingmoor Yard on 24 September 1962. Carlisle New Yard was designed to eliminate the need for such trips, and to speed up transits. The viaduct being used by the train was a wartime addition, in case of bomb damage to the girder bridge.
Derek Cross

Whitehaven, Egremont and Moor Row areas. This was really interesting stuff.

I was still 'learning the road' so the following week I came back from Luton on the 12.10am from Euston and went straight through to Carlisle. I had a first class compartment to myself so I had quite a good sleep. After breakfast in the station's Refreshment Room I met the Carlisle District Controller, Fred McNaughton, a man with a lifetime's experience and only a couple of months off retirement. To him I was just a lad. Anyway, he looked after me and showed me round the Control Office, which was upstairs in the palatial station buildings fronting onto the square. In the afternoon I met the Carlisle Goods Agent, who showed me round the goods yards and depots, of which there were still several, a relic of the pre-grouping days when Carlisle was served by no fewer than seven companies — the Maryport & Carlisle, the North British, the Glasgow & South Western, the Caledonian, the North Eastern, the Midland and the LNWR. Most of them had their own goods depot, engine shed, marshalling yard, etc, which was a very costly arrangement, but fortunately they all shared the passenger station. That was my next port of call. The Stationmaster was Jimmy Leslie, one of the old breed of SMs who upheld the old traditions. I was known to have come from the Eastern Region, which might not have gone down well, so I was at pains to point out my LMS parentage.

Still at Carlisle
I had stayed the night at Carlisle, at the Royal Temperance Hotel, so I was around bright and early next morning. Carlisle station had Assistant Stationmasters on all three shifts, which gives some indication of its importance. I was shown round the station, met the staff, visited some of the 30 signalboxes and ended up having a drink with Jimmy Leslie, who had his own supply in his office. Imagine that happening today! In the afternoon, being a fine warm day, the Goods Agent took me on a more in-depth conducted tour of his main yards and goods depots. It was quite an empire. Then back to the Royal Temperance Hotel for a second night, to prepare for a visit to the new marshalling yard in the morning.

Carlisle New Marshalling Yard

Bonfire night, but a mild day. After a good night's sleep and a hearty breakfast I was ready to spend a strenuous day exploring the several square miles that were the Carlisle New Yard. As I mentioned previously, Carlisle suffered from its heritage of being served by seven pre-grouping railways, which all built their own marshalling yards. The North British at Canal, the Caley at Kingmoor, the LNWR at Upperby, the North Eastern at London Road, the Midland at Durran Hill and some subsidiary yards. There were also motive power depots at all those places. Tripping wagons from one yard to another occupied several trip engines and caused delay to wagons in transit, because most of the wagons that arrived at Carlisle were for stations and yards in Scotland, or further south and east in England. The grouping took place in 1923, yet in the intervening 40 years little had been done to rationalise this very expensive organisation. Now it was to happen.

The BTC (British Transport Commission) bought a large area of land to the west of the main Glasgow line north of Kingmoor, measuring nearly three miles long by one mile wide. Construction of the yard began in 1959, and it was brought into full operation in June 1963. It was still settling down when I arrived there, but it had achieved a huge reduction in the number of trip engines required. The base had been formed from 750,000 tons of ironworks slag was brought in from West

Above: Stone traffic from quarries was big business in the Division, and one of the largest quarries was at Horton-in-Ribblesdale, the first station north from Settle. Diesel-electric No 40138 passes Horton signalbox with a Leeds-Carlisle service. The connections leading to the quarry are at the right hand side of the photograph. There is nothing there now, except the two main lines. The stone goes out in big lorries. *B. J. Beer*

Cumberland, and this was covered by 100,000 tons of ballast. Separate Down and Up yards had their own reception and departure sidings. There were 37 sorting sidings in the Down yard and 48 in the Up yard. Each half of the yard had a separate signal and control box, known as the Up Yard Tower and the Down Yard Tower, and controlled trains movements in the area as well as the hump shunting.

A 'Cut' card was compiled for each train in the arrival sidings, showing the destination siding for each wagon (or group of wagons for the same siding). This was despatched to the Tower by pneumatic tube, where the details were transmitted on to a punched tape and fed into the control apparatus. Everything was automatic from then on until each Cut had passed through both the primary and the secondary retarders. The degree of braking pressure was computed, based on the speed, the weight and the 'rollability' of the Cut, and the length of empty siding remaining. Manual override was available at any stage. Rollability was calculated by a radar device which measured how quickly the Cut accelerated once it was over the hump. The combined yards had a capacity of over 5,000 wagons being humped per day.

It was a giant sausage machine but it had the drawback that everything had to be processed through it. It was soon found that the overnight fitted freights coming up from Scotland via the three routes (G&SW, Caley and NB) arrived in a fairly close sequence which was faster than could be humped on arrival, and several hours could elapse before the wagons on those trains could be processed and emerge at the far end in a departing train. The train plan had to be revised to allow for this. Before the new yard opened, trains from Scotland were dealt with in a variety of smaller yards, which allowed for quick attaching and detaching, as happened at New England. Ironically, the new yard had been built to speed up wagon transit times, and in most cases it did, but the overnight fitteds needed a tailor-made service of their own.

The new yard quickly became a showpiece, and we received visitors from all over the place, both within the railway and from industry. We wanted to show it off and impress the latter. I recall one occasion when the railway marketing people wanted to capture produce from the Evesham area to Scotland, which was going by road. They arranged for some agricultural merchants to come to Carlisle to visit the new yard and see for themselves how expeditiously the traffic was now handled. A trial consignment was forwarded from Evesham and came to Carlisle on one of the fitteds, which arrived some time after midnight. I was sent to look after the party and fortunately all went well, after which we all went to a hotel in Carlisle for the remainder of the night (no doubt after a suitable nightcap).

A Little Diversion

Life in the Barrow Division was never dull and we must have spent half of our time travelling around the Division. One of the porters at Garsdale was retiring and it was decided that I should travel across there and present him with his long-service certificate. It was a whole day's job, of course, but I decided to head off in that direction the previous evening, which was an indication of the practical difficulties of travel to the further corners of the 'empire'. Rather than travel by car, which would be a nuisance the following day, I caught the 4.30pm from Barrow, then the 6.16pm from Lancaster to Penrith. Finally a bus took me to my ultimate destination, Appleby, where I arrived at

Below: During the summer season, excursions were run from Morecambe to Lake Windermere, using the branch from Plumpton Junction to Lakeside, followed by a cruise on Lake Windermere on BR boats. On 17 June 1962 a Stanier 2-6-4T, No 42136, is in charge of a six-coach train, also of LMS Stanier stock. The track appears to have been recently relaid. The engine was withdrawn six months later. *N. A. Machell*

Left: On 2 September 1965 an Ivatt Class 2 2-6-0, No 46441, works one of the regular timetabled trains that ran from Ulverston to Lakeside in connection with sailings. In this photograph it is passing Haverthwaite station, which is now the home of a preserved railway company.
D. A. Idle

Below left: An elderly ex-Midland 0-6-0 Class 2F, possibly No 58116 (LMS No 22902), shunts the yard at Haverthwaite on 4 May 1963. *Dr M. J. Andrews*

Bottom left: It would be hard to tell that, not all that long ago, a large ironworks existed here — Millom ironworks, built on vast deposits of high grade haematite iron ore. It was barely visible from the main line. Ex-LMS Class 4F 0-6-0 No 44311 has probably just arrived with a trainload of limestone on 14 July 1966. The locomotive will soon be joining the ironworks on the scrap heap; they closed in 1968. *RCTS*

Right: A lonely outpost in bleak territory? It might have seemed so if you had just arrived here from Ingleton and were waiting for a connection to Carlisle or Scotland. This is Low Gill, Westmorland, on a sunny day in about 1950 not long before it closed. The West Coast main line is at the other side of the island platform. The pair of lines in the centre are from Ingleton via Sedbergh. At one time this was the route that gave the earliest arrival in Glasgow from Leeds. But it was not for the faint-hearted. The route from Clapham and Ingleton was still open as a very useful diversionary route whilst I was at Barrow, but closed soon afterwards.
Author's Collection

9.0pm, to spend the night at the Tufton Arms Hotel. Fortunately they were still serving dinner. It was quiet there, as one would expect at the end of November.

Next morning, a beautiful sunny morning, I caught the train to Garsdale accompanied by District Inspector McHaffie, to visit the porter in his own home. He had just retired after over 50 years' service, all of it at Garsdale, so he said. He was over 70 years old and hadn't wanted to retire earlier, nor had he ever wanted to leave Garsdale. He and his wife were perfectly happy there. (There's a moral there somewhere.) He remembered well both the Hawes Junction (Garsdale) and Ais Gill accidents of 1910 and 1913 respectively and had a host of stories to tell. These days I would have taken along a tape recorder.

He lived in one of the row of cottages at the station and his wife received us with old world courtesy. On the dining room table there was a white tablecloth laid with best china and home-made cakes and delicacies. We sat and chatted for hours and I was quite touched. For them, the visit of the Assistant Superintendent from headquarters was a major event and I was glad that I had gone to present the old porter's certificate in person, rather than just posting it to his stationmaster. Duty done, I said my goodbyes and went forward to Horton in Ribblesdale, leaning over the rail of the brake van at the back of the local pick-up goods and surveying the scenery. And to think I was being paid for doing this! Arriving at Horton I had a tour of the local quarries, which in those days provided quite a lot of rail traffic. My guide was the area commercial representative for quarries and we finished up in Settle where it was time for a very late lunch. Finally, he took me to Clapham for a train to Carnforth, and thence to Barrow. Quite a round trip, but I was certainly learning the parish.

I Discover High Life in the Officers' Special
The inspection saloon belonged to the District Engineer but he lent it to us so that we could get round the parish more easily. The vehicle consisted of a saloon with table and chairs at each end, whilst in the centre were the toilet and the galley (a fully equipped kitchen for long days out). The galley was manned by an engineer's man who was a sort of cook/butler, and he was very good at his job. We were always well dined and watered. The saloon could either be propelled or drawn but, if it was being propelled, someone had to sit at the front window ready to sound the horn, or even to apply the brake. There was also a bell code buzzer to the footplate. The saloon was an excellent way of seeing the lineside — especially signals, crossover roads, level crossings of all types and wayside sidings and signalboxes. We had a lovely sunny autumn day for a saloon tour with the Superintendent and one or two assistants to Carnforth and the Lakeside branch. Bob loved to push the boat out and we had lunch at the Newby Bridge Hotel rather than on the saloon. The mountains looked splendid. What a way of earning a living!

Time to Take Charge
By Monday 2 December I had acquired a reasonable knowledge of the Division and took charge. Each morning the Divisions had a conference with the Line Office to discuss the current traffic position and any shortages of power or men etc. You also had to be prepared to answer for any shortcomings in train performance during the previous 24 hours.

The Control Office prepared all the necessary reports, so it was quite straightforward.

The following day we had the annual awards for the Best Kept Station and the Best Station Garden (for which Settle was always a strong contender). The function that year was held at the Olde England Hotel, Windermere, and all stationmasters attended, so it was quite a big gathering and a useful forum for a pep-talk or general discussion about issues of concern to stationmasters. This was followed by lunch. But it was now time to get down to some office work, of which there was plenty in the in-tray. However, a few days later I had a trip by freight train to Millom ironworks with Frank Upton. I don't remember much about it, and the ironworks closed a few years later. They were probably old-fashioned, and the iron ore on which they depended had always been mined locally, so perhaps it was becoming exhausted. I have been back to the site many times on bird-watching expeditions.

Things that go Bump in the Night

With 150 miles of main line over Shap and Ais Gill, accidents on those wild routes and heavy gradients were not uncommon, but nearly all of them concerned freight train derailments, especially on the downhill stretches. It was a period when such derailments were becoming more common and a source of some concern. Freight trains had run at speeds of up to 60mph for many years without any problems, but suddenly for some unexplained reason they had started to come off the rails at high speeds. The maximum permitted speeds had been reduced but it hadn't cured the problem.

I shared the 'On Call' duties with the Superintendent, and I was 'On Call' on 7 April 1964 when the phone rang just after 4.0am. It was the Control Office ringing to say that the 8.45pm Class 4 fitted freight from Manchester Ancoats to Carlisle had become derailed near Howe & Co's Sidings signalbox, just a few miles south of Carlisle and was blocking all roads. It's interesting how railwaymen have always referred to railway lines as roads, and probably still do. It's a shortening of the original name for railways as railroads.

The Control had swung into action and had started to divert trains away from the Midland line, but the two night expresses from St Pancras were trapped. The Edinburgh sleeper had been right behind the freight train and was stopped at

Armathwaite, only ten miles short of Carlisle. The engine ran round the train and took it back to Hellifield, ran round again, and was diverted to Carlisle via the Low Gill branch (which fortunately was still available), arriving in Carlisle nearly four hours late. The Glasgow sleeper was stopped at Appleby and was similarly dealt with. It lost 145 minutes.

The Kingmoor steam crane was ordered out straight away and arrived on site at 7.27am. Owing to the extent of the derailment the Skipton steam crane was also ordered out so that rerailing and clearance of the line could be undertaken from both ends of the site simultaneously. It was an education to see the breakdown gangs at work. They were well experienced in dealing with derailed freight trains and got on with it with the minimum of fuss as they had always done. The priority in those days was to get on with clearance of the line as quickly as possible so that the permanent-way engineer could then move in to restore the track and allow the line to be opened to traffic. This was the overriding priority — get the line reopened as soon as possible and no messing about.

I Make my Way There

One of my divisional inspectors gave me a lift from home to the site — a lovely run from home along Windermere and over Kirkstone Pass — and we arrived on site to be confronted by a heap of wreckage. The rear portion of the train, consisting of 16 vehicles and a brake van, had been derailed. Five were lying on their sides, two were upside down, and one van was in a field. The remainder were still more or less upright. It was a typical freight train derailment. The local movements inspector had been quickly on the scene and had ensured that protection had been carried out and that the safety of the line had been secured.

I was joined pretty quickly by colleagues from the P/Way and C&W departments and we set to work to find the cause. The permanent-way engineer examined the track leading up to the point of derailment and then made an assessment of the damage, and of the men and materials that he would need to repair it. The C&W engineer examined the wagons, and between us we identified the first wagon to have become derailed. It was a 12-ton empty shock-absorbing wagon.

A solitary British Transport policeman arrived from Carlisle to keep an eye on all the goods traffic that had been spilt from damaged vans and was lying around. We welcomed the presence of the police and regarded them as colleagues. They did not interfere in any way with the clearance of the line. I think they sometimes spent most of their time in the mess van which always accompanied the breakdown train, drinking cups of tea, but at least they were there if they were needed and we always tipped them off if the Inspector was on his way. We worked together as part of the railway family.

Feeding Arrangements

The mess van was accompanied by a fitter from the loco shed whose culinary expertise extended to keeping the kettle boiling and making sandwiches whose slices of bread were so thick that they could have been used to rerail the wagons. However, if spoken to nicely, mess van attendants would fry great platefuls of bacon and eggs and fried bread (white, of course), a sumptuous delicacy on a cold, wet morning after a long night's work. The word 'cholesterol' had not been invented in those innocent days and the breakdown crew would have reacted most unfavourably and with suitable invective if they had been offered muesli and yoghurt.

One of the most important duties of the operating department representatives on site was to ensure a plentiful supply of food. If the accident occurred out in the country a local farmer could usually be persuaded to part with quantities of ham, eggs and milk for a consideration (railwaymen were resourceful and inventive in those days and possibly still are) and one could usually obtain other supplies from a village shop. It was important to keep the breakdown crew well fed and happy so that they got the line cleared as quickly as possible.

This was achieved by 4.30pm the same afternoon, just over twelve hours after the derailment. The permanent-way people quickly got to work and reopened the up main line just after midnight and the Down main line at 3.20am, just in time for the 8.45pm from Ancoats! We had plenty of breakdown cranes in those days and plenty of motive power depots with the crane always in steam simmering away ready for instant use. Also plenty of fitters and shop staff who could be called on to turn out with the crane at short notice. It had always been like that. Everyone knew the routine and that made life a lot easier.

The Formal Inquiry

It was necessary to hold a formal inquiry into mainline derailments of this nature to identify the cause and consider whether changes of any sort should be made. Note well that it was not the purpose of the inquiry to apportion blame. The staff were aware of that and gave their evidence freely without the intervention of lawyers. They recognised that the purpose of the inquiry was to achieve a safer railway, which was in everyone's interests. Of course, one had to be aware of certain conventions. Firemen would nearly always support their drivers, and to a large extent guards would do the same, but I usually found that drivers were reliable and practical men, and straightforward under questioning.

Below: An ex-LMS Horwich 2-6-0, No 42878 from Springs Branch (8F), passes through Lancaster Castle station en route to Heysham at the head of a long semi-fitted freight train on 20 June 1964. *N. A. Machell*

Left: An almost unbelievable event but not entirely so, knowing the fearsome history of gales and storms at Ribblehead Viaduct. This was nature in one of its more playful moods. No one was hurt. This was the scene on the viaduct when day broke on Tuesday 8 December 1964. You couldn't have made it up, but none of the staff around seemed in the least concerned. *Author's Collection*

The inquiry was held two days later at Carlisle. It was the custom for the chair to be taken by the operating department, assisted by representatives from the various engineering departments concerned and from the locomotive running department. The witnesses had been assembled beforehand and were interviewed individually. In the case of this accident they consisted of the driver and fireman (from Lower Darwen Shed) of the derailed train, the guard (who came from Ashton Road depot, Manchester), the signalmen at Howe & Co's and Low House Crossing signalboxes, the local permanent-way inspector and the local ganger.

The train was 4L18 8.45pm from Ancoats to Carlisle and consisted of 32 vacuum fitted vehicles and a brakevan hauled by Class 9F 2-10-0 No 92161, a light load for such a powerful engine.

Its maximum permitted speed was 50mph although the line limit was 70mph. It appeared from signalbox records that the train was running between 55 and 60mph, but it was a dark night, the engine was not fitted with a speedometer and was very free running. In such circumstances it was very difficult for the driver to assess his speed accurately. The 17th vehicle was the first to become derailed and the train broke in two. The front portion ran forward for 580yd with the last two vehicles derailed before it came to a stand. Fortunately none of the traincrew suffered any injuries.

The C&W engineer had examined the first vehicle to become derailed and found that one of the springs was weak with almost an inch less camber than the diagonally opposite spring. This allowed a wheel to climb the outside rail on the right-hand curve past Howe & Co's signalbox. There was also a very slight track defect just before the point of derailment, but it was well inside laid down tolerances. This pattern of fairly minor defects in track and wagon combined with a train travelling at just above the maximum permitted speed was dynamite. The number of derailments each year had been hovering around the 200 mark for many years. Most of them were at low speed and a lot were on goods lines. Now we were beginning to see an alarming increase in the number of freight train derailments, many of them at speeds of 40/50mph travelling on main lines. The annual total reached a peak of 383 in 1969 but fell sharply afterwards, mainly because the maximum permitted speed of freight trains was reduced to 45mph. Wagon maintenance was also improved. It was a busy period for crash investigators and breakdown traincrews.

The Joint Inquiry report had to be agreed, and the conclusion had to be signed by all the departmental representatives on the panel. The panel was required to reach a conclusion based on the evidence, and there could be no ifs or buts. The report was then sent to Line Office, who ultimately passed it on to the Railway Inspectorate. The RI would already have decided whether or not to hold an inquiry from the initial reports which were sent to them, but they would not normally hold one until they had received the Joint Inquiry report. The RI did not normally hold inquires into freight train derailments unless passenger trains were involved also.

An Exciting Night at Ribblehead
However, not all mishaps resulted from such causes as the one at Howe & Co's Sidings. On Monday 7 December 1964 there was a strong south-westerly gale accompanied by heavy rain which continued into the night. Barrow sticks out into the Irish Sea and gets the full force of sou'westers. The wind howled around the house and rain lashed on the windows. Sleep was punctuated by the sound of crashing glass as the greenhouse was gradually demolished. I was not at all surprised to be woken at 4.0am (again!) by the sound of the telephone. This was before the era of bedside phones and central heating, and I crept downstairs in my dressing gown, standing shivering by the phone in the hall as the Control Office gave me a piece of quite astonishing news. 'You won't believe this,' said the voice of the Deputy Chief Controller at the other end of the line. 'I'm not having you on, but four or five brand-new motor cars are lying upside down on the Up line on Ribblehead viaduct. They've blown off the Luton-Bathgate car-carrier.'

I got dressed, had a quick cup of tea, then made my way to the office with difficulty against the howling gale, and picked up one of the pool cars. I then set off in the pitch dark to drive to Ribblehead along flooded roads littered with tree branches. It was a hair-raising drive and I didn't get to Ribblehead until 7.15am, just as dawn was breaking. I was met by the Stationmaster and taken into his cosy kitchen for a cup of tea. I expect his wife offered me breakfast too, but there was work to be done. I wanted to see this remarkable event for myself but I needn't have rushed. The Skipton steam crane didn't arrive on site until 10.0am because it had to collect some flat wagons on which to load the cars. By that time the wind had abated and the rain had ceased. The thought did enter our heads of just dumping the cars over the side of the viaduct, but there was no great urgency to clear the line and the National Park might have objected. Mornings were a fairly quiet time and trains were being diverted via Ingleton and Low Gill. Thank goodness we still had that facility; it closed shortly afterwards. TV crews came along during the morning and there was a photograph in one of the newspapers.

The line was cleared by 2.0pm and I had another cup of tea, c/o the Stationmaster's wife, before setting off for Ais Gill. The car train had been parked in the loop waiting for a loading inspector to come along and satisfy himself that all the cars were sufficiently secure. They were. I expect I had another cup of tea with the signalman. I made a

Below: A Stanier Class 5 4-6-0, No 45013, drifts through Ribblehead with what looks like the pick-up goods, calling as required. *Author's Collection*

Left: The first day of July 1964: another fine, clear and sunny day on the S&C. Wild Boar Fell fills the background as a Type 2 diesel, No D7581, passes Ais Gill with the 8.05am all-stations from Carlisle to Hellifield. If you miss it, there isn't another one until 4.37pm. *Author*

point of never refusing a cup of tea because you never knew where the next one was coming from in such a far-flung empire. All part of the railway family.

The Formal Inquiry — Events of the Night are Recalled

We had the formal inquiry three days later, at Skipton. We chose Skipton because it was easier of access for the witnesses. Our main concern was the method of securing the cars at Luton and we had the assistance of loading experts from the goods department. The cars had been secured only by metal chocks under the wheels, and they recommended suitable changes. The signalmen at Blea Moor, Dent and Garsdale were also witnesses and, so far as I recall, the signalman at Blea Moor had been peering out of his rain-streaked windows to observe the train go by and had noticed some gaps among the cars on the train. His suspicions were aroused and he phoned his colleague at Dent to have a good look at the train as it went by. The signalman there definitely spotted some gaps among the cars and arranged to have the train stopped at Garsdale for examination. I can't recall whether the signalmen were rewarded for their vigilance and quick thinking but they certainly should have been. If an Up train had run into those cars the consequences can best be imagined. The signalman at Blea Moor said that he had never known such a wild night in all his experience.

One can imagine the scene at Garsdale. The wind was still howling and the rain was still lashing down. Garsdale can be a bleak spot, halfway up the fellside and fully exposed to westerly gales. The signalman kept his signals at Danger, and when the train arrived he explained the situation to the driver,

who sent his secondman to fetch the guard and examine the train. They reported back that there were indeed gaps on the train and that there had been no gaps when the guard had joined the train at Leeds. So where were the cars? Signalmen further back along the line were telephoned to discover whether they had noticed anything amiss, but they hadn't, so it was necessary to start examining the line from Blea Moor back towards Settle.

The Stationmaster at Ribblehead didn't have far to walk before he discovered the cars. He was a brave man to venture on to that viaduct in the pitch dark and with the gale threatening to pluck him off it and hurl him hundreds of feet onto the bleak moorland below. But you had to be made of stern stuff to be a stationmaster on the wilder parts of the S&C. I wonder if there is any record of that night's stirring events in the new Heritage Centre at Ribblehead station. Some parts of that night's saga have had to be recalled from memory, with the help of Derek Soames, a retired signalman from Settle Junction who worked at Hellifield North signalbox at the time.

On the day of the Joint Inquiry we had steak and kidney pudding for lunch in Brown Muff's café in the High Street at Skipton. At these inquiries we always had two shorthand typists working in rotation because all the evidence was taken down verbatim and signed by the staff concerned as a true record. This avoided arguments afterwards. By coincidence, as Christmas was approaching, and to persuade the diners to part with some of their cash buying presents, models were parading around the restaurant in nighties and underwear. Fine for the typists, but it quite put us off our steak and kidney pud.

Fifteen

MORE TALES OF A HAPPY LIFE IN THE BARROW DIVISION 1963/65

Plans for the Closure of the Settle & Carlisle (S&C) Line as a Through Route

Almost the first day I arrived at Barrow I was shown a signalling plan for the closure of the S&C between Appleby and Ribblehead, which was of course the most expensive part of the line to maintain with its viaducts and tunnels. There was also very little passenger or freight traffic at the intermediate stations between Appleby and Ribblehead. Carlisle to Appleby would become a dead-end branch with a minimum passenger service, but there was quite a bit of freight traffic at Kirkby Thore and Long Meg. The military authorities also wanted access to their depot at Warcop. At the other end of the line, access would still be required to the quarries in the Horton area and at Ribblehead.

However, the Low Gill line (between Clapham and Low Gill) was allowed to close, which made the retention of the S&C more important as a diversionary route. Any plans for closure of the S&C were deferred so that it could be used as a diversionary route during the planned electrification of the West Coast main line, which was expected to follow from the completion of the Euston to Manchester and Liverpool section. However, when the route over Shap was relaid, no catch points were provided because they would be unnecessary in a few years' time when all loose-coupled wagons had been withdrawn. In the meantime, any Anglo-Scottish freight trains conveying loose-coupled wagons would have to travel via the S&C, and this continued for some years after completion of electrification to Glasgow

in 1974. The end of this story is well known, but hindsight is a wonderful thing. Who would have known of the huge resurgence of the line, many years later? So we must not criticise railway managers of that era, who were under orders from the government to reduce the subsidy.

A Birthday Treat

By 1963, the steam scene on the main lines was mainly Pacifics, 'Scots', 'Jubilees' and 'Patriots', Class 5s and 'Britannias'. Apart from Pacifics, any of these could be seen at Barrow. We now lived at Roose, the first station out of Barrow, in a house whose garden ran down to the railway. My young son loved it. The railway line was at a lower level than the house, but if you stood on the lavatory seat you could peer through the bathroom window and just make out the engine's number. The 7.0am from Barrow to Manchester usually had a 'namer' and its passing coincided with a visit to the bathroom by young son. Fortuitously the 8.34pm to London St Pancras, another 'namer', usually coincided with bedtime.

'Where would you like to go for your birthday?' I asked. 'Please,' he said eagerly, 'Can we go to Scout Green and watch the expresses?' His birthday is in July, so I made the trip coincide with the Saturday of the return Glasgow Fair traffic. Even as late as 1964, Glasgow Fair produced an enormous number of specials to London, Blackpool, Morecambe and other destinations, returning a fortnight later. Coupled with the normal summer reliefs and the summer dated extras, this resulted in virtually a continuous procession of

Above: Unusual power for a freight train: LMS Standard Class 2P 4-4-0 No 40695, a Barrow engine, engages in a most unlikely spot of shunting at Plumpton Junction in around 1960. *Dr M. J. Andrews*

Below: A 'Britannia' class Pacific, No 70022 *Tornado*, has just passed Furness Abbey, and in a couple of minutes will be passing the bottom of my garden, en route to Barrow in around 1964. *RCTS*

Above: A splendidly-clean 'Jubilee', No 45695 *Minotaur,* takes the Keswick three-coach portion of the 'Lakes Express' past Hay Fell, just north of Oxenholme, on 12 July 1963. *Derek Cross*

Below: A Stanier Pacific, No 46237 *City of Bristol,* passes Tebay's Down starting signal on its way north with a Down parcels train on Saturday 4 July 1964. *Author*

Above: On 9 September 1966, the photographer is at Scout Green, a little further up the hill, to see a Class 8F 2-8-0, No 48526, being banked by a 2-6-4T, No 42134. *L. A. Nixon*

Below: A reminder of happier times: a commendably clean rebuilt 'Royal Scot', No 46136 *The Border Regiment*, works hard up the grade after leaving Carlisle with the Sunday express from Glasgow Central to Liverpool Exchange and Manchester Victoria in October 1963. *Peter J. Robinson*

Above: An historic picture, taken in September 1963, of the junction at Oxenholme, with access directly from the main line to the Windermere branch. This was later removed although access remains at the south end of the station. A Class 5 4-6-0 is approaching on the Up Main line. I saw my first streamliner here is the summer of 1938. Such excitement! *Author's Collection*

heavily loaded expresses toiling up Shap or hurtling down it. Many, indeed most, of them were steam-hauled. On another occasion we camped out at Scout Green on the Friday night. I can't remember whether we had much sleep, but it meant that the boys could start train-spotting as soon as it became daylight. Such days are now the stuff of memories. In many ways, the WCML over Shap in 1964 was still very much a prewar railway scene. It wouldn't be for much longer.

Not satisfied, the boys wanted to go to Ribblehead to see the expresses toiling up the Long Drag, so on Saturday 25 July 1964 we motored across there and saw Nos 45705 *Seahorse,* 45697 *Achilles* and 45658 *Keyes.* The latter 'Jubilee' spent all its life shedded at Holbeck. Then we spent three

hours at Hincaster, just south of Oxenholme, on the way back.

The entire division had a prewar air. Almost all the stations were still open. Manual signalboxes and Absolute Block reigned supreme. Apart from 'Britannias' and 'Clans' on the main lines, almost all the engines belonged to the LMS era, especially at Barrow and around the coast line, with plenty of Standard Class 4F 0-6-0s and Standard 0-6-0Ts.

West Cumberland

Almost the whole of the Cumbrian coast line passed through an area of considerable interest to the student of industrial archaeology, based on iron ore. Huge deposits of haematite iron ore of very high quality, and said to be among the largest in the world at the time, were discovered in various places throughout the area in the mid-19th century, and these, coupled with locally available supplies of coal and limestone, led to the very rapid and intensive development of iron and steel making in the area. This in turn led to the development of a railway system to serve the industry, resulting in a tangle of lines and branches, some of which were built by independent concerns. Barrow itself

Above: A undated general view of Moor Row station, the signalbox, the yard, and the engine sheds on the left. A very elderly-looking goods engine is approaching the signalbox. The whole layout here was the property of the Whitehaven, Cleator & Egremont Joint Railway, a wholly-owned enterprise of the Furness and LNWR railways. In its heyday before the First World War, this whole area was a very complex network of different companies, with some duplication.
Author's Collection

Below: A little further along, beyond the buildings, the complexity of routes can be appreciated. The line curving round to the right leads to Sellafield, the line straight ahead leads to Frizington and Rowrah, whilst the line curving round to the left leads to Workington over the metals of the Cleator & Workington Junction Railway. Judging by the wagons, this could be a 1950s photograph, although it is undated.
Dr M. J. Andrews

Above: A photograph taken on 7 May 1963 shows an LMS Ivatt Class 4 2-6-0, No 43004, at Cleator Moor goods station with a mineral train from Rowrah to Moor Row. *N. A. Machell*

became an important industrial town and port almost overnight. The decline came almost as quickly, and by the 1930s much of the area was one of the most seriously depressed parts of Britain.

However, by 1963 when I went to the Barrow Division, many of these lines and branches were still in situ, although some saw little use, but they were of great interest, especially in the hinterland of Workington and Whitehaven. There were still five working collieries in that area, but steel-making was more or less confined to the great steelworks at Workington. Further south, Barrow ironworks had closed a couple of years earlier, and Barrow's prosperity now seemed to depend on the building of nuclear-powered submarines. Millom ironworks, based on the Hodbarrow mine deposits of iron ore, were still in business, but they too were to close in 1968. Now, Hodbarrow is an RSPB bird reserve. The birds seem to revel in the remnants of the industry.

Travelling Around the Division by Train

The Barrow Division contained some of the finest countryside in Britain, but communications across the area from Barrow were poor. A day in Carlisle meant the 7.0am from Barrow, changing at Carnforth into the 6.0am from Warrington and arriving in Carlisle at 9.57am. The return journey was usually on the Perth-Euston leaving Carlisle at 4.0pm and changing at Lancaster, arriving in Barrow at 7.3pm if you were lucky. The train from Lancaster was usually in the incapable hands of one of the notorious D5700s, those Metro-Vick Co-Bos which were hopelessly unreliable. The whole class of 20, built in 1958/59, had been dumped on Barrow in 1962, Barrow being the farthest-flung corner of the LM empire. Quite clearly the authorities didn't dare risk a scandal by just scrapping them, so they sent them to where they thought they could cause the least harm.

Appointments at Carlisle meant a 12-hour day, of which six were spent travelling. It was marvellous for a railway enthusiast, and scenically it was one continuous delight. It was also a good way of seeing what the railway was doing, so it was by no means time wasted. It could be seen even better from the front end if the train happened to be diesel-hauled and I had many such journeys over the

WCML on one of the EE Type 4s, the D200s. Steam enthusiasts will not forgive me, but travelling as a passenger on a steam loco on an express was not one of my favourite activities. You couldn't see anything, it was too noisy to talk, you had to keep jumping out of the way of the fireman, and you were frozen at one side and scorched at the other. It was also an advantage to be dressed for the job. By 1964 many steam locos were being run down ready for scrapping and were rough riders. So the buffet car won, with afternoon tea at 2s/3d.

Travelling Around the Division by Car

As an alternative, especially if you were being accompanied by non-operating types who found train travel less exciting than you did yourself, there was always the car. There were various routes by car from Barrow to Carlisle and all of them passed through the heart of the Lake District, but the favourite was probably via Windermere, over Kirkstone Pass to Patterdale, then along Ullswater and the back roads to Carlisle. Except during the heart of the tourist season it could easily be done in less than two hours. Stations on the S&C were even less accessible and if there were two or three places to be visited, a car was almost essential.

As an example — on one occasion I left home at 7.30am, called at Oxenholme, Tebay, Shap, Kirkby Stephen, Appleby, Penrith and some of the stations on the Cockermouth, Keswick & Penrith (CK&P). I had a meal near Cockermouth, then set off for home. It was now getting dark (it was 18 September) and I decided to make for home over the fells. It was a thrilling and anxious journey on a pitch-dark night on a narrow, winding mountain road, but it was quicker than sticking to the main road which wandered all around the coast. I did wonder what I should do if the car conked out on one of the more remote stretches. Our pool cars were not 100% reliable but this one kept going and got me home at 10.0pm. We used Humber Hawks, which were splendid, elegant vehicles no longer required elsewhere on the Region, so Barrow got them.

Doing it the Hard Way

On another occasion I needed to visit two or three places on the S&C, so I left home after tea and spent the night at an hotel in Carlisle. Next morning, with the sun rising into a clear blue sky, I met one of my inspectors and we travelled in the brake van of the local pick-up to Appleby, then crossed over to the old North Eastern line and proceeded to Warcop, which was an army depot, and on past Kirkby Stephen to the end of the line at Hartley Quarry. Quarry traffic had ceased and that end of the line was soon lifted, so I was glad to have had the chance to revisit it for the last time. We were back at Appleby in time for the Up 'Waverley' so, greatly daring, I decided that I would have a footplate trip to Hellifield on one of the ex-LNER Pacifics which had been transferred to Holbeck and were held in high regard as good riders. Holbeck had about eight of them at one time, both 'A1s' and 'A3s'. They tended to be used indiscriminately on both passenger and freight jobs, especially as time went by and diesels become more common. However, to return to my story, when the train ran into Appleby I saw that there were already four people on the footplate of the 'A1', and I rapidly decided that I would not be welcome. Instead, I remained at Appleby and visited the Express Dairies Depot. For many years they had sent several milk tanks to London every day and at one time these were attached to the rear of the 4.0pm Glasgow to Leeds, but in recent years they had been worked into Carlisle to join the tanks from Aspatria.

The Divisional Organisation on the London Midland Region

In many ways, the Divisional HQ was in the wrong place. Carlisle would have been more appropriate, especially from an operating point of view, and most of the Division was far more accessible from Carlisle than from Barrow, but for commercial and political reasons Barrow was chosen. The Division had been created in 1963 with the fusion of the former District Traffic Offices at Carlisle and Barrow, as part of the LM Region's latest reorganisation, but it was fairly clear that the Barrow Division could only continue to exist until all the proposed rationalisation and closure schemes of both passenger and goods depots had been achieved. Barrow was merged with the Preston Division not long after I left, and Preston itself was merged with Manchester in due course. Life was never boring in railway management circles. It has not changed. But such changes are expensive.

When I went to Barrow in October 1963 most of the branches were still open too, including Silloth, the Lakeside branch, and the whole of the

Cockermouth, Keswick & Penrith. The latter was a jewel and even had through coaches to Euston during the summer months, starting from Workington. Can you imagine that now? Workington, with through coaches to Euston (and St Pancras) both via Barrow and via Penrith. Look at it now. *Sic transit gloria mundi* and a half! The branches closed quite soon afterwards, victims of the government's demands for economy. Beeching wasn't to blame, although he shouldered most of it. It was government policy and he was just the agent. No one could foresee the resurgence of the railways and the wish that we hadn't closed Penrith-Keswick.

Windermere had excellent mainline services, with through trains to Liverpool and Manchester, as well as a 9.25am to Euston, the summer-only 'Lakes Express' at 11.5am and an 8.30pm to St Pancras via

Above: In the early 1960s, the Eastern Region transferred a number of their Pacifics, made redundant by the introduction of diesels on the East Coast main line expresses, to work over the Settle & Carlisle line on the Anglo-Scottish expresses. They were also put to more mundane use, as seen here with Class A1 No 60154 *Bon Accord* at the head of a Class D Carlisle to Stourton freight, passing Delaney's Sidings signalbox on 8 August 1965. These sidings, situated between Skipton and Gargrave, served a local quarry. *Author's Collection*

Below: A Workington-based LMS Ivatt Class 2 2-6-0, No 46432, runs into Keswick station past Keswick No1 signalbox. There are those who believe strongly that the Penrith to Keswick portion of the route should not have been closed. *RCTS*

Crewe (the Barrow/Windermere sleeper was temporarily diverted to St Pancras during the modernisation and electrification of the southern part of the WCML). Those through services were killed off by electrification of the main line, which precluded passenger-friendly multi-portion trains, although Windermere now has a very good DMU service to Manchester and its airport.

The Settle-Carlisle line stations had never had a frequent service; indeed, there were only two all-stations trains between Hellifield and Carlisle, which was probably sufficient for the sparse traffic. However, they provided a tremendous variety of motive power, both steam and diesel. 'Clans' were often seen. They were probably the least successful of all the BR steam locos, but they were quite sufficient for three coaches on an all-stations train. The local stations had been proposed for closure under the Beeching plans, but the Minister refused to give his consent. They were closed later, but the station buildings and platforms remained and were used in due course by the 'Dalesrail' weekend trains. Most of them were reopened and refurbished in grand style under Railtrack, and they now have the most frequent service they have ever had.

Settle had the 'Waverley' in both directions and the 4.10pm from Glasgow (St Enoch, of course). Appleby did even better; it had the St Pancras to Edinburgh Waverley night sleeper in both directions and the 10.25am Leeds to Glasgow as well. One of life's delights was to travel back from Glasgow on the 4.10pm and have dinner in the dining car after it left Carlisle. As I recalled earlier, the diner was a 12-wheeler of LMS vintage, a splendid vehicle with a splendid crew who looked after you well. Imagine sitting in a warm and comfortable train feeding your inner self with a good meal, washed down with half a bottle of good wine, whilst feasting your eyes on the wild surroundings as the train heaved itself up Mallerstang. On a dirty night, with the rain lashing down, the contrast between the outside world and the warm, comfortable coach with its contented and

Below: A 'Jubilee' 4-6-0, No 45729 *Furious*, lives up to its name as it storms past Stainforth Sidings signalbox, north of Settle, with a Down express. The sidings served a large, now closed, quarry. *Author's Collection*

A Railwayman's Odyssey

well-fed passengers was enormous. On a lovely summer evening with the setting sun highlighting the tops of the Pennines in all their rich colours it was truly a delight.

The Level Crossing Problem

Level crossings have always been the bane of the operator's life, expensive to man and always a source of potential danger. Fortunately there were only three public ones on the WCML and the S&C, but there were plenty on the coast line, of infinite variety and a source of never-ending delight to a student of level crossings. Level crossings worked from signalboxes and protected by fixed signals were reasonably safe, but those which were worked by crossing keepers who lived in a cottage next to the crossing were less so. The real mavericks were those private level crossings known as occupation crossings which had only had light traffic but which for some reason had seen a sudden increase in use by heavy road vehicles. There was one at Waterslack Quarry whose only access was over the railway line between Silverdale and Arnside. We began to receive reports from engine drivers about near misses and something had to be done quickly. A meeting was arranged with the quarry owner and we came to an agreement as to the arrangements needed for ensuring safety. Occupation crossing 'owners' are responsible for the safe use of the crossing, but we wanted to be sure that our trains and passengers were safe.

The quarry owner was a rough and ready sort of chap, but he talked sense and at the end of the meeting he said, 'Come on, I'll take you out for a meal. We'll go in my car.' It would have been churlish to refuse, so we followed him to his car. We couldn't believe our eyes. It was a spanking new Rolls-Royce. Such luxury! Nor did we go to the local pub, but to some posh hotel where the staff treated him with great reverence. He was obviously a good customer, and what is more, he knew his wine.

The Best Kept Station and the Best Station Garden, Competitions

One of the more arcane customs of the railway was the Best Kept Station Competition, and all the stations in the Division had to enter. There was also the Best Station Garden competition, but this was voluntary. For judging purposes all stations had to be visited twice a year, in April/May and in August/September, and it was customary to use the

Below: An 'Austerity' 2-8-0 heads a mixed freight through Ulverston, heading towards Carnforth. *Dr M. J. Andrews*

inspection saloon for this purpose. It couldn't really have been done otherwise. Judging 80 stations in such a far-flung empire was no easy task, and even working out the programme was a work of art to avoid too much back-tracking.

In 1964 it took three days at the beginning of September, setting off at about 8.0am each morning. The Divisional Superintendent had just been promoted and I was acting in the vacancy, so I was in charge of all the arrangements. Each day a number of other divisional officers and heads of section would come along because it was an excellent way of seeing the Division and meeting the outside staff. We were blessed with fine weather throughout. On Day 1 the saloon was propelled up the coast via Millom, Whitehaven, Workington and Maryport to Carlisle, calling at every station, depot, signalbox and level crossing en route. It was hard, tiring work but the views were superb. The Lake District mountains stood out in all their impressive array and across the sea the Isle of Man was clearly visible. We could have sold tickets for the trip at £50 a time. The saloon was equipped with a kitchen and a steward, and we put ourselves away into a siding somewhere for a hot lunch, making sure that the train crew and the local Stationmaster had their share. At Carlisle we called it a day and came home non-stop via the WCML and Carnforth. It wasn't

politic to visit the Silloth branch; it closed the following weekend.

On Day 2 our route took us along the coast to Carnforth, then down the WCML to Oxenholme and Windermere. The fine LNWR signalbox at the latter had a superb view across the lake to the Langdale Pikes. Windermere was quite a big station in those days, with plenty of sidings for stabling coaches. Back to Oxenholme, then down the WCML again to Penrith before the *pièce de résistance* — all the way along the CK&P, under the shadow of Blencathra and Skiddaw to Keswick, then along the shore of Bassenthwaite Lake to Workington; a superb journey and one which wouldn't be available for much longer.

Day 3 took us to the S&C, starting off at Settle. The Stationmaster, Mr Taylor, was a gardening expert and won the competition every year. He told us that he planted out 6,000 bedding plants and I could believe it as I surveyed the platforms. It was a long day but we were well fed and watered, with a noggin or two on the way home when the day's work was over. I kept pinching myself to make sure that I wasn't dreaming it all.

The awards took place later in the year at the Pheasant Inn, Bassenthwaite, where all the stationmasters and other local officials assembled. I didn't count them but it was quite a gathering.

A Railwayman's Odyssey

I suppose it was an expensive event but it was a social gathering too and an encouragement for those who maintained a station garden mostly at their own expense and in their own time.

It was also the end of an era, a glorious end. Change was coming rapidly. Diesels were replacing steam in ever-increasing numbers, freight was declining, branch lines and local stations were closing, stationmasters were being replaced by station managers and area managers with larger areas of responsibility, and economy was the watchword of the day. But it was great while it lasted. However, there was a brave new world to come, full of interest and excitement (and challenges). New pastures beckoned. But I doubt that there would ever again be a period of such delight as running the Barrow Division.

Below left: A Fowler Class 4 parallel-boilered 2-6-4T, No 42319, comes off the Arnside Viaduct and approaches Arnside station with the 1.20pm from Barrow to Crewe on 5 July 1963.
G. T. Robinson

Above: Settle Junction and signalbox, with the line to Morecambe bearing left under the bridge and the line to Carlisle bearing round to the right. Undated. *Courtesy John W. Holroyd*

Below: John Taylor, Stationmaster at Settle, was again the winner of the station garden competition. He won the competition every year helped, no doubt, by his wife. The presentations were held at the Pheasant Hotel, Bassenthwaite. *Author*

Left: A few years earlier I had been making my way back from Glasgow Central and, as usual in those days, one walked up to the front end to see what was on that day. Very suitably, it was a Stanier Pacific, No 46243 *City of Lancaster,* a Crewe North engine, at the head of the 'Mid-day Scot'. For some reason that year, it had been retimed to depart at 3.0pm, which was not a success. After departure I walked down the train to see how many passengers we had. There were twelve! *Author*

Below: I can't recall any suggestion that the Waverley route was under threat whilst I was at Barrow; in fact, it was a main freight route from east Scotland to northwest England via the newly-built Millerhill Yard and the equally new Kingmoor Yard. A Thompson 'B1' 4-6-0, No 61354, a St. Margaret's (64A) engine, in fine condition, leaves Galashiels on a train from Edinburgh Waverley to Hawick on 23 July 1964. *(no attribution)*

A Railwayman's Odyssey

Sixteen

BARROW TO NOTTINGHAM 1965 — FROM THE FRINGE TO THE CENTRE

Tying Up the Loose Ends

I hadn't been at Barrow for all that long, but clearly the powers-that-be thought that I was enjoying myself too much and needed to get my hands dirty. It wasn't really true — we were busy not only with the normal day-to-day work of running a widespread division but also with implementing the many changes that were coming along. However, it was 'intimated' to me that I ought to be looking ahead to working in a larger Division, and it just happened that a vacancy had suddenly arisen in the Nottingham Division for the Assistant Movements Superintendent, owing to the untimely death of the incumbent. The same job but in a higher grade, and on my old stamping ground — the Midland line. It was an opportunity too good to miss, so I 'intimated' in turn that I was willing to be considered for the position. That was the beginning of January 1965,

It was a busy time at Barrow. On 4 January I went to Line HQ at Manchester to discuss new arrangements for controlling the movement and disposition of diesels. On the 7th I went to Carlisle for a meeting with the Scottish Region about the timings for the block trainloads of limestone from new Shap Quarry at Hardendale to the new Ravenscraig steelworks at Motherwell, based on the daily tonnage to be moved, the maximum capacity of a loaded train over that route, the number of wagons and trains needed, and the timings to fit in with loading and unloading arrangements at the two ends. Quite complicated. Train paths then needed to be organised by the Timing Offices at Crewe and Glasgow. It was

exciting to be dealing with new traffic, and I had already had a visit to Ravenscraig to be shown round by the local rail manager and the steelworks manager. Hardendale Quarry is still in business, but sadly the steelworks have long gone.

Proposals to withdraw the local passenger train services between Crewe and Carlisle

To end a busy week I attended a meeting at Preston to discuss with the various staff Representatives concerned, under the Joint Consultation procedures, the withdrawal of local passenger train services between Crewe and Carlisle, and the closure of the stations concerned. In my case, that involved the stations at Milnthorpe, Tebay and Shap, which had only a limited service in any case. At this stage the consultation procedures were mainly concerned with the arrangements made for dealing with the redundant staff, and the Personnel Department had already taken the necessary steps. So, apart from the obligatory denunciation of management by the staff representatives, the whole thing was over quite quickly, in order to enable the staff reps to get their trains home. I got home 2½ hours late — the loco pulled the train in two at Lancaster, then failed at Furness Abbey. Needless to say, it was a Metro-Vick Co-Bo, not one of BR's best diesel designs.

Closure of several Signalboxes on the Settle & Carlisle line

There was something even more interesting the following week. I had been reviewing the need for all the signalboxes on the S&C line, and had

Left: Three northbound mainline trains served Tebay — the 6.0am Warrington to Carlisle (probably the old parliamentary train), the 9.25am Crewe to Aberdeen and the 10.40am from Euston to Windermere and Carlisle (the erstwhile 'Lakes' express). There was a motive power depot here, mainly to provide bank engines to northbound trains ascending the four miles at 1 in 75 to Shap. The shed is behind the wall on the left. The line curving in on the right is the old North Eastern branch from Kirkby Stephen. The train in the photograph has Pacific power. *Author's Collection*

Below: Farewell to the delights of the Barrow Division, symbolised by this delightful picture of a two-car DMU gently making its way down the coast from Seascale to Barrow, and off to the grime and graft of the Nottingham Division. *W. A. Sharman*

A Railwayman's Odyssey

concluded that several could be closed in view of the decline in the number of trains using the route. Before implementing the closures I needed to discuss them with the Train Timing and Timetabling people at the Manchester Line Office to make sure that they could path all the trains without the signalboxes which were to be closed. They could, so the closures went ahead, after the appropriate staff consultation, of course. The savings in signalling costs were assessed at £15,000 a year, quite a tidy sum at the time.

Spanish Railway Officials Visit Carlisle New Yard

The following day I was engaged in showing a party of Spanish railwaymen round Carlisle New Yard. In those days we had something to show them; now it's the other way round. It wasn't a good day for such a venture — there were sleet and snow showers, then a gale sprang up and damaged

signalling equipment in the Carlisle area, as I was told by Carlisle Control at 1.30am and 5.0am. It was also very windy at Barrow — the remainder of my greenhouse blew down, and I could hear sounds of breaking glass whilst I was on the telephone, shivering in the cold. No central heating in those days. But the real excitement started on the Saturday morning.

Things Start Hotting Up

Mr Grainger, my Divisional Manager, informed me that the Line Manager, Derby, wanted to see me the following Tuesday, about the Nottingham job. So off I went on the 7.0am train via Manchester and met both Mr Cowell, the Line Manager, and Mr Bellamy, the Nottingham Division Movements Superintendent. They were both very friendly and looked pleased when I told them I was interested in the job. I didn't have long to wait for further developments. The following morning, Mr Gray, Divisional Manager, Nottingham, rang to ask when I could start, and the following morning there was a letter from him welcoming me to his Division. I felt that was a good start. It was arranged that I would transfer on Monday 1 February 1965.

It was a wrench to leave Barrow. I had made some good friends and I was sorry to leave them. I was also sorry to leave the Lake District. On the following Monday, after a meeting with the Atomic Energy people at Sellafield, I had a trip up Wasdale to say goodbye to the mountains. It was a lovely,

Below: I arrived at Nottingham too late to see one of the last Garratts, such as this one, at work, working north between Clay Cross and Hasland. They were all withdrawn quickly in the mid-1950s. No 47967 was the first of a batch of 30 built in 1930 by Beyer Peacock. Hasland (18C) had quite a good number, whilst Westhouses (18B) and Wellingborough (15A) had a few from time to time, but Toton (18A) had the lion's share. *G. H. Burton*

Left: One for Midland enthusiasts: the passenger service between Nottingham Midland and Mansfield/ Worksop was withdrawn in 1964, but before then ex-Midland Class 3F 0-6-0s were sometimes pressed into service on the route. No 43727 is seen in full cry passing the Midland signalbox at Basford Sidings with a train for Worksop. Note also the fine Midland signal on the Up line.
E. C. Haywood

Centre left: During the Second World War, quite a number of ex-London, Tilbury & Southend 4-4-2Ts were transferred to the Nottingham and Leeds areas, among others. No 41947 stands in Mansfield Town station with a train for Worksop.
J. Cupit

Below left: At the beginning of 1965, the Great Central route was still quite busy, but it wasn't to last. Here Class V2 2-6-2 No 60963 heads an empty stock train near East Leake. The 'V2s' were the LNER's and BR's maids-of-all-work.
T. G. Hepburn/ Rail Archive Stephenson

clear day, and the tops of Scafell and the Pike were streaked with snow glistening in the sun — it was beautiful. I seemed to spend the rest of my last week travelling around the Division saying goodbye to colleagues.

A New Venture Begins — the Area Covered by the Division

The Nottingham Division had three main lines, some secondary routes, and some cross-country routes. It contained the Midland main line from just south of Chesterfield as far as Loughborough, both direct via the Erewash Valley and Toton, and also via Nottingham. It also had the West of England main line from the junction at Clay Cross to just north of Tamworth, via Derby and Burton on Trent. And it had the Peak Forest route to Manchester from the junction at Ambergate to a point near Millers Dale, via Matlock and Bakewell.

The main cross-country route was Crewe-Stoke on Trent-Derby-Trent-Nottingham-Newark-Lincoln. It entered the Division between Uttoxeter and Tutbury and left it on the approach to Newark.

There were several important freight-only routes, such as the Leen Valley from Nottingham to beyond Mansfield, and the route from Kirkby on that line, to the Erewash Valley main line at Pye Bridge, and thence to the West of England main line via Butterley, joining it at Ambergate. There were also quite a lot of relatively short but interesting colliery branches. In addition, there were the former GN lines and yards around Nottingham, all ripe for closure.

I was surprised to find that part of the former Great Central main line was also in the Division. This ran from south of Chesterfield, past the major marshalling yards and engine shed at Annesley, and on through Nottingham Victoria station towards Leicester Central. My office was at Nottingham Victoria station, on the first floor of the clock tower, with a bay window overlooking the square in front of the station. It was quite a large, imposing office, with sloping desks and rows of drawers underneath on three sides. I opened one, and files almost burst out, as the drawer was full. I tried another one. The same. They were all the same. They were not labelled and there was no index. My predecessor, Reg North, had died on the job, and the office was more or less as he had left it. Fortunately, being in lodgings, I had time to sort through all the files,

and identify those that needed action. It was just the job for the dark evenings. The Nottingham Control Office and the Trains Sections were also located at Nottingham Victoria. There was still a Control Office at Derby, and a District Controller with support staff, but not for much longer.

My first priority was to get to know the Division, so I spent much of the first few weeks visiting the more important parts of it and meeting the local managers, and also making contact with the local firms, especially collieries, power stations and steelworks.

The Passenger Business

Nottingham was not a busy passenger division and the main flows of longer distance traffic were to London, to Manchester via Peak Forest, to Birmingham, the West Country and South Wales, and northwards to Sheffield, Leeds, Bradford, Scotland, York and the North East. Neither Derby nor Nottingham had a heavy commuter traffic.

Despite the changes caused by the former Midland main line being split between three Regions (London Midland, Eastern and North Eastern), the pattern of express passenger trains had not changed greatly since nationalisation. There were still four expresses from Bradford Forster Square to St Pancras, via Nottingham, Manton and Kettering: there was roughly an hourly service on the North East/South West route, from Newcastle, York, Bradford Forster Square, Leeds and Sheffield to Birmingham, Bristol and Cardiff. The time-honoured 'Devonian' still ran from Bradford Forster Square, but only as far as Paignton. The two daytime and two night-time Anglo-Scottish services still ran to and from St Pancras.

The main surprise was the expanded St Pancras–Manchester Central service via Leicester, Derby and the Peak Forest, which had been augmented to run almost hourly to allow the West Coast route service to be reduced whilst electrification work was taking place. This provided some interesting motive power at times, including 'Royal Scots'. There was also the 'Midland Pullman', a first class only diesel 'de luxe' express service from Manchester Central at 7.45am to St Pancras in 3hr 10min, returning from London at 6.10pm. It called only at Cheadle Heath.

The relatively few local and cross-country services were in the hands of the ubiquitous diesel multiple-units.

The express service on the former Great Central (GC) was, from memory, mainly in the hands of former LMS types, mostly Class 5 4-6-0s and 'Royal Scots', but it was withdrawn not long afterwards to allow the complete closure of most of the GC. The Manchester services had already been withdrawn, but there was still a sporadic service between Nottingham and Marylebone. However, there was still one real express — the 8.30am Newcastle to Bournemouth — a 10hr 20min journey into history, suitable only for railway fanatics wanting a last journey over the GC. The splendid cathedral that was Nottingham Victoria station had a dying air about it, as though it

recognised that its destruction could not be far away. Within a few years it had become yet another shopping centre — a sad end.

The real meat of the Division was coal, iron and steel and general merchandise, as we shall see in the next chapter.

The Organisation

At the head of the Division was the Divisional Manager, who reported directly to the General Manager and his many minions of the London Midland Region at the Holy of Holies — Euston. Under him were all the various departments — Movements (a fancy name for Operating),

Above left: A much-photographed train of the time, summer 1966, because it it was a regular 'Jubilee' turn. This was the Bradford to Poole (SO) train, headed on this occasion by No 45562 *Alberta, p*assing the old coaling plant at Nottingham 16A shed. Notice how busy the goods yard was (but not for much longer).
J. Cupit

Below left: A 'Peak' class Type 4 diesel, No D99, has just backed on to train No 1S68, the Down 'Thames-Clyde', at Nottingham Midland on 2 July 1966. *J. Cupit*

Above: On the Great Central, a Class B1 4-6-0, No 61192, heads a stopping passenger train, the 1.30pm from Nottingham Central to Marylebone, between Whetstone and Ashby Magna on 24 March 1962. *M. Mitchell*

Passenger Commercial, Freight Commercial, Motive Power (now known as Maintenance) and the Central Services Offices, which served all the main departments. They dealt with Staff, Works and Finance.

The layer below the Division was filled by Stationmasters (soon to be replaced by Area Managers), Yard Masters, Goods Agents and Shedmasters. During the 1960s the organisations were in a state of flux, mainly responding to changes in traffic levels and the effect of modernisation, especially dieselisation. And to the pressing need to cut costs.

The Divisional Movements Superintendent had an Assistant (me), two District Controllers, an Inspectorate and the Sections for dealing with passenger train working, freight train working, signalling and accidents. There was a Chief Inspector, with a number of Signalling Inspectors, Freight Train Inspectors and Passenger Train Inspectors. They were the eyes and ears of the Division. We had two Control Offices (under the respective District Controller), which were remnants of previous organisations, one at Derby and one at Nottingham. They would be merged at Nottingham in due course. They were open continuously and were responsible for monitoring the current state of train working and freight traffic, and making appropriate arrangements and changes where necessary.

I hope that's all clear, but major changes were not far off.

What was in the Division

Many small stations had already closed under the Beeching plan, and many local train services had been withdrawn; in fact, there were very few left. The small stations that survived were mainly on the Derby-Nottingham-Newark line, and on the Derby-Manchester line via Matlock. A visit to Monsal Dale signalbox was a pleasure to be reserved for a sunny afternoon.

Being a large freight Division, there were marshalling yards at Avenue (Clay Cross), Tibshelf, Blackwell (Westhouses), Toton (by far the largest and the only modern yard), Beeston, Bestwood

Left: This is a 1950s' view of the Peak Forest route between Chinley and Derby, as Compound 4-4-0 No 41185 runs gently into Matlock with an Up local train. A Derby (17A) engine, No 41185 was withdrawn in 1957. *D. Sellman*

Centre left: The Peak Forest route was heavily used for freight. A class 8F 2-8-0, No 48745, runs through the picturesque station at Cromford with an Up freight on 7 October 1961. *Ian Allan Library*

Below left: Westhouses shed (18B) was set well back from the Erewash Valley main line, so could not be seen from the train. Several BR 2-10-0s were allocated there, including this one, No 92104, in June 1963. *RCTS*

Park, Kirkby, Chaddesden (Derby) and Burton on Trent. We also had Annesley on the GC, bu I only had time to visit it on two or three occasions before it closed in the summer of 1965. Beeston (Nottingham) was in process of closure and Rowsley had just been closed. By 1970 they had nearly all gone — victims of changes in traffic levels and traffic flows. Toton reigned supreme. The yards in the Division collectively dealt with about 350,000 wagons in a four-week period, of which Toton handled over 150,000.

There were steam sheds at Nottingham, Kirkby, Derby, Burton, Toton and Westhouses. Also Annesley GC, soon to be closed. Nearly all the passenger services were by now diesel-hauled, or worked by DMUs, but with the exception of a few of the overnight merchandise fitted freights, all the freight trains were still steam-hauled, and most were loose-coupled, which caused some difficulties when diesels took over. Yet within a couple of years all the steam sheds had closed, with the footplate staffs being located at signing-on points, mainly at major passenger stations and at Toton. It was a major upheaval and the rate of change was astonishing. Maintenance was then carried out at a new maintenance depot at Toton, and there were refuelling facilities at Derby and Nottingham.

There was a Freightliner Terminal at Beeston, of which more later.

The Freight Traffic Producing (and Receiving) Areas

Nottingham was the main merchandise area, with Boots, Raleigh Cycles, Plessey and Players cigarettes. There was a large goods yard and depot, and several fully fitted express freight trains departed each evening. The other place of some traffic significance was Burton on Trent, famous for its beers. In the old pre-grouping days it was served by the Midland, the Great Northern, the North Staffs and the LNWR, each with its own facilities and each wanting as big a share of the traffic as possible. There was a positive tangle of railway-owned lines and junctions and signalboxes as well as warehouses, engine sheds and marshalling yards. On top of all that, the various breweries mostly had their own internal siding layouts, often running through the streets. By the 1960s, rationalisation of the breweries was taking place, and there was less use of the internal layout.

The BR layout was also in the planning process of rationalisation.

The main traffic in the Division was undoubtedly coal, which was produced in huge quantities from about 40 collieries. There was a west to east shift in the coal measures. Collieries in the west, in Derbyshire, were being worked out and closed, whilst in the interwar period several new collieries were opened in an area to the east of Mansfield. Even after the war, new collieries had been opened near Nottingham, at Calverton and Cotgrave.

The pattern of coal train working was really quite simple. Each colliery was served from a local marshalling yard (and often from a local engine shed). At the local marshalling yard, outwards traffic was shunted into trainloads for one destination or yard as far as possible, with the residue been tripped to a larger yard, such as Toton. The main destinations outside the division were Gowhole (for Manchester etc), Sheffield, Peterborough/Whitemoor, Wellingborough and Washwood Heath. There were still a few collieries on the line between Derby and Clay Cross, but there were a lot on the Erewash Valley line and its branches, and many on the Leen Valley line from Nottingham to Mansfield and beyond. As the weeks passed into months and then into years, I visited every colliery (and some several times), and probably ate my lunch in the colliery canteen at most of them.

Many of the collieries were also served from branches laid down by the Great Northern Railway, with the workings being centred on Colwick, one of the largest yards on that company, and still part of the Eastern Region. In effect, therefore, each colliery had four fans of sidings — two for the empty wagons being delivered (one from each company, or later each Region), and two for the outgoing loaded wagons. This suited the colliery managements, because they had two strings to their bow. But it was an arrangement that was to be short-lived, as we shall see.

Much of the coal traffic was destined for electricity power stations in various parts of the country, but since the war and the nationalisation of electricity generation, several large power stations had been built along the River Trent, at Castle Donington, Repton and Willington, Staythorpe, and Drakelow Nos 1, 2 and 3. The internal track layout at Drakelow was so complex that it had its own CEGB power signalbox. By arrangement with the collieries, the coal was usually turned out in block trainloads for power stations, bypassing marshalling yards.

Mention ought to be made of the major iron and steel works known as Stanton and Staveley, just north of Toton, which produced major traffic flows of raw material inwards and finished products outwards. The iron ore came from High Dyke, on the GN main line south of Grantham, and arrived at the works from a connection with the ex-GN Nottingham to Derby line. Here was another example of double-servicing, which was also to be short-lived. The speciality of the works was large-diameter iron pipes.

On the Domestic Front

For the first fortnight I was entitled to hotel expenses, which gave me time to look round for some good, homely digs. A chap in the office told me that he was staying in some very good digs and there was a spare bedroom, so I arranged to join him, at Mrs Butenko's. She was married to a Polish chap, who didn't say a great deal. It was fine, the meals were good, and she was used to people coming and going at irregular hours.

On the housing front, I soon discovered that there were plenty of houses for sale in my price range, and after several weeks of intensive searching I found a very nice three-bedroomed detached in West Bridgford, which was really a suburb of Nottingham on the south side of the Trent. It had gas-fired central heating, was newly decorated and spacious, and my offer of £3,950 was accepted. There was only one snag — this was 5 March and possession would not be available until 21 June. This gave plenty of time to sell our house at Barrow, which was taking a little while. A change of agent speeded things up. Val came to see the house and liked it. We moved in on 18 June. Everywhere seemed to be a mass of blossom on trees and in gardens, and Nottingham prided itself on being the 'Queen of the Midlands'. It also had a reputation of having the prettiest girls, and it had an engine named after it — No 46251 *City of Nottingham*. It was indeed a fine city.

Whilst lodging I had travelled home after work on Friday and returned to Nottingham on Monday mornings, but I had to do my share of 'On Call', which meant staying in Nottingham some weekends. I normally went backwards and forwards by car, an Austin A40, which was OK up to 50mph but started to vibrate a bit at 60mph. Barrow to Nottingham was about 200 miles and a fairly slow journey, which took five or six hours, but the car was useful for house-hunting, a daunting task, as there was so much choice over quite a wide area. I was glad to be settled in our new house! Domestically it was fine, too, for the boys' schooling. They were five and ten years old and within a five/10 minutes' walk there was a grammar school, a technical grammar school and a junior school.

A Timetable of Events 1965

• There were 11 car-carrying (motorail) services in 1965, 80,000 cars had been carried in 1964, which was an increase of 20% over 1963.
• A new, 10-year, contract had been signed nationally for the carriage of newspapers, magazines, etc.
• January – The Nottingham Division had 46 'Peaks', 15 Brush Type 4s and 85 Type 2s. There were very few steam workings south and west of Toton, but steam was common north of Toton
• February 1 – I began a five-year stint at Nottingham.
• February 20 – A new spur was installed at Netherfield and Colwick to connect the former-GN with the former-Midland and enable trains from the GN section to access Nottingham Midland station when Nottingham Victoria closed.
• March – Fitted freights and fish trains were diverted from the GC route to other routes, mainly the Midland.

The Nottingham Victoria to Marylebone passenger trains were worked mainly by ex-LMS and BR Class 5 4-6-0s
• April – Steam allocations in the Nottingham Division were as follows:
16A Toton
2-8-0 Class 8F — 5,
2-6-0 Class 2MT — 3
16B Annesley
ex-LMS 4-6-0 Class 5 — 18,
ex-LMS 2-8-0 Class 8F — 13,
2-10-0 BR — 29
16C Derby
2-6-4T — 1,
ex-LMS 4-6-0 Class 5 — 11,
ex-LMS 2-8-0 Class 8F — 24.

A Railwayman's Odyssey

BR 2-6-0 Class 2MT — 3
16E Kirkby
ex-LMS 0-6-0 Class 4F — 7,
ex-LMS 2-8-0 Class 8F — 36
16F Burton
ex-LMS 4-6-0 Class 5 — 14,
0-6-0T — 4,
ex-LMS 2-8-0 Class 8F — 16
16G Westhouses
ex-LMS 0-6-0 Class 4F — 11,
ex-LMS 2-8-0 Class 8F — 24,
0-6-0T — 4.
The Division still had 118 Stanier Class 8F
2-8-0s.
• June 14 – All Annesley-Woodford freights were
withdrawn. They were known as 'windcutters', as
they ran in accelerated timings when Class 9F
2-10-0s were introduced, and became a legend.
• June 24 – There were 71 steam locos at Toton.
• June – All track in Rowsley marshalling yard
had now been lifted.
• July 13 – The last steam loco, 0-6-0T No 47645,
was towed away from Nottingham shed.
• August – Annesley and Beeston (Nottingham)
marshalling yards were closed.
• September 5 – There was a high speed freight
train derailment on plain track at Castle
Donington, between Trent and Burton. I was
called out in the middle of the night. It was a
typical derailment of a fast freight on plain line,
occurring in the middle of the train, and as usual
there was a heap of wreckage. I took the formal

Above: A Brush Type 4, No D1516, leaves
Nottingham Midland station with a London
St Pancras to Sheffield Midland train, No 1E19,
on 29 May 1969. *David Percival*

inquiry a couple of days later, the conclusion
being the usual fatal combination of train speed,
track condition and wagon condition, none of
which were in themselves especially dangerous.
• September 6 The Pye Bridge to Kirkby
passenger service was withdrawn.
• September 27 – eight Britannias were allocated
to Banbury for working Marylebone-Nottingham
and Rugby-Nottingham passenger services.
• October 30 – The Nottingham Division now had
154 mainline diesels — 40 'Peaks', Brush Type
4s — 38, Type 2s — 76.
• Colwick Yard was very busy. Queues of coal
trains were waiting to get into the yard from the
north.
• November 6 – My office moved from
Nottingham Victoria station to the new Divisional
Headquarters at Furlong House, on the site of the
old engine shed at Nottingham Midland. My new
office was functional but not so spacious as my
former, grand quarters.
• November – The remodelling of Burton
Marshalling Yard was in progress.
• December – Annesley shed finally closed.
• 90-ton bogie tank wagons were being
introduced by Shell-Mex and BP Ltd. Maximum
speed 60mph, air-braked.

To trespass a little into 1966, on 3 January, the London Midland Region, Nottingham Division, took over the following Eastern Region lines:
• Trent Lane Junction (Nottingham) to Bingham, including Colwick Yard, Colwick Motive Power Depot and the Cotgrave Colliery Branch. All LNER locos were transferred away except for five 4-6-0 Class B1s.
• Carlton & Netherfield to Newark (exclusive).

The St Pancras expresses were diverted from the Nottingham-Melton Mowbray-Manton-Kettering route to run via Leicester.

A merger of the Nottingham and Leicester Divisions took place the same day, with HQ being in the new, purpose-built offices at Furlong House, Nottingham. My job as Assistant Divisional Movements Superintendent was split into two. One for forward planning and one for current operations. I was given the forward planning job, much to my delight. I was going to be very busy and could concentrate on the job without worrying about what was going on currently.

The extended boundaries of the Nottingham Division, having merged with (or more accurately swallowed up) the Leicester Division, were Ketton (on the Peterborough line), Sharnbrook (just north of Bedford), Nuneaton (exclusive both via Market Bosworth and via Hinckley), and Northampton (exclusive), plus the rump of the ex-GC. There was clearly going to be a lot of travelling and a lot of long days. Much of it would have to be by car in the absence of a passenger train service.

Above: On 5 February 1964, a BR Sulzer Type 4 Diesel, No D90, with an empty stock train, passes Beeston marshalling yard. The yard will shortly be the first one to close in the Nottingham Division and will become the site for a new Freightliner Terminal. *J. S. Hancock*

Acquiring Driving Skills

Riding around on the footplate of steam locomotives gave little practical benefit. As the third man you could see ahead only with difficulty, and conversation was near-impossible owing to the racket. But once diesels came along it was a different world. You could see the line ahead in comfort and it was quiet enough to talk. It was also smooth enough to make notes.

One day a clerk from the Motive Power Department came into the office and said quite casually, as though passing the time of day, 'The Motive Power Department is closing down and the footplate staff are being transferred to the Operating Department, and into your tender care. We shall transfer a clerk to you (with all his files) and the Locomotive Inspectors.' This was great news, but what a sad end to the Motive Power Department, with its long and proud history. With the closure of all the engine sheds, the footplate staff transferred to new signing-on points at the main centres, such as Nottingham, Derby, Burton, Kirkby, Toton, Leicester, Coalville and Wellingborough (from memory) and came under the Area Managers, who received an additional assistant. All maintenance

Above: On 19 September 1964, the Locomotive Club of Great Britain (LCGB) ran a special railtour through the Division. 'Royal Scot' class 4-6-0 No 46155 *The Lancer* passes Market Harborough No 3 signalbox with the train from St Pancras. *G. D. King*

Below: Leicester Goods Depot looks busy on 1 July 1969, but a major change is afoot. BR's goods depots are being handed over to a new organisation called National Carriers Ltd, part of another new organisation called the National Freight Corporation. In the meantime, no changes are apparent as one of BR's early 'Peak' class Type 4s, No D8 *Penyghent*, comes gently past an adverse distant signal with a loaded coal train from Toton to Brent. Note also that the driver has conscientiously set his headcode for a mineral train, using a disc. *J. H. Cooper-Smith*

Left: One of Kirkby's stock of Class 8F 2-8-0s, No 48119, sets out from an unidentified marshalling yard with a Class H freight train. The engine was one of a batch turned out by Crewe just before the outbreak of the Second World War. *Ian Allan Library*

work on diesel locomotives was transferred to a new purpose-built depot at Toton, whilst DMUs were dealt with at Etches Park, Derby. There were refuelling and stabling facilities at the main centres and at carriage sidings. A new post of Divisional Maintenance Engineer was created.

The closure and winding up of the Motive Power Department and the closure of all the sheds was an event of epoch-making proportions, yet it hardly raised a ripple. New accommodation had been created at the signing-on points and, if truth be told, locomen were glad to move into decent accommodation. But there were long-term implications. The locomen had lost their own private home — the engine shed — and their boss — the Shedmaster. Area Managers and their assistants were not always a good substitute, and some of them knew little about motive power affairs. Understandably, the locomen sometimes felt cast adrift into an organisation that knew little of their problems. I was determined to do my bit to make them feel welcome.

From now on I rode in driving cabs whenever possible, because it gave such a good view of the line ahead and to the side. It was an excellent way to learn the layout in detail, and to note what was going on out there. I soon came across the Locomotive Inspectors, and one of them said to me, 'You'll learn a lot more sitting in that seat,' pointing to the driving seat. I jumped at the chance, and whenever I had a spare day or was travelling to a meeting I would phone him up and say, 'Where shall we go today?' He would find a driver who was happy to let me sit in his seat, and off we would go. Actually, it's not as difficult as it might seem. I already knew the road, the signals, the speed

restrictions, etc and the Rules. Now I needed to know how to drive, how to handle loose-coupled freight trains (a skill in itself) and how to react to signals, speed restrictions, station stops, etc. I needed to get a feel for the things that were of concern to drivers. The Inspector said to me, 'Any fool can start a train. The skill is in stopping it.' We went on passenger trains to Birmingham and Sheffield, and on parcels and freight trains to various places. It was very valuable experience when holding inquiries into mishaps and signals passed at Danger, and even in train timing.

It was also important that the Locomotive Inspectors should feel at home in the Operating Department, and I made a practice of consulting them on every suitable occasion. I would invite them onto the panel at inquiries, or when dealing with disciplinary matters concerning drivers. We held periodic meetings with all the Inspectors present (just as we did with the Operating Department Inspectors). After such meetings the Inspectors would repair to the local pub, and I would join them there. On other occasions there would be a buffet lunch. No problems about drinking on duty in those days. Those men were invaluable, and had always come from the footplate grades. They were now out-based at the various signing-on points, and an important part of their job was to know their drivers. They examined footplatemen rising through the ranks to driver, but once a man had become a driver he was not examined again. He was trusted to keep up his knowledge of the Rules and Regulations, and it generally worked. The Locomotive Inspectors were re-christened Traction Inspectors, to recognise the change from steam to diesel and electric.

Seventeen

TALES OF THE NOTTINGHAM DIVISION — INTO THE NEW ENLARGED DIVISION 1966

Point-to-Point Train Running Times

Seven minutes were allowed for a Type 4 diesel on an express passenger train from Kettering to Wellingborough, start to stop. The distance is seven miles. Trains consistently lost time over that section so the Traction Inspector and I decided to have a look at it. Cyril, the Inspector, was a bit of a fire-raiser, and his ploy was to get on board at Kettering and challenge the driver to do it in seven minutes. None of them could. Cyril then determined to have a go himself. He picked an amenable driver and set off from Kettering like a rocket. We were soon doing 90, but even then it looked as though he wasn't going to manage it. We were still doing 90 racing past Neilsons Sidings, the marshalling yard just north of Wellingborough, with the station just round the next corner, so to speak. At the last minute he flung the brake handle to full service position and we hit the end of the station platform still doing 50mph. We screeched through the platform to the astonishment of the waiting passengers and ground to a halt with half the train off the platform. Almost exactly seven minutes, but hardly appropriate for everyday use. Another minute (or maybe two) was added in the next timetable. Footplate riding was excellent for checking that the timetabled running times were appropriate. And it was enjoyable too. It was also good to be seen to be out and about.

Below: One of BR's experiments with Franco-Crosti boilers, which was ultimately abandoned, No 92029 was photographed at Kettering shed (15B) in October 1962, by which time the Crosti boiler had been removed. Nos 92020 to 92029 were equipped with the Franco-Crosti boiler from new in 1955. Locomotive engineers never stopped trying to improve the efficiency of the steam locomotive, even at the eleventh hour. *RCTS*

How Were Point-to-Point Running Times Arrived At in the Steam Era?

In steam days there was a very well established procedure for setting point-to-point running times. These were done by the Chief Mechanical Engineer's Department for every running line on the system, for each type of motive power likely to be used and for every type of train that might be run. There were also various categories of point-to-point times — such as start to stop, start to pass, pass to stop and pass to pass. These timings had been established over many years and only had to be reset when new types of traction were introduced, or when there were other changes, such as when maximum allowed speeds over particular sections of line were increased.

Drivers of passenger trains worked to the timings shown in the Passenger Working Timetables, which included passing times at junctions etc. They knew from experience just how fast they would have to go in order to arrive at the next stopping point on time. The timings allowed for the maximum loads or tonnages diagrammed to be conveyed on those trains, and there were different categories of timings, such as full load, limited load (faster), special limit (faster still) and XL limit (look out!).

Drivers of freight trains had to have regard to the amount of brake power available, and to any restriction of speed required by particular types of wagon or load, which would be notified to them by the guard. Drivers of heavily loaded trains needed to approach Distant signals at a speed that would

Above: An excellent photograph, which illustrates very well the size of Wellingborough engine shed and yard. A Stanier Class 8F 2-8-0, No 48467, works a southbound ballast train on 19 April 1963. The marshalling yards — known as Neilsons — were just off the left-hand side of the photograph. *Colin Boocock*

allow them to stop their trains safely at the 'Stop' signal ahead. Express freight trains, either fully fitted or with at least a third fitted, tended to be driven more like passenger trains, within the maximum speeds laid down for their class of train.

On some companies, signalmen at regulating signalboxes had copies of the timing booklet for their particular area so that they could regulate slower trains when being closely followed by faster ones. The details in these booklets were refined in other booklets, known as 'Margins' booklets, which showed the actual time margin that signalmen should work to, to allow for trains being slowed to turn onto goods lines etc. On other companies, the timings were published in the Working Timetable. In practice, signalmen had to use a certain amount of judgement and experience. They were not to know the particular type of locomotive being used on a train that day. A lightly loaded goods train might run faster than a more heavily loaded one. Signalmen had to take into account that a goods train signalled by the bell signal 'four-pause-one' (through mineral or empty wagon train) might have

Above: The Saturdays Only summer special that ran from Leeds and Bradford to Poole and back has just passed Lenton North Junction, in July 1966. The engine is 'Jubilee' No 45562 *Alberta,* one of a small number of 'Jubilees' that kept the steam flag flying until almost the end of steam. Based at Holbeck, they also worked Saturdays Only expresses between Leeds and Carlisle, watched by legions of fans. *G. G. Stanley*

fifty wagons of coal or fifty empties. They knew only from experience which it might be. Regulating (or margining, as it was known) was a fine art. And after all that, not all drivers ran at the laid down point-to-point times. Some drivers of unfitted goods trains liked to get a move on; others ran more slowly. The engine might have leaking tubes, or a tender full of slack. Some drivers would co-operate by running on a tight margin if they were given the tip by the signalman. They often disliked being put inside (eg onto a goods line). Signalmen had a feeling that some drivers wanted to get a move on, whilst others would dawdle a little in order to get put inside and earn overtime. They might phone a colleague further back and ask, 'How's so-and-so doing?'

Point-to-Point Timings in Diesel and Electric Days

When particular lines were being electrified, the CME usually had plenty of time to establish the running times, and only a relatively few types of traction would be involved. The same applied to the introduction of diesel multiple-units. However, the introduction of diesel locomotives of several types with wide route availability and standard capability, being introduced over a short timescale, was a different matter. Detailed timings were quoted for passenger and fast freight trains, based on the number and types of train expected to be run, and the types of diesel expected to be used. Timings were also quoted for freight trains of lower classification, either unfitted, or with a fitted head (ie next to the engine). Timetablers had to have regard more to the braking power of a locomotive than to its pulling power. And braking power had to have regard to poor railhead conditions. But there was one saving grace for train timers — diesel locomotives had a much more predictable and consistent power output than their steam counterparts. Local freight trains were generally not timetabled, and drivers took what they thought they could pull and stop.

The Calculation of Freight Train Loads

The method of doing this went back to the earliest days of railways, based on the obvious fact that an engine could pull more empty wagons than loaded wagons. But loaded wagons could be full of coal, or full of empty boxes, or any state in between. Simple systems were introduced, such as one wagon of coal = three units, one wagon of merchandise = two units, and an empty wagon = one unit. In the 1960s

Above: Withdrawal of ex-LMS Class 4F 0-6-0s was on a small scale until almost the end of the 1950s, and there were still plenty to be seen in 1955, such as this example, No 44369, a Derby engine, approaching Market Harborough with an Up freight train. *P. H. Groom*

this was refined. Wagons were classed as heavy, medium, light and empty and labelled accordingly. They were then assigned a nominal tonnage, eg 23, 17, 11 and 8, so that the yard inspector and the guard could calculate the load of a train in tons. The driver was then given a note stating the tonnage being conveyed and the brake power. Fitted wagons had a nominal brake power based on their category of load: H, M, L or E. Freight Train Loads books were published, giving the maximum loads for each type of diesel over each section of line, taking into account the amount of brake power available from the locomotive and the wagons. The system was designed to allow the maximum capability of the locomotive to be used, without any risk of overloading, and the maximum safe speed, without risk of passing signals at Danger. Special training sessions were organised so that drivers, guards and yard staff knew what was required. It was a major change.

The Scheme for Rapid Loading and Rapid Unloading of Power Station Coal

This scheme was first devised by people on the Eastern Region (who traditionally were always first in the field with ideas for improving freight train working). It eventually consisted of permanently coupled trainsets of high capacity, air-braked hopper wagons, of 29/32 tonnes capacity, loaded from overhead bunkers at collieries and being unloaded at power stations through the bottom doors onto conveyor belts. BR was particularly interested in this scheme for use at the new power stations being planned, because it would bring considerable economies in the number of wagons required.

The Central Electricity Generating Board were also very interested, because it would lead to considerable economies for them also when building new power stations, avoiding the need to buy many acres of land to provide the loaded wagon and empty wagon sidings that would be needed under conventional methods of operation. All that would be necessary were rapid unloading facilities from hopper wagons, and conveyor belts to take the coal away to stacking grounds or directly to the furnaces, plus a very simple track layout. The new power station to be built at Ratcliffe was already in the design stages, and was opened in August 1967.

The National Coal Board were rather less than happy, and would have to be sweetened by lower carriage charges, based on tonnages forwarded, to compensate for the cost of erecting bunkers and conveyor belts. But they would have the advantage of a guaranteed supply of empty wagons, and agreed to co-operate; in fact, they became quite

Above: Saxby Station Junction signalbox controlled the junction between the former LMS main line from Nottingham to Kettering via Melton Mowbray and Oakham, and the line to the M&GN via Bourne (the left-hand line with a light engine, No 48182, on it). The M&GN could be quite a busy line on summer Saturdays, but would be closed within a couple of years. A Class 8F 2-8-0, No 48029, takes a trainload of empty coal wagons back to the Nottinghamshire coalfield on 23 June 1956. *J. F. Oxley*

enthusiastic. The NCB knew that increasing quantities of their coal output would have to be in small pieces, suitable for power station use. The house coal market had almost dried up.

The main principles, and especially the carriage charges, were agreed at HQ level between the BRB, NCB and CEGB. The details of track arrangements were left to be dealt with at Divisional level. Happily, with the prospect of more colliery canteen lunches, this was well within my remit, and I met an NCB chap from East Midlands HQ who was as keen as mustard on the new system. He had details of all the collieries that might supply coal to Ratcliffe power station and between us we visited all those collieries and jointly decided exactly where the bunker should be located and the changes in track layout required to enable it to be served in the most efficient and practicable manner. Normally, empty trains would run straight from the main line to the bunker line, then the wagons would

be loaded on the move whilst the train was slowly drawn forward. The bunker had an intricate device to enable this to be done. After loading, the diesel loco would run round the train, couple up, test the brake, and return to the power station. Loading time would be 45-60 minutes. The NCB immediately began to build bunkers at several collieries.

The arrangements at the power station were similarly quite simple. The train would run into the power station to the unloading point and pass through it at a steady half-a-mile per hour (using specially modified locos able to do so) whilst the wagons were being unloaded. Unloading time of a train was between 35 and 45 minutes, depending on the number of wagons. Devices, known as 'Daleks', were located at the entrance to the unloading hopper, which tripped the safety catch and opened the bottom doors, whilst similar devices performed the opposite function at the exit. The wagons were examined before departure by a C&W examiner to ensure that they were all suitable to be reloaded. A siding was provided into which any defective wagon could be detached. From memory, Ratcliffe power station required 24,000 tons of coal per day, about one train per hour, and one trainset of 36 wagons could do four round-trips per day, given the short distances from the collieries to the power station. Six trainsets would be required, plus spares: about 250/300 wagons. If the power station had been served conventionally, about 5,000 standard wagons would have been required. The scheme was a huge success and was applied to all

Above: There was a tangle of lines and there were many collieries in the North Leicestershire coalfield between Burton-on-Trent and Leicester. The main line between those two towns ran via Coalville and Ashby-de-la-Zouch. In this photograph, a BR/Sulzer Type 2 diesel, No D7558, passes Gresley on 16 October 1965 with a trainload of power station coal, probably bound for one of the Drakelow power stations near Burton. *Brian Stephenson*

Below: Derby Road signalbox, on the ex-North Stafford Railway Derby to Stoke line a mile from the main northeast/southwest line, controlled a level crossing over the A38 trunk road, and the signalman was having increasing difficulty in closing the gates across the busy road. As I recall, it was an early candidate for automatic half barriers. The date is 30 May 1965. *P. H. Wells*

A Railwayman's Odyssey

new power stations and to several existing ones. It was called 'merry-go-round'.

The Enlarged Nottingham Division — a Wider Sphere of Interest and Activity

The year 1966 in the Nottingham Division was to turn out to be one of the most eventful in modern railway history, so far as changes were concerned. Here are some of the major changes in which we would be involved, many of which entailed site visits and meetings:

Preparations for Trent and Derby power signalboxes
Colliery bunker loading schemes
Diesels replacing steam north of Toton
Closure of steam sheds
Modernisation of level crossings
Closure of marshalling yards
National Freight Train Plan
Single-servicing of collieries and Stanton ironworks
Closure of the GC north of Arkwright Junction Nottingham
Closure of all remaining GN lines apart from Nottingham to Grantham

January 1966

27   A review with the Divisional Civil Engineer of the 1967 permanent-way renewals programme. This entailed a certain amount of crystal-gazing on our part and depended on many of the items listed above being achieved in the agreed timescale. In addition, there were reductions in running lines. Mainline renewals were planned at HQ level.

February

15   There were site visits to Silverhill, Teversall and Pleasley collieries regarding bunker loading schemes.

28   Burton New Yard opened. There was an urgent need to concentrate all shunting and sorting of wagons in one place, which had traditionally been done in several for historical reasons, going back to pre-grouping days. As the workload had declined considerably from those days, it had become possible to modify one of the existing yards and modernise it. Unfortunately, by the time it opened, the number of wagons of beer being forwarded had declined still further, mainly owing to changes within the structure of the brewing industry, or so it was believed.

March

18   It was intended to introduce bonus incentive schemes for traincrews working freight trains. There was nothing new in this system, as it had been operating successfully for many years in parts of the North East, but it was fraught with problems. How would signalmen and yard staff react? Would they demand a share of the benefits? Under the consultation procedure, we had to go through a series of lengthy meetings with the local staff reps at each traincrew depot which worked freight trains in the slower categories, mainly coal and empties. The men were not unnaturally sceptical at first, seeing it as a means of reducing the staff, but when they grasped what it was all about, and that it would mean more money in the wage packet, they became more enthusiastic. The Work Study Department had to establish a datum time for every terminal, with bonus being paid for quicker turn-rounds. The payments were not great, and the benefits to management quite small. I seem to recall that the scheme was abandoned at the next annual wage increase, to sighs of relief all round, with a nominal amount being included in the wage increase.

19   We had the first of many meetings about the National Freight Train Plan. The BRB had decided to divert all heavy freight from the GN line south of Doncaster and route it via the Midland into Toton. Wagonload freight was declining and this seemed a sensible development.

23   The Division was running 'Courtesy Courses' for staff in contact with the public. They were held in a local hotel, with buffet lunch.

27   I attended a very interesting meeting at Ambergate with the East Midlands Gas Board, which revealed its plans for a new works there to produce gas from naphtha. Two to four trains of naphtha per day were expected, and we were asked to plan the necessary track layout and determine how trains were to be worked in and out. This

was a very exciting project but was knocked on the head by the development of North Sea gas before work began.

April

4 Leicester West Bridge Goods Depot closed, including Glenfield tunnel.

18 A new passenger timetable was introduced, incorporating major changes. Several St Pancras to Manchester expresses were returned to the newly electrified West Coast route, a not unexpected development. The Bradford Forster Square/Leeds to St Pancras service was reduced in frequency, and a new semi-fast service was introduced between St.Pancras and Leicester/Derby/Nottingham.

Wellingborough steam shed was closed.

A two-road diesel depot was planned at Burton, near the old roundhouse.

May

I attended a fortnight's Work Study Techniques course at The Grove, a large country house in an extensive estate near Watford, which had been bought by the LMS in 1938 as its wartime HQ. It had a bar, too, and a snooker room. It was now used for various training courses. The Grove was set in many acres of parkland, which was at its best in May. I can't recall that we worked very hard, and probably thought that the whole thing was really a bit of a waste of time, but it was good to have a chat with colleagues from the whole of BR.

31 51 steam locos were noted at Colwick, mostly Class 5s and '8Fs'.

June

19 There was a meeting with the signal engineers to discuss their 1967 Works Programme. This was a mechanism that gave the signal engineers the opportunity to find out what we would be up to next year, and which of their proposed work could be deferred or even dropped altogether. These meetings with the technical people were of great value to both sides.

July

7 We had a meeting at Stanton ironworks to discuss single-servicing via the Midland route to allow Victoria station to be closed. This was part of the plan to close all GN lines in the division except the Nottingham to Grantham line. The main traffic flow via the GN was iron ore from High Dyke, south of Grantham, and it was proposed to run these trains via Nottingham Midland station and Toton. The ironworks people were very amenable to our proposals, although I did have some concern about the availability of paths through Nottingham station. In the event, it worked well. A visit to the ironworks was always worthwhile, because the managers there were very hospitable. If this diversion had not been practicable the developers of the Nottingham Victoria

Below: 'Jubilee' class 4-6-0 No 45626 *Seychelles* removes a train of empty stock from Platform 6 at Derby Midland station on 31 August 1963; this was the occasion of the Works Open Day.
T. Boustead

Above: Seychelles also worked a Newcastle to Bristol express from Derby Midland station. This was also a Works Open Day, but not necessarily the same day as the previous photograph, as the engine looks cleaner in this photograph. *J. Cupit*

station site would have had to build a tunnel through the area to provide for the iron ore trains and return empties. We saved them the need to do so, and to celebrate they took us out to lunch, and BR was handsomely rewarded. It was a good day's work.

9   I accompanied an enthusiasts' railtour, just for the fun of it. The train consisted of 12 brake vans, hauled by a specially cleaned Class 5, and we visited colliery branches and Stanton ironworks.

11   There was a meeting at Euston to discuss route rationalisation. It sounded very important, but I can't recall anything significant affecting us.

21   A late-evening DMU ran into three horses between Beeston and Attenborough, and I was called out. There was no derailment, but we had to summon a vet to help us to clear the line, as we quickly discovered that dead horses can be very heavy and cumbersome.

28   I took a brake van trip on a coal train from Kirkby to Burton via Pye Bridge and Ambergate. This was quite exciting, as Kirkby is at the top of a hill, whilst Pye Bridge is at the foot, resulting in a steep falling gradient. We had had excitements there before (and were to have some more).

August

9   It was time for the Station Cleanliness and Tidiness competition. I visited all stations between Clay Cross and Loughborough (by car), whilst other people covered the remainder of the Division.

September

12   We had a meeting with the staff representatives regarding the closure of Kirkby steam shed.

15   I held a Joint Inquiry into the derailment of a coal train between Kirkby and Pinxton. It was the same old problem, with the driver attempting to keep his speed down and causing buffer-locking. The performance of 60 unbraked, loaded coal wagons on a steep, falling gradient, with the driver trying to maintain a constant speed not exceeding 10mph, was an object lesson in mechanics. In theory, the driver should collect all the wagons together, buffer to buffer, at the top of the incline, and keep them like that all the way down, but in practice it was different. The front of the train could be almost stationary whilst the rear was racing downhill at up to what felt like 20mph. The guard just screwed his brake on as hard he could, and then braced himself for the impact.

18   A coincidence. I met an Inspector Farnell,

Above: A long train of iron ore, probably from High Dyke on the East Coast main line, is taken through Nottingham Midland station by a pair of English Electric Type 1s, en route to the Stanton and Staveley ironworks, just north of Toton. The locomotives are Nos D8046 and D8186 and the date is 5 August 1968. *David Wharton*

Below: A former Midland Railway 0-4-4T, No 58065 (old LMS No 1367), runs into Nottingham Midland station on 4 November 1957 with its single push-pull coach. It normally worked the Southwell branch from Rolleston Junction. These engines were introduced by Johnson in the 1880s and, therefore, were now 70/75 years old. *T. G. Hepburn/Rail Archive Stephenson*

who had been Stationmaster at Battyeford in 1939 and lived in the same house as I lived in 12 years later.

19   I carried out investigations into last week's derailment, and made various tests. It was agreed that the practical solution was to increase the speed restriction on the incline from 10mph to 15mph. It was unscientific, but it worked. The problem arose when drivers attempted to keep the speed of their engine below 10mph, resulting in surges through the train which in turn caused buffer-locking and derailment.

20   I attended site visits to level crossings on the Nottingham to Newark line to see which were suitable for conversion to automatic half-barriers (AHBs). The BRB had a very ambitious programme to convert a large number of manned public level crossings to unmanned crossings with automatic half-barriers, and had made money available for it to be done Quite a number of crossings in the Division were converted before the whole project came to a shuddering halt following the fatal collision between an electric express and a massive road transporter carrying a 120-ton transformer, at Hixon, Staffordshire, on 6 January 1968. The British public had always been suspicious of AHB crossings, and loved the old-fashioned gates, and their fears appeared to have some substance. In the event, hardly any more conversions to AHB were done in the next 10 years.

October

10   We had a saloon tour with the Divisional Manager. Out via Oakham to Wellingborough. Lunch at Higham Ferrers. Back via Leicester. Three Lt-Cols in the saloon — the DM himself, the Divisional Movements Superintendent and the Divisional Commercial Manager. The bar opened promptly at 12.00 noon. Strict military discipline was observed. I probably hid on the loco, being an airman. The DM, Bobby Gardiner, was a martinet, but probably the best manager I ever came across. It was a time of prodigious change, but under his management we achieved all we had to. His system was to leave his officers to get on with running their departments, provided they achieved the desired results. He also acted as an umbrella, and sheltered us against any complaints that might come from Crewe or Euston. I think that they were afraid of his ire too. If I recall correctly, some of the top men at Euston were also Lt-Cols.

12   I met Col Reed, an Inspecting Officer of the MOT, and took him to level crossing site meetings at Beeston and Long Eaton.

The same evening, my lecturing career began. I was asked at fairly short notice to give a talk on 'Railways and the Coal Industry' to a fairly prestigious coal industry audience. It seemed to go well, and was reported in both morning and evening Nottingham papers. I later discovered that I had stood in for George Brown, Secretary of State for Economic Affairs who was 'indisposed'.

13   There was a meeting with the local staff representatives regarding the closure of the Cromford & High Peak line.

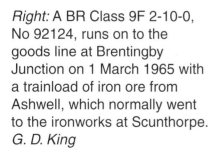

Right: A BR Class 9F 2-10-0, No 92124, runs on to the goods line at Brentingby Junction on 1 March 1965 with a trainload of iron ore from Ashwell, which normally went to the ironworks at Scunthorpe. *G. D. King*

17   The Gas Board's plans for its new installation at Ambergate were firmed up, but before any track or signalling work began, the whole scheme was abandoned in favour of North Sea gas. We had done a lot of work on the scheme, and the technical departments were not pleased.

19   Run down of Colwick yard began.

November

14   Iron ore traffic from High Dyke and Belvoir to Stanton ironworks, which had run via the GN route, was diverted to run via Nottingham Midland station and Toton. The developers of the Victoria station site paid us £50,000 for doing this. I travelled on the first train to see what sort of a run we had. It worked OK.

December

8   There was a big meeting with NCB at Area HQ level to develop bunker loading schemes, which must have been a success because they gave us a splendid pre-Christmas lunch in their mess.

Derailments of 10ft Wheelbase wagons on Express Freight Trains

Some of these have already been mentioned, but the problem was a national one. Following the derailment of an empty banana van on the Western Region on 21 January 1966, BR took the highly restrictive step of reducing the maximum permissible speed of all trains conveying 10ft-wheelbase wagons to 45mph, even though it was known that this would have a most serious effect on traffic movement. However, despite this action the number of freight train derailments continued to increase apace, from 259 in 1966 to a peak of 393 in 1969. It was eased thereafter by improved wagon maintenance and the rapid rundown of short-wheelbase wagons, caused by losses of traffic in general, but particularly after National Carriers took over responsibility for BR's former merchandise traffic in 1968, and transferred most of it to road, or so it appeared to us.

There were several separate causes for the increase in derailments, all disconnected but potentially dangerous when they all came together. It was suggested that wagon designers perhaps didn't appreciate that when they built wagons with steel underframes instead of timber, the wagons would be more rigid. It may not have worried them if they had. Civil engineers laying concrete sleepers and long-welded railways probably thought that the stiffer track would be beneficial and give a smoother ride, which it did, but the more flexible track of bull-head rails on timber sleepers had allowed the hunting and oscillations of wagons to be absorbed, which stiffer track did not. And perhaps planners of dieselisation didn't appreciate that diesels pulling freight trains and running deceptively easily at higher speeds than steam engines had done might lead to derailments. Why should they? But taken together, a difficult and intractable problem was created. The BR Research Department set about designing a longer-wheelbase

Below: The frontage of Nottingham Midland station forms a backdrop to a double-headed train of iron ore on its way from Belvoir Junction to Stanton and Staveley ironworks. The locomotives are English Electric Type 1s Nos D8112 and D8184 and are seen on 20 November 1969. *R. Elsdon*

wagon with improved suspension, but it came too late. The traffic had gone and the problem with it. By 1971 the number of derailments had gone down to 225, and to 140 by 1976.

Yet another line closure

On 1 August, the line from Wellingborough London Road (LNWR) to Northampton closed completely. The chord line from Wellingborough London Road to the Midland station remained in use for two trains of iron ore per day, which were loaded at London Road and departed at 14.00 and 17.05 to West Hartlepool.

At the end of 1966 there were more than 400 oil trains per week, one of the unsung successes of the Reshaping Plan. It was becoming clearer that block trainloads were the way forward for the railway industry, carrying such commodities as coal, coke, limestone, cement, iron ore, aggregates, petrol and oil, and motor cars. New wagons, with long-wheelbase or bogies, air-braked, and often provided by the consignor, were coming increasingly into use. Merchandise was to be transferred to the new Freightliner container service where possible.

On 5 December Colwick Motive Power Depot was closed without any fuss.

INTO 1967

Consideration began to be given to the staffing of the new power signalboxes to be opened at Derby and Trent in 1969. The signalmen's control panels would be split into three sections at Derby and four at Trent, and there would be a need for one or more controllers/regulators to take overall control and

Above: This photo is included because it shows the 1.50pm local train from Wellingborough Midland Road to Northampton Castle on the last day of the service, 2 May 1964. The engine is a Class 2MT 2-6-2T, No 41225. *J. A. Powell*

liaise with the Divisional Control Office. In manual signalboxes, the signalmen report directly to the section controllers in the Control Office in order to keep the Control Office up to date regarding the running of trains, but that would not be practicable in a power signalbox. It was therefore decided that we would have one or two out-based Control Office staff in the power signalboxes for this purpose, to ensure close liaison. They would be transferred from the Control Office.

There was one snag. Signalmen belonged to the NUR and were wages staff; controllers belonged to the TSSA and were salaried staff. In concept there was a gulf the size of the Grand Canyon between the two groups. Unwittingly we found ourselves sitting on a keg of gunpowder. However, staff in the Nottingham Division were pretty reasonable on the whole, and we persuaded the signalmen (and the Unions) that the controllers would only perform Control Office functions and would not touch the signalling panels. I tried to persuade HQ that all posts in power signalboxes should be of salaried status, but open also to signalmen, but I'm afraid that that was a bridge too far at the time.

On 31 March 1967 the Minister of Transport opened a new £2¼ million Design and Development extension to the Engineering Research Laboratories at the Railway Technical

Centre at Derby. The Centre had six main buildings on an 8½ acre site, and became one of the finest railway research centres in the world. It was destroyed after privatisation, in a supreme act of vandalism. All that experience and technical know-how thrown to the winds.

On 29 June 1967 the first meeting was held to plan the closure of Colwick Up Sidings. The GN access into the collieries which were served from both the Midland line and the GN line and which fed their GN coal traffic into Colwick were in the process of closure, and the coal traffic was to be diverted into Toton via the Midland access.

On 20 July 1967 an Up Midland express hit a derailed goods wagon near Kettering, breaking all the windows on one side. The Joint Inquiry was held at Kettering the following day. Unfortunately, no further information is available.

On 2 September 1967 Nottingham Victoria station closed for good. The only passenger services still using it were the trains from Grantham and the Rugby-Nottingham service. The Grantham service was easily diverted to use the Midland station, and the Rugby service terminated south of the tunnel at the southern end of Victoria station, at a reopened Arkwright Street station. To access this station, the DMU had to be driven into the tunnel to clear the junction, then reverse out of the tunnel into the platform. An interesting manoeuvre. The station site was sold for £¾ million pounds (which sounds rather cheap because it was a huge site plumb in the centre of the city). Demolition of the station began only 10 days after closure. The clock tower at the front of the station was retained as a memorial, together with my erstwhile office.

On 26 October 1967 there was the first of several meetings about reducing running track mileage. This initiative had originated in the Department of Transport, when probably one of its special advisers said that we had too much track. The Department then established a 'Surplus Capacity' fund to pay BR for the costs of taking out track which BR declared to be surplus to their requirements. First attention was centred on the goods lines between Wellingborough and Bedford. Money was also paid if BR closed signalboxes or installed AHBs, so it was quite popular. We were being paid by government for doing what we would have done anyway under normal good housekeeping. Unfortunately, as always happens, there was pressure from HQ to seek out every yard of track which might possibly be declared surplus.

On 2 November 1967 there was a meeting at Euston to discuss an astonishing proposal, to divert permanently into Euston the Midland line expresses which currently ran to St Pancras. They would be diverted after the Leicester stop. This proposal had two purposes: to run more trains over the electrified lines into Euston; and, to improve the economics of the West Coast electrification scheme, which were under attack from the Department of Transport. It will be remembered that the first sections of electrified line were from Liverpool and Manchester to Crewe, and the WCML scheme halted there in about 1960 whilst a government-appointed committee examined the economics of continuing to Euston. Fortunately, common sense prevailed, but apparently it was a close-run thing. HQ was anxious to improve the economics to justify the extension of electrification to Glasgow.

The likely route for the diversion appeared to be from Wigston Junction, just south of Leicester, then along the line a couple of miles towards Nuneaton to a spot where that line crosses under the former GC main line. A chord would then be built there to take trains on to the GC (which fortunately was still open) and down the GC to Rugby, where another chord would join the WCML just south of Rugby station.

Semi-fast trains between St Pancras and Leicester/Nottingham/Derby would continue to use St Pancras. Suburban services would also do so. However, the seeds were sown as to the possible closure of St Pancras, with diversions a few miles north of the capital into King's Cross and/or Euston. That would be expensive, but St Pancras could be demolished, with savings in staffing, maintenance and potential land sales. At that time, just before the 1968 Transport Act, nothing was ruled out.

On 8 December 1967 Henry Johnson (later Sir Henry) was appointed Chairman of the British Railways Board. He had been General Manager of the LM Region and had overseen much of the WCML electrification. He succeeded Stanley Raymond, who had been 'removed' by Barbara Castle, the fiery Minister of Transport, after an argument.

Eighteen

THE EVENTS OF 1968 AND BEYOND
GOODBYE, STEAM — THOU FAITHFUL SERVANT

Into 1968 — The State of Play

The year started on a high note for me. Most of the major planning developments over the last two years had either come to pass, or were well on the way to it. The phasing out of steam was complete and much of the rationalisation work had been done, although there was still some to do. The easing of the planning workload enabled me to take on responsibility for current performance, with an increase in both grade and salary. It meant that I could do more riding around the Division, keeping an eye on what was going on currently (swanning around really and learning how to drive diesel locos and DMUs — but it had a serious purpose).

External Influences

The most important national development in 1968 was undoubtedly the Transport Act of that year, introducing major policy changes. In many ways it could be said to be the most important Act of the century, until the railways were sold off in 1996. The 1921 Railways Act had created the Big Four, but the railways were still privately owned and continued as before. The 1947 Transport Act had nationalised the railways but the main changes were that Regions replaced railway companies, and the government became the sole shareholder. The 1955 Modernisation Plan was just that — it modernised the way we did things. It didn't change them. The 1963 Act led to the simplification of the railway map and introduced liner and company trains, but the 1968 Act contained more radical changes.

The 1968 Transport Act

The most significant part was a resolution of the age-old question as to whether the railways were a public service or a commercial concern. It was now firmly declared that they were, in effect, a public service, and that their losses in operating

Right: A 'Peak' class Diesel, No D155, prepares to depart from Nottingham Midland station with the 07.45 from St Pancras to Sheffield, on 5 August 1968. *David Wharton*

uneconomic stopping passenger trains would be borne by the government. BR were required to submit details of all such lines and the losses sustained, and a grant (not a subsidy) would be paid to enable BR to continue to provide such services. From this date onwards there were very few new closures. At last, the railway map was stabilised.

Almost as important was the creation of Passenger Transport Authorities (PTAs) in each conurbation outside London. PTAs had to decide what passenger services they wanted, and apply to the government for a grant to cover the cost. This was passed on to BR. The PTA set the timetable and the fares and was also required to co-ordinate buses and trains, and road traffic planning, car parking policies, etc. They rapidly became very rail-orientated, but it should be noted that policies in relation to local passenger services were no longer the concern of BR. That was a fundamental change.

The Sundries Division, which ran all the goods depots and handled all less-than-wagonload traffic (a major loss-maker for BR) was transferred to a new company, National Carriers, part of another new company, the National Freight Corporation (NFC). All the goods depots and warehouses were also transferred and there was a legal transfer of the land on which they stood. That didn't matter at the time, but once they ceased to be used for goods traffic, the land on which they stood (and in some cases the buildings) became a valuable asset, but access was a problem — they were oases of land surrounded by BR land. A lovely opportunity for lawyers.

Within a short time, BR's pride of the line — the overnight fully-fitted express freight train network more or less disappeared, together with the yards and sidings which had supported it. But the losses incurred by the Sundries business also disappeared from the BRB balance sheet. However, BR lost Freightliners, because the government thought that NFC would encourage more containers by rail. There was no evidence that it ever happened. Governments are not renowned for their skills in such matters, to put it gently.

January
A series of meetings was held at Euston and Crewe regarding the proposal to divert Midland expresses into Euston from Leicester and to electrify Leicester to Rugby, which was referred to in the previous chapter.

February
I was still giving lectures on the new Freight Trains Loads book.

We toured the Division, looking in every corner, every nook and cranny, for surplus capacity in track and signalling, and the money it would bring.

March
A quite serious safety issue had developed at Lincoln Street level crossing, Nottingham. The Corporation complained about delays to buses caused by the gates being closed for lengthy periods. The surrounding road layout was very complex, and it was agreed that traffic lights would

be installed to control road junctions and across the level crossing. When the signalman wished to close the gates, he would simply put the appropriate road traffic signals to Red, then close the crossing. It sounds simple, but the phasing of the traffic lights and the separate provision for right-hand/left-hand turns over the crossing made it quite complicated.

Several meetings were held at Euston: (1) commissioning Trent and Derby power signalboxes; (2) Beeston Freightliner terminal — track layout and signalling; (3) use of high capacity coal wagons. Each of these was a major issue on its own.

There was a large meeting with Sectional Councils 1, 2, 3, 4 and 5 regarding the closure of the GN lines around Nottingham. It took two days but was ultimately successful, and was the conclusion of six separate meetings with the staff representatives.

Below left: Turning the clock back to 1964, a member of that ubiquitous and versatile class of LMS Class 4F 0-6-0s, No 44139, waits for departure time at Nottingham Midland station with a local train on 26 August. Sadly, the engine, allocated to Nottingham 16A, looks to be in poor condition. *V. C. K. Allen*

Above: Turning the clock back even further to 1954, a well-cleaned Class 8F 2-8-0, No 48384 of 1944 vintage, approaches Market Harborough with a mineral train bound for Wellingborough. The engine was allocated to Toton. *David Clow*

Below: On Sunday 9 February 1969 English Electric diesel No D8175 trundles down the Erewash Valley with wagons of coal for signalboxes. This was a vital duty — two days earlier there had been a massive blizzard with drifts a foot deep, followed by a hard frost with temperatures down to 20° F, causing a certain amount of chaos on both road and rail. ·
V. Bamford

April

The end of my Railway Operating Course. No fewer than 48 members of staff entered for the examinations, which was very encouraging. Unfortunately, I had to mark all the papers, which was quite a task.

May

The Royal Train with HM The Queen came to Nottingham, hauled by Nos D5223 and D5226. It had stabled overnight at Old Dalby, on the disused line from Melton Mowbray Junction.

Plans were being developed for the ultimate closure of Wellingborough yards.

On Sunday the 26th, two major events took place. All the GN lines in the Division were closed except the line from Grantham to Nottingham Midland. However, the line from Derby to Egginton Junction was retained for the BR Research Department. Secondly, the Ministry gave authority for the closure of Trent station, which allowed us to make considerable improvements to the track layout and incorporate them in the forthcoming power signalling scheme. The decision was just in time.

Trent was an unusual station — it stood at the centre of a tangle of lines and had access to all of them — to and from Derby, Nottingham, the Erewash Valley and to the south. It had very little passenger traffic of its own, its main purpose being to allow connections to and from Derby and Nottingham with Midland main line expresses

which bypassed both. But Trent rose from the ashes in the shape of the new power signalbox which was built alongside the main lines.

June

A contract was signed with Rootes for £650,000 to transport car bodies from Coventry to Linwood for three years. Twenty-two two-tier bogie wagons were built for the traffic.

At 16 June, the Nottingham Division had an allocation of 140 Peaks (including Nos D1 to D10), 29 Brush Type 4s, 132 English Electric Type 2s and 82 English Electric Type 1s.

The 29th — the Matlock to Peak Forest line was closed completely. I rode over it in the cab as far as Chinley. In many ways, it was a sad day for me as

Below: Trent was an unusual station — it served to provide connections for Derby and Nottingham passengers with long distance expresses that ran via the Erewash Valley and served neither. It had a most complex layout and a splendid array of Midland Railway vintage signals. The station closed in 1968, just in time for the layout to be rationalised and simplified under the Trent power signalbox scheme. In this photograph of LMS Class 4 260 No 43002 departs from Trent station and heads off towards the Erewash Valley with a Warwickshire Railway Society special on 12 February 1966. *G. D. King*

A Railwayman's Odyssey

Above: In fine early spring sunshine, an LMS Class 4F 0-6-0, No 44421, climbs through the closed station at Great Longstone, on the Peak Forest route, with a Down freight train on 23 March 1964. The engine was allocated to Rowsley (17D), and the train was likely to have been a Rowsley to Gowhole Sidings freight. Rowsley marshalling yard closed a month later, on 27 April 1964, and the engine shed closed on 3 October 1966. *Ian Allan Library*

an old LMS (Midland Division) man, but a lesser-known part of the Beeching Report had examined duplicate routes and decided that five trans-Pennine routes were too many, and Derby to Manchester was selected for closure. It was said that with an excellent electrified service from London to Manchester, there was no need for a parallel service from St Pancras. That was largely true, but it completely overlooked the needs of intermediate stations such as Leicester, Nottingham and Derby, as well as a number of smaller ones, which were then cut off not just from Manchester but from the whole of the North West. Buxton also suffered, being cut off to the south. The Peak Forest route, as it was known, had to remain open from Derby to Matlock for the local passenger service, and from Peak Forest onwards for the very valuable limestone traffic, so the only saving was less than 20 miles. In retrospect it was a bad decision, forced upon the railways by the government, but it was in line with the attitudes of the times.

July

I visited Cotgrave Colliery with the BRB/NCB Movements and Technical Group, to give them a demonstration of the new rapid loading bunker, which was working very successfully.

The Divisional Manager, knowing that I had been running operating courses, asked me to run a one-day course, with him in the chair, on 'Leadership', for 10 senior area managers from the Region. This was a most interesting diversion, and I was under instructions to put them under pressure. So I did my best, but it didn't win me any friends, although it possibly increased my standing with the DM, which turned out to be quite useful.

September

There was a runaway at Tibshelf with a loaded coal train coming down the branch. It ran into the sidings and crashed into some wagons standing there. The driver baled out and injured himself. The use of diesels on such trains on steeply graded downhill lines and colliery branches was causing new problems. The wagons were all unbraked and loose-coupled, and in time-honoured fashion going back to the 19th century, the guard pinned down the wagon handbrakes as the driver slowly drew his

train out of the colliery sidings onto the incline. When the driver felt that he had the train under control, he would sound the whistle, and the guard would jump in his van. It worked perfectly well with steam locos, but diesels were a different matter. We conducted trials to see how it could be done safely.

The procedures at the top of the incline still worked quite well with diesels, but we discovered a problem about halfway down the hill. Owing to subsidence, a hollow had developed, which initially steepened the gradient at that point and required the driver to brake more severely. However, at the other end of the hollow, the downhill gradient lessened and the driver had to ease the brake to get his train over the 'lip', then increase it at some stage. We found that if the speed of the train exceeded 15mph at any point it was in danger of running away. It could be quite exciting to be in the cab with 60 wagons of coal pushing you and the speedometer gradually rising to 16, then 17, and so on. The branch line terminated in Tibshelf Sidings, and we made sure that the points were set for an empty siding. I doubt that we could have got away with such questionable operations in today's ultra-safe world, but these were more 'robust' times.

Social Affairs

One Saturday the Nottingham Control Cricket Club held its annual dinner and dance. Val and I were invited, as the club had invited me to be its President. I had played in the team for a couple of years but only to make up the number, as they had only 10 regular players. I was very much out of practice, not having played for many years, but they

Above: By 15 May 1968, when this photograph was taken, diesels reigned supreme. No D5399, a Type 2 BRC&W loco of 1962 vintage, heads a trainload of power station coal near Donisthorpe. The passenger station, which closed in 1931, lay on the joint LNWR and Midland line from Nuneaton via Shackerstone and Measham to a junction near Overseal and Moira with the line from Coalville to Burton-on-Trent. Donisthorpe colliery remained in production until 1980.
M .Mitchell

capped me when I made my highest score, which was probably into double figures. I enjoyed it, but I retired at the end of the season. We played on Sunday afternoons against other clubs (mainly non-railway) within about a 20-mile radius, some of whom had their own sports grounds, 20 overs each side. In those days there was still a good social life within the railway industry, with dinners, dances, sports, etc and we enjoyed it very much.

October

A diesel-hauled, loaded, unbraked coal train to Staythorpe power station (on the Nottingham-Newark line) ran past a signal at Danger and through some level crossing gates. The question to be answered was whether the driver had braked inadequately, or possibly too late, to stop at the signal, or was there some other cause? On a Sunday we carried out braking trials to see what needed to be done or whether the driver had been slow in responding to the Distant signal. We used the same driver, and he accepted that he was at fault. Drivers were generally very decent at owning up if they had made an error, and we were pretty lenient in such cases if the driver had a good record. The early days of diesels on freight trains created quite a learning curve for all of us.

November
2.15am on the 26th. A phone call from the Control Office. A Kirkby to Lloyds (Corby) coal train had become derailed in running near Stoneyford on the Erewash Valley. A Kettering to Tees iron ore train had run into the wreckage. All four lines were blocked. There was a tremendous pile of wreckage mixed with coal and ironstone, and a big clearance job for the breakdown crews and the permanent-way staff. The goods lines were reopened at 6.0am next day but the main lines were blocked until 4.0pm on the 28th. I held the Joint Inquiry on the 28th. The cause was a broken wagon spring.

The State of Play — 1969
The rationalisation of marshalling yards, stations and track, which had kept us so busy, had by now been largely completed. Steam had been phased out and all motive power depots had been closed, with signing-on points (SOPs) being established at several traffic centres. The grade of Stationmaster had been abolished and replaced by Area Managers (with assistants) covering much larger areas.

Westhouses SOP had 38 turns, using Type 1s. Kirkby SOP had 64 turns, almost all using Type 1s. Colwick SOP had 17 turns, Type 1s. Burton SOP had 8 Type 4 turns and 7 Type 2 turns. It had become customary to use Type 1s in multiple, marshalled nose to nose, to increase braking power.

The main task for 1969 was preparing to bring into service two major power signalboxes at Derby and Trent in the summer and autumn respectively,

and then for detecting and ironing out any problems, both for the operators and the signal engineers. On most weekends there were stage works to be carried out, and signalling staff had to be selected and trained.

Goods depots had been transferred lock, stock and barrel to National Carriers, and the new Freightliner depot at Nottingham (Beeston) had been transferred to the National Freight Corporation (NFC). Output from the goods depots declined and the Freightliner depot failed to prosper as expected. The government had assumed that the NFC would encourage containers from private hauliers into what was now their own terminal but it didn't happen. What do governments know about these things?

The NCB had been carrying out its own rationalisation of collieries, resulting in several closures of pithead installations, with coal being taken underground to an adjacent colliery, where it was dealt with at the washery there. It had the welcome effect of simplifying our trip workings. Merry-go-round working to Ratcliffe power station was now in full swing.

Perhaps it wasn't appreciated at the time, but these changes, especially the use of Area Managers, and the opening of power signalboxes, had reduced the workload of the Divisional office, and perhaps its role as well. The railway was becoming over-managed and there were too many layers —

Below: An English Electric Type 1, No D8066, heads north through Shipley Gate, on the Erewash Valley, with the Toton breakdown crane on 24 July 1968. *V. Bamford*

Headquarters (the British Railways Board), the Regions (remnants of the old companies) and the Divisions — all wanting a slice of the action. The Regions and the Divisions should have merged into units that were larger than Divisions but smaller than Regions. Nottingham could easily have merged with Sheffield and St Pancras and created a Midland Line office, free from Regional control. Strangely, a proposal for something similar to that on a national basis was to emerge some years later, but it was killed off, or so it was said, by the opposition of the strongly entrenched Regions, which the Board had the power to deal with but failed to do so. The cost of staff redundancies, resettlements and removals also frightened the Board.

The Events of 1969 (Accidents will be dealt with separately)

In January the Nottingham Division had 121 'Peaks', 43 Brush Type 4s, 128 Type 2s and 82 Type 1s. The latter were mainly worked in multiple on coal traffic.

Also in January, proposals for the closure of Chaddesden (Derby) marshalling yard were coming to fruition and there were several meetings with local staff representatives.

There were two bad snowstorms in February, disrupting traffic working. On the 7th there were drifts a foot deep and I had to stay in the Control Office until 11.0pm, helping to organise snowploughs. It was followed by a severe night frost, with temperatures down to 20° F. The combination of the two resulted in a lot of frozen points. Two weeks later we had more snow, up to 5in deep. The next day No 4472 *Flying Scotsman* passed through the Division on a mystery tour and was banked up the hill from Pye Bridge to Kirkby.

Also in February a newly appointed Inspecting Officer of the MOT, Lt-Col Tony Townsend-Rose, spent two days in the Division and I showed him round. For whatever reason, we immediately struck up a relationship that lasted for many years. He spent the night at the George Hotel in Nottingham and we had dinner together. The following day he travelled with the guard at the back of a Toton to Washwood Heath freight.

Cab riding on diesels was not being neglected, and I travelled around with my mentor, Traction Inspector Cyril Jones, whenever time permitted. It allowed me to learn about driving a loco and get a feel for the driver's job, but it also enabled me to get out and about and see what was happening around the Division. On 20 April I drove a freight train from Toton to Spring Vale (West Midlands) and back (type of loco not recorded).

In April it was stated that research on the gas turbine train at Derby Railway Technical Centre was well advanced and it could be in service by 1972. Maximum speed 150mph. This developed into the electric Advanced Passenger Train (APT).

On 5 May the Rugby-Nottingham DMU service on the old GC route was withdrawn, and the line was closed completely between Rugby and East Leake. It remained open between Nottingham Weekday Cross Junction and East Leake to serve the latter depot and Ruddington. The idea of using part of the line for a diverted Leicester to Euston service seemed to have been shelved. The heat was off for three reasons — half of the Board's capital debt was written off under the 1968 Transport Act and a quarter was placed in suspense. Interest had therefore to be paid henceforth on only one-quarter of the previous capital debt. Secondly, grants were to be paid for all loss-making passenger services which the government decided should be retained (which was almost all of them). Thirdly, the creation of PTAs gave those authorities jurisdiction over which passenger services in their areas they wished to retain, with the government paying a grant to cover losses. For the Board, it was a win-win-win situation. It also paved the way for the extension of West Coast main line electrification from Weaver Junction to Glasgow.

The Beeston Freightliner Terminal, planned and developed by BR, became fully operational in July and was handed over to the National Freight Corporation, to the chagrin of the Board. And us.

Swanwick colliery, served by a branch from the Pye Bridge to Ambergate line, closed. As this was the only terminal on the line, and as there was now no through traffic, the line was placed out of use, and later became a well-known preserved line.

Signalmen normally routed trains according to the train's identity, as displayed in its headcode and in the Working Timetables. However, the local trips, of which there were many, only had a trip number identity, and the destination of its next trip was telephoned from the Control Office (which organised the trip working) to the signalmen. The introduction of centralised power signalboxes required a different method to be devised, and each

Right: In 1966 there was still a through service from Nottingham to Marylebone on the GC (but not for much longer). A Stanier Class 5 4-6-0, No 45426, accelerates from the Leicester Central stop with the 5.15pm from Nottingham Victoria on 23 June that year. *J. H. Cooper-Smith*

terminal destination in the Division was given a unique number, between 50 and 99, to be displayed in the loco headcode box and telephoned to the power signalbox. The number was also carried in the Train Description apparatus on the power signalbox control panels.

Derby power signalbox was opened in three stages, normally from 10.0pm on Saturday to 6.0am Monday, during which the line was closed to most traffic. The stages were at fortnightly intervals from mid-June to mid-July. There were some problems with track circuit and other S&T failures after the first stage, but the other two stages were completed smoothly. I spent many hours in the signalbox during this period, and it was very satisfying to see several years of preparation come to successful fruition.

Trent power signalbox, a rather larger installation, opened similarly between late September and early December. The S&T acquitted themselves well, but the third stage included the very complex Toton

yard area and was accompanied by fog and minimal hours of daylight. As a result, drivers ran more cautiously and the working became sluggish during what was normally a heavy period for coal traffic. It took a few days for the working to settle down, and for HQ to calm down. HQ obviously didn't appreciate all that was involved, and the effect of fog. Fortunately it didn't snow, although it had done so during November.

In November I had a meeting with the NCB at their Eastwood offices, and they took me to lunch at the Sun Inn, Eastwood, which proudly boasts of having been the birthplace of the Midland Railway.

More quarry closures took place. The Twywell and Cranford quarries closed, which resulted in the complete closure of the Twywell branch from Kettering Junction. This was the remains of the old Midland line from Kettering to Huntingdon via Thrapston and Raunds, and the haunt at one time of elderly Midland 2-4-0s. Incidentally, we used it on the night of 26/27 June 1969 to stable the Royal

Right: A reminder of the days when Skegness was a very popular holiday destination for people living in the East Midlands. Day excursions were also popular, as seen here with Class 5 4-6-0 No 44776 coming off the Burton branch at Knighton North Junction, Leicester with an excursion train for Skegness on 6 August 1963. *G. D. King*

Train on a journey north. The train arrived at 3.15am and departed at 8.0am, conveying the Duke of Edinburgh. I was on duty to see it arrive and be put safely away, which required another loco to be attached at the rear to draw the train on to the branch, and stop at a suitable point chosen beforehand (we never propelled the Royal Train). I stayed there until the train had gone on its way, then I went home to bed.

Finally, as winter approached, we checked that our plans were ready for dealing with the winter coal traffic. Although the amount of coal being conveyed in less than trainloads had diminished, Toton had become the focal point for coal from all points north. Toton then sorted it and sent it forward to Whitemoor, Wellingborough, Northampton and Washwood Heath. During the miners' so-called 'bull weeks', when output was higher than normal, we were unable to move it all currently and it accumulated towards the weekend. A special train programme was then arranged for Sunday, with several dozen special trains being run, which brought back empties. Local trips cleared the collieries of loaded wagons and took them to Toton, returning to the collieries with empty wagons ready for Monday morning. Those power stations still using conventional wagons were one of the sources of empty wagons, because they were unloading coal all weekend. Fortunately, the programmes had all been carried out in previous winters, so we had a lot of experience to call on and we weren't starting from scratch.

ACCIDENTS

1 January at Crich Junction, on the Clay Cross to Ambergate line, a loose-coupled Up goods train became divided in running when an instanter coupling became disconnected as the train braked for a 20mph permanent-way speed restriction (PWS or PSR) and the wagons buffered up quickly. The guard had not applied his handbrake. The signalman at Crich Junction, having received the 'Train Divided' bell signal, decided to allow the first portion of the train to proceed and gave the appropriate handsignal to the driver (a green handsignal waved slowly from side to side). Despite this, the driver stopped his train and the second portion ran into it, derailing three wagons. The guard was unaware that the train had become divided.

In another accident, the crew of a train consisting of 35 empty oil tank wagons omitted to carry out a brake test on the front portion of 18 fitted vehicles, which would have indicated that the brakes were inoperative. When coupling up the loco, the guard had opened up the steam heater cock on the diesel loco instead of the airbrake cock. With the fitted head out of use, the driver was unable to stop the train in time at the Home signal at danger at Hilton level crossing and he crashed through the gates, fortunately without injuring anyone.

At **Codnor Park,** on the Erewash Valley line, a load of strip steel on a wagon loaded at Immingham shifted, causing the wagon to become unbalanced and derail.

At **Wingfield,** on the Clay Cross to Ambergate line, a 9in piece of rail broke off at the end of the rail above a bolt hole and derailed two vehicles in a parcels train.

Left: A BR/Sulzer Type 2, No D7631, passes through Loughborough Midland with a test train from Derby on 14 September 1965. The Brush works are on the right of the picture.
J. H. Cooper-Smith

Above: 4,600 h.p. of super power for a load of 21-ton hoppers. Two of the original 'Peak' class diesels, Nos D1 *Scafell Pike* and D2 *Helvellyn*, show off their paces near Barrow-on-Soar in the summer of 1967. One wonders if this spectacular marshalling had been prearranged at Toton. All 10 of the first batch of 'Peaks' were transferred to Toton in early 1962, as they were non-standard amd only Toton men knew how to drive them, which ensured that they weren't 'borrowed' by other Regions. *Graham Wignall*

At **Sawley,** between Trent and Derby, a signalbox was being demolished near an automatic half-barrier level crossing and the workmen were relying upon the road warning bells at the crossing to alert them to an approaching train. A workman was using a petrol-driven saw to cut a large piece of timber and did not hear the bells. He was struck by a train and killed.

At **Kettering,** an empty Brute parcels trolley with side curtains was blown off the platform into the path of a goods train. We were becoming aware of a new hazard, with the air turbulence caused by a train passing through a station at high speed. (Brute — British Railways Universal Trolley Equipment.)

At **Derby LNWR Junction,** a 45-ton tank wagon loaded with kerosene was derailed and fell onto its side, blocking the Up and Down main lines. The cause was said to be tyre wear and a worn switchblade, both just within permissible tolerances. It raised an interesting question — a degree of tolerance may be acceptable in one piece of equipment, but should it be reduced to cater for the effect of multiple pieces of equipment acting together?

Between **Repton and Willington,** a herd of cows escaped onto the line from a flooded field by breaking through the railway fence, and were run into by a goods train.

At **Thurgarton** level crossing, on the Nottingham to Newark line, the resident crossing keeper was putting the gates back across the line after the passage of a Down train but failed to notice the approach of a train on the Up line. It struck the gate and a piece of it injured the crossing keeper.

On the **Swanwick branch,** a single line off the Codnor Park to Ambergate line giving access to Swanwick colliery, there was a head-on collision on a blind bend between a train and a light engine. The driver of the light engine was going too fast in the circumstances. An Employment Inspector of the MOT held an inquiry into this accident.

On 23 January at about 10.30pm I was riding in the cab with an inspector on an express from St Pancras to Nottingham, when the driver ran past the Home signal at Danger at Mansfield Junction by half a train's length. The driver had applied the brake as soon as he saw the Distant signal at Caution and was driving within the permissible line speed. There had been no problem with the brake when stopping or reducing speed earlier in the journey. I decided to re-create the circumstances

Above: A trainload of empty iron ore tippler wagons passes through Nottingham Midland station on 8 July 1969, then past the carriage sidings and on to the GN, en route to, probably, High Dyke for a refill. *J. H. Cooper-Smith*

after the passengers had disembarked at Nottingham, so we ran round the train and took it back to Trent for another run. Arrangements were made for the Mansfield Junction signalman to keep his Distant signal at Caution as we approached at line speed. Despite the driver making a full brake application as soon as he saw the adverse Distant signal we still ran past the Home signal. We had two choices: (1) to move the Distant signal further out — not really an option as the signal would be removed when power signalling was introduced later that year, and (2) to reduce the line speed from 80mph to 70mph. We adopted the latter. The driver was absolved from blame. But the niggling thought remained — why had no other driver been similarly caught out? Or had our presence affected the driver's concentration? Probably the latter.

The following day two permanent-way men were knocked down and killed by an express at Mountsorrel, near Leicester. I took the Joint Inquiry with the District Engineer and it was followed later by an inquiry by an Employment Inspector from the MOT. Although the workmen concerned belonged to the District Engineer, it was the practice for the Operating Department to chair an inquiry if a train was involved.

Three days later there was another inquiry, into an accident to a shunter at Nottingham station. That was followed in due course by an Employment Inspector's inquiry.

The following day there was yet another fatality and another formal inquiry, this time to a male member of the public, crossing the line at a public footpath crossing near Sutton Junction. The Coroner held an inquest a few weeks later. BR were held to be not to blame.

It should be mentioned that a report in the prescribed format was compiled and signed after each formal inquiry and sent to Crewe, which then forwarded it to the Railway Inspectorate. For legal reasons, the report did not contain any recommendations — these were sent separately. The report contained a question and answer statement of each witness, who signed it afterwards as a true record. Shorthand typists took it all down in relays.

On 25 February there was an inquiry into yet another fatal accident, this time to a goods guard. Such a string of fatal accidents was unusual, but did not lead to a raft of changes.

On 3 March there was a Joint Inquiry into a freight train derailment at Croft (on the Leicester to Nuneaton line). The wagon concerned was an empty 16-ton mineral wagon, and the accident was caused by the driver going too fast (as proved by the signalbox train registers).

On 6 May there was a freight train derailment at Beeston South Junction.

On 11 June there was a Joint Inquiry into a derailment at Derby.

On 4 July there was a freight train derailment at Barrow upon Soar (between Trent and Loughborough). Two 'Hyfit' wagons were derailed. They had been loaded with ingots, which had shifted during the journey, causing the wagons to become unbalanced. The remainder of the train was taken back to Toton so that the loads could be examined before being worked forward.

On 17 September there was a Joint Inquiry into a fatal accident at Leicester Humberstone Road. There was an MOT Employment Inspector's inquiry a couple of months later.

On 3 December a DMU ran past a signal at Danger at Branston Junction (Burton) and was diverted by the lie of the points onto the opposite running on which a freight train was approaching, fortunately at low speed. The DMU driver quickly brought his unit to a stop and the freight train driver saw the signal ahead go back to Red. He managed to stop clear. The following day I held an inquiry and decided to do a re-run early the following Sunday morning, using the same unit and the same driver. The driver admitted that he must have run past the signal at Danger. It was very necessary to go to these lengths, because there had been mutterings among locomen about suspected wrong-side failures of the new colour light signals which had come into use a few months earlier as part of the Derby power signalling scheme. There had been some signalling failures in the early days of the power signalbox, but they were always right-side failures, ie the signals went back to Red to protect the equipment failure. But such events made locomen a bit uneasy.

On 16 December I was called out by Control at 11.0pm because Stoneyford Junction signalbox (on the Erewash Valley line near Codnor Park) was on fire and the power signalbox cable had been damaged. The signalbox had been taken out of use a few weeks earlier under one of the commissioning stages of the Trent power signalbox. Damage to the power signalbox cable would normally put all signals to Danger and a form of handsignalling had to be introduced to keep trains moving. Points had to be worked by hand by Inspectors or relief signalmen. I didn't get home until 8.0am the following morning, for a big breakfast.

The old year went out in style. I drove a Type 1 on a train of empties from Toton to Clipstone Colliery

Below: An LMS Mogul 2-6-0 (otherwise known as a Horwich Crab), No 42855, passes Basford Sidings signalbox (Nottingham) with an excursion from Mablethorpe on 27 July 1963.
Ian Allan Library

and back with loaded wagons. Under the guidance of Traction Inspector Cyril Jones, of course.

Looking Back

The year 1969 had been an exciting one, particularly with the commissioning of Derby and Trent power signalboxes. What new challenges would there be in 1970? I had now had five years at Nottingham and it was a vastly different railway from the one which existed when I first arrived in the Division. All steam gone, two new power signalboxes had been successfully commissioned, several hundred manual signalboxes had been taken out of use, most marshalling yards had closed, several branch lines and some main lines had been closed, stationmasters had replaced by area managers, freight sundries had been handed over to National Carriers, there had been a big reduction in staff numbers, and merry-go-round working had been introduced from collieries to power stations. Had there ever been such a period of change? The NCB had been carrying out their own rationalisation of collieries, closing several and merging others. The ill-fated freight train bonus scheme had come, and had quickly gone, consolidated into a pay award. What a waste of time and effort that had been.

The former Nottingham and Leicester Divisions had been merged four years previously, and the workload of the new Nottingham Division had since been quite substantially reduced, although we had been very busy making the changes. The time was ripe for a further merger. Or better still, the sweeping away of an administrative layer. But that would mean a huge upheaval.

Into 1970

The major upheavals of the last few years were by now almost behind us. Line closures, power signalling, elimination of steam, rationalisation of marshalling yards and track layouts, all less-than trainload traffic channelled through Toton, expansion of merry-go-round working and many minor changes had all been achieved. Now the emphasis was to be on seeking economies and maintaining high standards of operational performance.

Financial Affairs

We had been introduced to the terrors of **the**

Budget. We had thought, in our innocence, that this was the province of the Chancellor and only heard of once a year, but now we were required to forecast our total expenditure in staff costs for the following year in great detail, and to achieve a saving of X% over the previous year. A new Finance Section had been created to assist with this, but they only did the number-crunching and it was up to the operators to seek economies, better known as staff cuts.

The savings in staff costs over the previous five years had been quite enormous, but had been achieved mainly through changes in freight traffic patterns and through the application of technology. Now we were going to have to look elsewhere and a great deal of time and effort was expended on this. The fact was that BR had to meet their target, imposed by the government, and as HQ's expenditure was relatively small, the Regions were given their targets. The Regions didn't spend much, so the Divisions (which is where staff costs mainly occurred) were given their share, and that meant putting pressure on the poor unfortunate area managers. Just like the army. Promotion depended on achieving that share. Cutting costs became top priority.

Some Interesting news

Cab riding was much more fun than cost-cutting. This was the real railway and was far more interesting than being closeted in some smoke-filled room trying to squeeze another job out of the system. I was doing my share of this in order to maintain standards when some interesting news emerged about a vacancy for the post of Divisional Operating Superintendent (DOS) at Birmingham. Bobby Gardiner, my Divisional Manager, told me that I was being considered for the post. Great excitement. Even my wife was moderately excited. This was 22 January 1970. Ever since I became a stationmaster I had set my sights on being a DOS. They were plum jobs.

The Chain of Events

On 26 January I was called for interview at Regional HQ, Euston, to be seen by Dougal Fenton, Assistant General Manager, LM Region, John Pollard, Divisional Manager, Birmingham, and some staff folks. I had known Dougal Fenton when he was on the Eastern Region and I was one of the Yard Masters. I had not previously met John

Above: Let's conclude this last chapter with a bit of nostalgia. On 10 June 1950 W. A. Camwell captured this moment for posterity of a former Midland Railway Class 1P 0-4-4T No 58055 (formerly LMS No 1342) departing from Stretton & Clay Mills Halt with a local service between Tutbury and Burton-on Trent, all of 5¼ miles. The engine was withdrawn shortly afterwards; it achieved some 65 years of service.
W. A. Camwell/SLS

Below: These LMS Class 5 4-6-0s have featured throughout these pages, covering a period from 1934 to 1968, so here is a last look at one as No 44915, a Rugby (2A) engine, runs into Rockingham station with the 12.40pm from Harwich Town to Rugby Midland on 18 May 1964. Rockingham lay between Seaton and Market Harborough. Despite carrying an express passenger train headcode, the train called at all stations between Peterborough East and Market Harborough. No wonder the journey from Harwich to Rugby took five hours. *G. D. King*

Pollard, but he seemed very friendly and was a pal of Bobby Gardiner's (they had both been Lt-Cols). It was a genial interview and I went home feeling that things had gone well. I recognised, of course, that a genial interview can mean one of two things — either they want you and there's no point in wasting time, or they don't want you and ditto. But which one was it?

A few days later news came that Bobby Lawrence, General Manager of the LM Region, wanted to see me. He was another member of the ex-army clan. So, on 10 February, I travelled to St Pancras in the driving cab with Inspector Cyril Jones, my footplate mentor, because I had found from experience that it put me in the right mood for a critical interview. I can't remember much about the interview, except that the GM had been at pains to stress that Birmingham was the most important Division on the LM Region, and the job was the most demanding. I don't know what happened in the next 10 days, but on 20 February Bobby Gardiner called me into his office and told me unofficially that I had got the job. Three days later it was official. To say I was overjoyed would be a massive understatement. DOS's posts were probably the most coveted jobs in the Operations Department. You were still sufficiently near the ground to be able to keep in touch with what was going on. You could walk into a signalbox. You could climb into the driving cab. You were amongst the rough and tumble. But you were also part of senior management with all the status that that implied.

I had had two ambitions in my railway career. I hadn't been long in the service when I decided that I wanted to be a stationmaster, and I achieved that in 1951 when I was appointed at Battyeford. It was only a small station, but it was a start. Then it was a question of climbing up the ladder to more important SM posts. Ambitions of being a DOS were too far in the distance at that stage. However, it came within the bounds of possibility when I was selected for the Management Training Scheme. After that I did set my sights on becoming a DOS. And finally, fortune had favoured me. And, I suspect, Bobby Gardiner, who I am quite sure backed me all the way with his pals. He was a martinet, but a first-rate manager and let you get on with the job. And now I was off to a new life in the Birmingham Division. But that's another story.

And finally, a Leeds to Skipton DMU passes the photographer, W. Hubert Foster, between Bingley and Keighley. This picture has special nostalgic associations for me. All my schoolboy lineside observations were made in and around Bingley — including this spot — and I joined the London, Midland & Scottish Railway Co Ltd at Keighley as a junior booking clerk in 1943. Finally, Hubert Foster used to join us for a spot of train-watching on summer evenings and sell us his photographs at twopence or threepence a time. I still have them all. And John Holroyd, who has the care of Hubert's collection, and is a very proficient photographer in his own right, is also a valued friend. The photograph is undated, but is probably mid-1950s. *W. Hubert Foster*